GCSE
Core Science
Foundation Workbook

This book is for your foundation level **GCSE Core Science** year 10 exams.

It's full of **tricky questions**... each one designed to make you **sweat** — because that's the only way you'll get any **better**.

There are questions to see **what facts** you know. There are questions to see how well you can **apply those facts**. And there are questions to see what you know about **how science works**.

It's also got some daft bits in to try and make the whole experience at least vaguely entertaining for you.

What CGP is all about

Our sole aim here at CGP is to produce the highest quality books — carefully written, immaculately presented and dangerously close to being funny.

Then we work our socks off to get them out to you — at the cheapest possible prices.

Contents

Section 6 — Chemicals from Oil

Section 7 — Heat and Energy

Section 8 — Electricity and Waves

Section 9 — The Universe

Published by CGP

Editors:
Joe Brazier, Emma Elder, Ben Fletcher, Helen Ronan, Hayley Thompson,
Jane Towle, Julie Wakeling.

Contributors:
Mark A Edwards, Paddy Gannon, Rebecca Harvey, Frederick Langridge, Paul Warren.

ISBN: 978 1 84762 203 7

With thanks to Katherine Craig and Dawn Wright for the proofreading.
With thanks to Jan Greenway, Laura Jakubowski and Laura Stoney for the copyright research.

Graph of sulfur dioxide on page 46, source ww2.defra.gov.uk © Crown copyright reproduced under the terms of the Click-Use licence.

Every effort has been made to locate copyright holders and obtain permission to reproduce sources. For those sources where it has been difficult to trace the originator of the work, we would be grateful for information. If any copyright holder would like us to make an amendment to the acknowledgements, please notify us and we will gladly update the book at the next reprint. Thank you.

Groovy website: www.cgpbooks.co.uk

Printed by Elanders Ltd, Newcastle upon Tyne.
Jolly bits of clipart from CorelDRAW®
Based on the classic CGP style created by Richard Parsons.

The Nervous System

Q1 Suggest why it is important for animals to be able to **detect changes** in their surroundings.

....

Q2 **Tick** the box next to the correct statement below.

- [ ] Light receptor cells contain a nucleus, cytoplasm and a cell wall.
- [ ] Light receptor cells have the same structures as plant cells.
- [ ] Light receptor cells contain a nucleus, cytoplasm and a cell membrane.

Q3 Which of the following is **not** an example of a **stimulus**? Underline your answer.

pressure   change in body position   hearing   change in temperature   chemical

Q4 **Circle** the correct answer to complete each of the following sentences.

a) You have **three** / **five** / **seven** sense organs.

b) Cells called **receptors** / **sense organs** detect stimuli.

c) **Balance** / **Light** receptors in the ear detect changes in **sound** / **body position**.

d) Receptors in **hair** / **skin** detect **temperature** / **time** changes.

e) Neurones transmit information as **chemical** / **electrical** impulses.

f) Light receptors in the **ear** / **eye** detect **light** / **taste**.

g) The **vertebrae** / **CNS** coordinates a response.

Q5 Some parts of the body are known as the **CNS**.

a) What do the letters CNS stand for?

....

b) Name the two main parts of the CNS.

1. ....

2. ....

The Nervous System

Q6 A **gland** is an **effector**.

a) Name the **other type** of effector.

....

b) What substances are secreted by **glands**?

....

Q7 Which of the following describes the **path** taken by a **nervous impulse**? Underline the correct answer.

effector → sensory neurone → CNS → motor neurone → receptor

receptor → sensory neurone → CNS → motor neurone → effector

receptor → motor neurone → CNS → sensory neurone → effector

synapse → receptor → CNS → sensory neurone → effector

Q8 In each sentence below, underline the **sense organ** involved and write down the **type of receptor** that is detecting the stimulus.

a) Tariq puts a piece of lemon on his tongue. The lemon tastes sour.

....

b) Siobhan wrinkles her nose as she smells something unpleasant in her baby brother's nappy.

....

c) Xabi's ears were filled with the sound of the crowd cheering his outstanding goal.

....

d) Lindsey feels a wasp sting the skin on the back of her neck. She screams very loudly.

....

Top Tips: An adult human brain weighs about 1.4 kg — it's an incredibly complicated system of about 100 billion nerves, and if you could unravel them all, they'd stretch to more than 150 000 km. You don't need to know any of that, but I reckon it's pretty interesting stuff...

Synapses and Reflexes

Q1 **Circle** the correct answer to complete each of the following sentences.

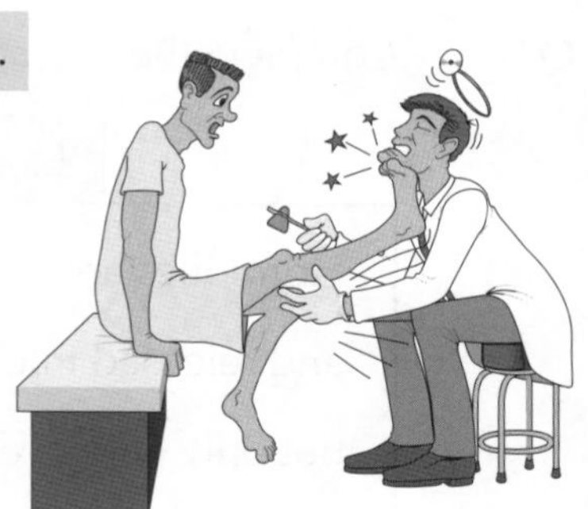

a) Reflexes happen more **quickly** / **slowly** than considered responses.

b) The main purpose of a reflex is to **protect** / **display** the body.

c) Reflexes happen **with** / **without** you thinking about them.

d) A synapse is a connection between two **effectors** / **neurones**.

e) **Chemicals** / **Impulses** are released at synapses.

Q2 When you touch something hot with a finger you **automatically** pull the finger away. The diagram shows some parts of the nervous system involved in this **reflex action**.

receptor in skin

V

W

X

Y

Z

muscle

spinal cord

a) Draw lines to match up the names below to the correct letter shown on the diagram.

V

W

X

Y

Z

relay neurone

motor neurone

synapse

sensory neurone

Some names can be used more than once.

b) Draw a ring around the correct word in the sentence below.

Information is carried **electrically** / **chemically** along neurone **X**.

c) Complete these sentences:

i) In this reflex action the muscle acts as the ....

ii) The muscle responds by ....

Q3 Explain how a nervous impulse gets across a **synapse**.

....

....

....

Hormones

Q1 Complete the passage below about **hormones**. Use the words in the box to fill in the gaps.

blood	chemical	target	glands

Hormones are .... messengers. They are produced in ....

and released into the .... They are carried all around the body,

but only affect certain .... cells.

Q2 Label the diagram by naming a **hormone** produced by each body part.

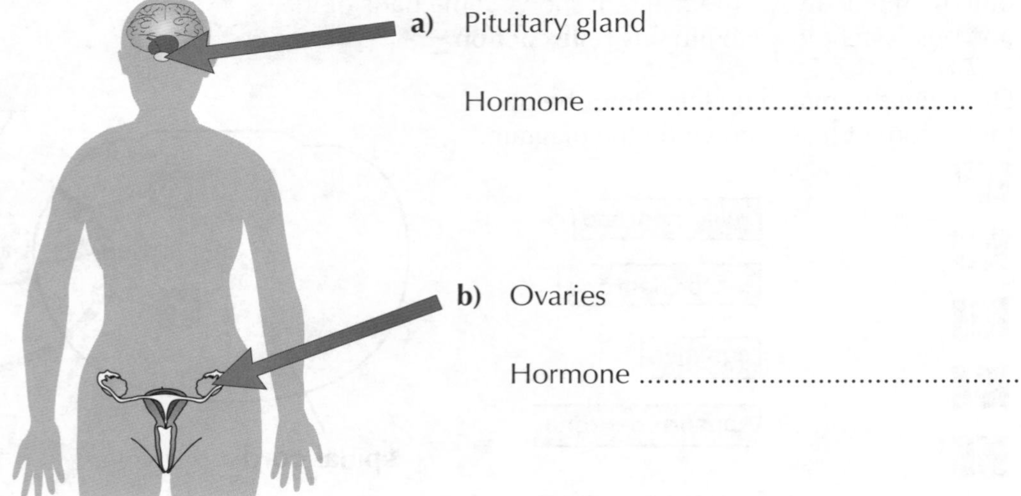

a) Pituitary gland

Hormone ....

b) Ovaries

Hormone ....

Q3 Circle the correct words in each sentence to show the differences between **hormones** and **nerves**.

a) Hormones are generally **faster / slower** than nerves.

b) Hormones tend to act for a **shorter / longer** time than nervous impulses.

c) Hormones usually act **on a precise area / in a general way**.

d) Nerves act **on a precise area / in a general way**.

Q4 Fit the answers to the clues into the **grid**.

a) Transports hormones around the body.

b) A hormone produced by the ovaries.

c) A hormone produced by the pituitary gland.

d) Hormones are secreted by ___________.

e) A hormone involved in the menstrual cycle.

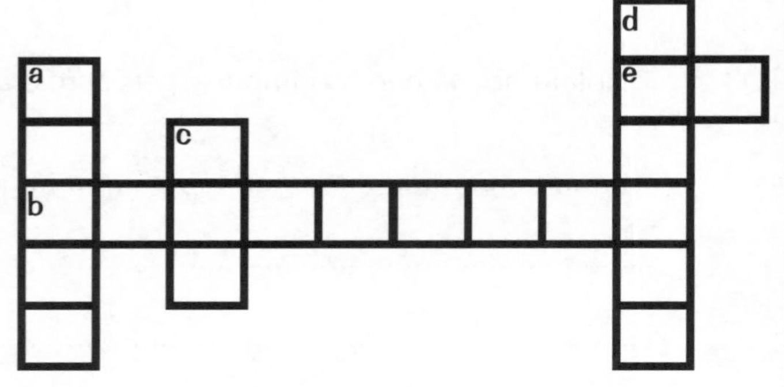

The Menstrual Cycle

Q1 Hormones are involved in the **menstrual cycle.**

Complete the table to show **where** in the body each hormone is produced.

HORMONE	WHERE IT IS PRODUCED
FSH	
oestrogen	

Q2 **FSH**, **LH** and **oestrogen** have specific functions in the menstrual cycle.

a) Draw lines to match each hormone with its function.

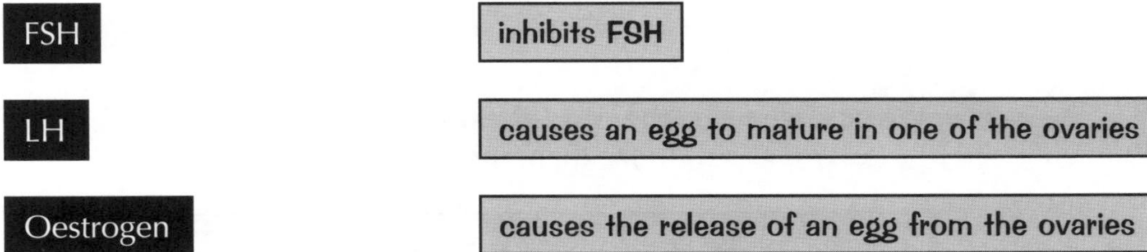

b) Which hormone causes the ovaries to produce oestrogen?

....

Q3 The diagram below shows how the **uterus lining** changes during the **menstrual cycle.**

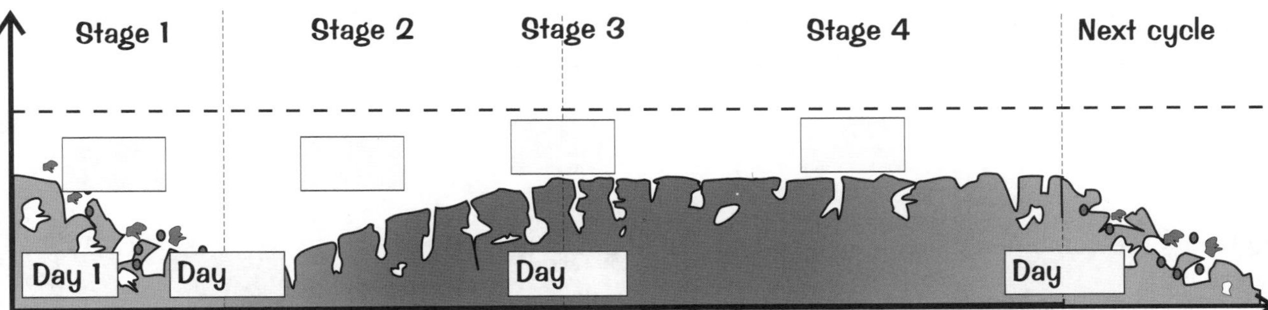

a) Fill in the **day numbers** in the boxes where they are missing.

b) Write the **correct letter** in the each of the remaining boxes, using the labels below:

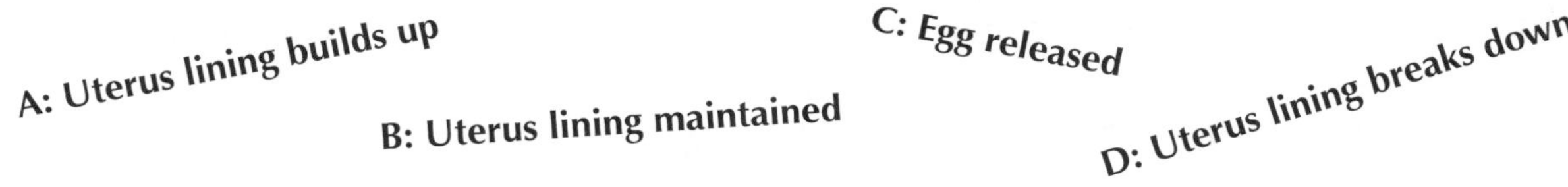

Controlling Fertility

Q1 Hormones can be used to **increase fertility**. Complete the following sentences by writing in the correct words from those listed below.

a) Some women have levels of FSH that are .... to cause their eggs to mature.

too high too low

b) FSH and LH can be injected to .... egg release in a woman's ovaries.

prevent stimulate

c) FSH and LH help a lot of women ....

to get pregnant to not get pregnant

Q2 Fill in the gaps in the passage using the words below. You might need to use some words **more than once**.

lower high blood clots side effects contraceptive progesterone

The pill is an oral .... The first version of the pill contained .... levels of oestrogen and .... However, there were concerns about a link between oestrogen in the pill and ...., such as .... The pill now contains a .... dose of oestrogen so has fewer ....

Q3 The **combined pill** contains oestrogen and progesterone.

a) State **two benefits** of taking the combined pill.

1. ....

2. ....

b) Suggest why a woman might take a progesterone-only pill, rather than the combined pill.

....

Controlling Fertility

Q4 Fertility can be reduced through taking the contraceptive pill or increased through injections of FSH / LH. Complete the table below to show the **disadvantages** of these treatments.

	Possible disadvantages
The contraceptive pill	1. .... 2. ....
FSH / LH	1. .... 2. ....

Q5 **In vitro fertilisation** (**IVF**) can help couples to have children.

a) Write numbers in the boxes to show the correct order of events to explain how IVF works. The first one has been done for you.

[1] FSH and LH are given to the woman to stimulate egg production.

[ ] Once the embryos are tiny balls of cells, one or two of them are transferred to the woman's womb.

[ ] The woman's eggs are collected from her ovaries and fertilised in a lab using a man's sperm.

[ ] The fertilised eggs are grown into embryos.

b) Discuss the **advantages** and **disadvantages** of in vitro fertilisation.

....

....

....

Top Tips: Sometimes, it's haaard to be... a womaaan... Or a man, if you're trying to learn all this. But sometimes you've just got to bite the bullet and get on with it. It's a tough old life.

Plant Hormones

Q1 Tick the correct box to show whether the following statements are **true** or **false**.

		True	False
a)	Plant shoots grow away from light.	☐	☐
b)	The response of plants to light is called phototropism.	☐	☐
c)	Plant roots grow towards light.	☐	☐
d)	Plant roots grow in the same direction that gravity acts.	☐	☐
e)	The roots of plants are positively geotropic.	☐	☐
f)	Growth towards light decreases a plant's chances of survival.	☐	☐

Q2 The growth of plants is controlled by plant growth **hormones**.

a) **Fruit ripening** is an example of plant growth controlled by hormones. Give **three** other examples of plant growth controlled in this way.

....

....

b) **i)** Name the group of **hormones** involved in the growth responses of plants to both **light** and **gravity**.

....

ii) How do plant hormones move through the plant? Circle the correct answer below.

by blood　　　in solution　　　as electrical impulses

Q3 Suzanne is doing an **experiment** to investigate the response of plant **shoots** to **light**. The equipment she uses is shown below on the left.

a) Draw how Suzanne could set up her equipment for this experiment in the box below.

lamp
plant shoots
cardboard box

b) Describe what will happen to the plant shoots during this experiment.

....

Commercial Use of Plant Hormones

Q1 Describe **four** ways in which **plant hormones** can be used **commercially**.

....

....

....

Q2 Barry is investigating the effect of a **plant growth hormone** on the **growth of the roots** in some identical plant cuttings. His measurements are shown in the table.

a) Complete the table by calculating the increase in root length at each concentration.

Concentration of growth hormone (parts per million)	0	0.001	0.01	0.1	1
Length of root at start of investigation (mm)	20	20	20	20	20
Length of root 1 week after investigation started (mm)	26	32	28	23	21
Increase of root length (mm)					

b) On the grid to the right, plot a bar chart of the increase in root length against the concentration of plant growth hormone.

c) Which concentration of growth hormone caused the biggest increase in plant growth?

....

Q3 Sanjay owns two fields — **Field A** and **Field B**. The fields are identical except that Sanjay uses a **weedkiller** on **Field B** but **not** on Field A. The weedkiller contains plant growth hormones.

This table shows the yields (amounts produced) of barley for both fields.

Year	1998	1999	2000	2001
Barley yield from field A, kg/ha	35	33	37	34
Barley yield from field B, kg/ha	48	44	49	43

a) What effect did the weedkiller have on the **crop yield** of Field B, compared to Field A?

....

b) Explain how the weedkiller works.

....

....

Homeostasis and Body Temperature

Q1 Put ticks in the boxes to show whether each technique helps to **warm up** or **cool down** the body.

		Warm up	Cool down
a)	Shivering.	☐	☐
b)	Increasing the blood flow near the surface of the skin.	☐	☐
c)	Exercising.	☐	☐
d)	Putting on more clothes.	☐	☐

Q2 **Homeostasis** is an important process in the human body.

a) Tick the box next to the best definition of homeostasis.

☐ The maintenance of a person's balance.

☐ The maintenance of control systems in the body.

☐ The maintenance of a constant internal environment in the body.

b) Why is homeostasis important for **cells** in the human body?

....

c) Hormonal communication systems are involved in homeostasis.
Name the **other** type of communication system involved.

....

d) The automatic control systems that keep the body's internal environment constant are made up of three parts. Draw lines to match each part with its correct function.

Receptors	produce the response to the change.
Processing Centres	detect a change in the internal environment.
Effectors	receive information on the change in the internal environment and organise the response.

Q3 The human body is usually maintained at a **constant temperature**.

a) What temperature is the human body usually kept at? ....

b) Name **one** condition you can get if you're exposed to:

i) **high** temperatures for a long time. ....

ii) **low** temperatures for a long time. ....

c) Explain how **sweating** helps to lower your body temperature.

....

....

Controlling Ion Levels and Water Content

Q1 Ronald eats a meal that is **very high in salt**. Which of the answers below explain correctly how Ronald's body **gets rid** of too much salt? Tick **one or more** boxes.

- ☐ Ronald's liver removes salt from his blood.
- ☐ Ronald loses salt in his sweat.
- ☐ Ronald's kidneys remove salt from his blood.
- ☐ Ronald's saliva becomes more salty, and the salt is lost when he breathes.
- ☐ Ronald gets rid of salt in his urine.

Q2 The body needs to **balance** its water input and output.

a) Why is it important to maintain a balanced water level?

....

b) Name three ways that water is **gained** by the body.

1. ....

2. ....

3. ....

Q3 The concentration of a person's urine depends on the **concentration** of their **blood plasma**.

a) List three things that affect the concentration of **blood plasma**.

1. ....

2. ....

3. ....

Concentrated solutions contain less water than dilute solutions.

b) Complete the following sentences by circling the correct word(s) from each pair.

i) When you drink too little you will produce **concentrated** / **dilute** urine.

ii) On a hot day you will produce **more concentrated** / **less concentrated** urine than on a cold day.

iii) Drinking a lot of water will produce a **large** / **small** amount of urine.

c) Why does **exercising** mean that you produce concentrated urine?

....

....

....

Controlling Blood Sugar

Q1 a) Name the **main hormone** involved in controlling blood sugar level.

....

b) i) Give the name of the **organ** that produces this hormone.

....

ii) Circle the **position** of this organ on the diagram on the right.

Q2 Use all of the words below to fill in the gaps in this passage about the control of diabetes.

pancreas insulin two diet sugary foods rise

There are .... types of diabetes. Type 1 diabetes is where the .... can't produce insulin. Type 2 diabetes is where a person can't respond to insulin. In both cases the blood sugar level may .... to dangerous levels. People with type 2 diabetes can usually manage their disease by controlling their ...., particularly by avoiding .... However, people with type 1 diabetes also have to inject .... at mealtimes.

Q3 The graph shows the **blood sugar level** of a healthy person over a period of 5 hours.

a) The blood sugar level rose quickly at **point X**.
What could have caused this **increase** in sugar level?

....

....

b) Why does the body's blood sugar level need to be **kept constant**?

....

....

Top Tips: Although diabetes is a serious disease, many diabetics are able to control their blood sugar levels and carry on with normal lives. Sir Steve Redgrave even won a gold medal at the Olympics after he had been diagnosed with type 1 diabetes.

Mixed Questions — Section 1

Q1 **Hormones** are chemical substances.

a) How do hormones travel around the body?

....

b) Tick all the factors below that describe how hormones work.

- [ ] slow response
- [ ] response lasts for a long time
- [ ] response lasts for a short time
- [ ] acts on a very precise area in the body

c) **Plants** contain hormones too.

i) Fill in the missing word to complete the sentence below:

> The group of plant hormones responsible for phototropism and geotropism are called ....

ii) **Phototropism** and **geotropism** are the responses of plants to light and gravity.
Draw lines between the boxes to complete the sentences. One's already been done for you.

Positive phototropism is when...	plant shoots grow towards the light.
Negative phototropism is when...	plant roots grow in the direction of gravity.
Positive geotropism is when...	plant shoots grow away from gravity.
Negative geotropism is when...	plant roots grow away from light.

Q2 The diagram represents the **menstrual cycle** in a particular woman.

a) What is the length of the **complete menstrual cycle** shown?

.... days.

b) What happens on **day 14** of this woman's cycle?

....

c) **Oestrogen** is one of the main hormones that control the menstrual cycle.
Name **one** other hormone involved.

....

d) Briefly explain how the **oestrogen** in the contraceptive pill **prevents** pregnancy.

....

....

Mixed Questions — Section 1

Q3 The diagram shows a **runner** waiting to start a race in the **Olympic Games**.

a) Give **one sense organ** that the athlete is relying on at the start of the race, and state the **type of receptors** it uses.

....

b) When the athlete starts the race, information will travel around his body along **neurones**.

i) What is the difference between motor neurones and sensory neurones?

....

....

ii) What is the name given to the **gap** between neurones?

....

Q4 **Water** is **lost** from the body in different ways.

a) For each of the parts of the body listed below, explain how water is lost.

i) Skin ....

ii) Lungs ....

iii) Kidneys ....

b) Let's suppose I put my annoying uncle on a treadmill to practise his running. I turned the setting to high (just to keep him quiet for a bit).* Compared to sitting still, will my uncle lose **more** or **less** water from the following body parts? Explain your answers.

i) Skin

....

....

ii) Lungs

....

....

iii) Kidneys

....

....

* Don't try this at home (I got into trouble).

Diet and Metabolic Rate

Q1 **Protein** is an important part of a balanced diet.

a) Circle the group below which needs to eat a **high protein diet**.

Office workers   Teenagers   The elderly

b) Why does this group need to eat a high protein diet? Circle the correct answer below.

They have busy jobs.   They're old.   They're still growing.

Q2 Use the words in the list to fill in the gaps in the sentences below.
Each word may be used **more than once**.

minerals   energy   warm   build   tiny   repair

a) Protein is needed to .... and .... cells.

b) Carbohydrates provide much of your ....

c) Fats are needed to keep .... and to release ....

d) Vitamins and .... are needed in .... amounts to stay healthy.

Q3 Answer these questions about **metabolism**.

a) Circle the **correct words** in the sentence below to explain what 'metabolic rate' means.

Your metabolic rate is the **time** / **speed** at which all the chemical **reactions** / **explosions** that take place in your body happen.

b) Circle **three** of these factors that will affect a person's metabolic rate.

proportion of muscle to fat in the body   proportion of hair to bone in the body   inherited factors   amount of exercise   number of brothers and sisters

Q4 Read each sentence below. In each case, **name** the person you would expect to have the **higher metabolic rate** and **explain why**.

a) Alice works as a **gardener**, while Emily works in an **office**.

....

....

b) Steven has **more fat** than muscle. His brother David has **more muscle** than fat.

....

....

Factors Affecting Health

Q1 Draw lines to match the **start** of each sentence below with its correct **ending**. The first one has been done for you.

Eating an unbalanced diet can cause	... malnutrition.
Eating too much fat or carbohydrate can cause...	... deficiency diseases.
Not eating enough vitamins or minerals can cause...	... type 2 diabetes.
Obesity can cause...	... obesity.

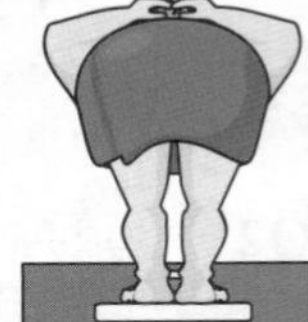

Q2 Complete each of these sentences by choosing the **correct word** from those listed below.

a) i) Some people are born with a low metabolic rate, so their cells use less .... than normal.

energy heat fat

ii) This can cause ....

obesity scurvy heart disease

b) i) Some .... factors increase blood cholesterol level.

contagious inherited limited

ii) This can increase the risk of ....

ear ache scurvy heart disease

Q3 **Fill in the gaps** in the passage below using the words in the box.

muscle	fat	healthier	energy	less	obesity	metabolic

People who exercise regularly are usually .... than those who don't. Exercise increases the amount of .... used by the body and decreases the amount stored as .... Exercise also builds .... so it helps to boost your .... rate. So people who exercise are .... likely to suffer from health problems such as ....

Top Tips: Everyone needs a balanced diet — but not everyone needs to eat exactly the same stuff. And even if you eat loads, you can still be malnourished if you don't eat the right balance of food.

Evaluating Food, Lifestyle and Diet

Q1 Circle the correct words to complete this passage on **weight loss**.

To lose body mass, a person needs to take in **more** / **less** energy than they **use** / **store**.

Eating **more** / **less** fat and carbohydrate means the body takes in less energy.

Exercise **increases** / **decreases** the amount of energy used by the body.

Q2 The **nutritional labels** of two different burgers are shown below. Both burgers have the **same weight**.

A:

NUTRITIONAL INFORMATION	per burger
Energy	2538 kJ
Protein	33 g
Carbohydrate	51 g
of which sugars	12 g
Fat	30 g
of which saturates	7 g

B:

NUTRITIONAL INFORMATION	per burger
Energy	2718 kJ
Protein	19 g
Carbohydrate	56 g
of which sugars	16 g
Fat	39 g
of which saturates	12 g

a) Which is the most **unhealthy** burger?

....

b) Explain your answer to part **a)**.

....

....

Q3 Two reports on **how to lose weight** were published on one day.

Report A was in a teenage magazine. It said that eating the cereal 'Crunchie Bites' helps weight loss because the girl band Kandyfloss had lost weight by eating it.

Report B was in a science journal. It reported on a big study of 6000 volunteers. They had lost weight while taking part in a clinical trial to test a new weight-loss drug.

a) Which of these reports is likely to be the **most reliable**?

Draw a ring around your answer. **Report A** **Report B**

b) Give **two reasons** for your answer.

1. ....

2. ....

The Circulatory System

Q1 The **heart** keeps blood pumping around the body.

a) The heart is a **double pump**. Circle the correct word from each pair in the sentences below to explain what this means.

i) The **left** / **right** side of the heart pumps blood to the lungs.

ii) The **left** / **right** side of the heart pumps blood around the rest of the body.

b) i) What type of cells make up the heart? Circle the correct answer.

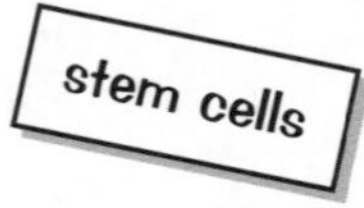

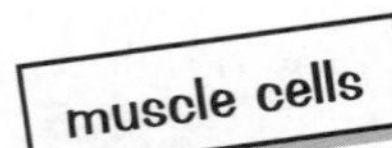

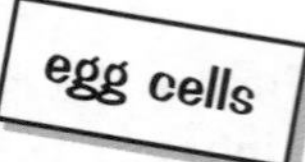

ii) Why is a blood supply to the cells in the heart essential?

....

....

Q2 The pictures below show cross sections of three **blood vessels** — an artery, a capillary and a vein.

A

B

C
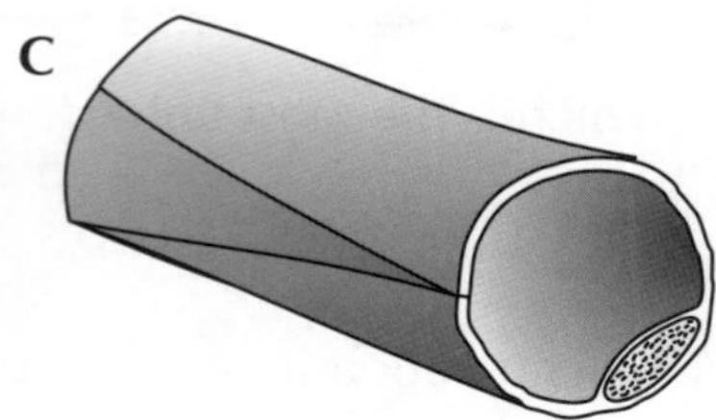

a) Write the name of each blood vessel by the correct letter.

A = ... B = ... C = ...

b) Explain how the following structures are related to the **function** of the blood vessel.

i) Strong and elastic walls of arteries

....

....

ii) Walls one cell thick in capillaries

....

....

iii) Valves in veins

....

....

Heart Rate and Blood Pressure

Q1 Fill in the blanks in the paragraph using the words in the list below.

higher relaxes artery two

Blood pressure measurements record the pressure of the blood on the walls of an .... When a doctor measures your blood pressure, ... readings are taken. The .... pressure is the pressure when your heart contracts. The other reading is the pressure when your heart ....

Q2 You can measure your **heart rate** by recording your **pulse rate**.

a) What is meant by the term 'heart rate'?

....

b) Explain why pulse rate can be used to measure heart rate.

....

....

Q3 The table below shows the blood pressure measurements of five adult men. **Normal blood pressure** is in the range of **90/60** to **120/80**.

	Blood Pressure
Chris	110/80
Dan	85/50
Steve	120/80
Ahmed	120/80
Nigel	150/95

a) How many men have blood pressure in the normal range?

....

b) Explain why normal blood pressure measurements are usually given as a range of values.

....

c) Which of the men has high blood pressure? ....

d) High blood pressure can damage arteries and cause the build up of fatty deposits. Explain how a **fatty deposit** in an artery could cause a **heart attack**.

....

....

....

....

Factors Affecting Heart Disease

Q1 Each of the factors below **increase** the **risk** of heart disease. Tick the correct boxes to show whether each factor is a **lifestyle** factor or **non-lifestyle** factor.

		Lifestyle	Non-lifestyle
a)	Poor diet	☐	☐
b)	Excessive alcohol intake	☐	☐
c)	Family history of heart disease	☐	☐
d)	Smoking	☐	☐
e)	Stress	☐	☐

Q2 Circle the correct word to complete the following sentence.

Infrequent / **Regular** moderate exercise reduces the risk of heart disease.

Q3 Heart disease is more common in **richer** countries than in **poorer** countries. Tick the box next to the explanation(s) below that you think are valid, reasonable explanations for this.

☐ People in poorer countries eat less junk food and so have a lower fat diet.

☐ Poorer people in poorer countries will have to walk more because they cannot afford cars and so they get more exercise.

☐ Poorer people in poorer countries cannot afford the treatment for heart disease and so are more likely to die of it.

Q4 a) What are **epidemiological studies**?

....

b) Suggest how an epidemiological study could be used to work out which lifestyle factors increase the risk of heart disease.

....

....

....

Drugs

Q1 There are many different types of drugs.

a) Which of the following statements best describes what a **drug** is? Circle the correct answer.

A chemical that is better than the other chemicals in your body.

A chemical that alters the reactions in your body.

b) i) What does it mean if you are addicted to a drug? Tick the boxes next to the correct answers.

- [ ] You want a drug really badly.
- [ ] You need to get a prescription for the drug.
- [ ] You can get withdrawal symptoms if the drug is not taken.

ii) Give **one** example of a drug that is very addictive. ....

c) **Statins** are a prescribed drug. What are statins used for?

....

Q2 Some athletes use **performance-enhancing drugs**.

a) Name **two** performance-enhancing drugs.

1. .... 2. ....

b) Circle any ethical arguments **against** an athlete using performance-enhancing drugs.

They may not know all the health risks.

It makes sporting competitions unfair.

Sport isn't really fair anyway.

Q3 A drug trial involved 6000 patients with **high cholesterol levels**. 3000 patients were given drugs called **statins**, and 3000 were not.

Both groups made lifestyle changes to try to lower their cholesterol, based on advice given. The decrease in the patients' cholesterol levels is shown on the graph.

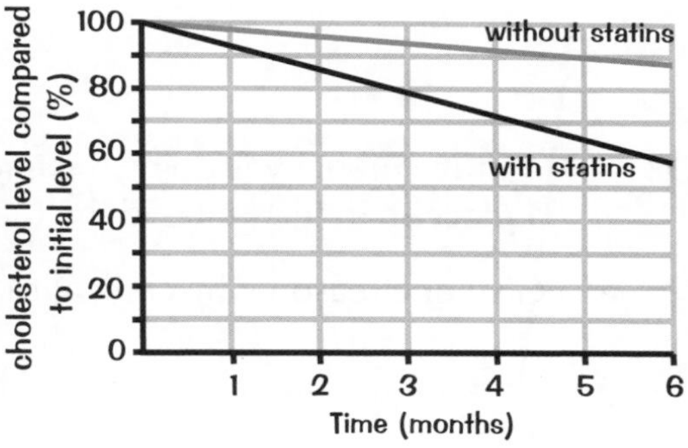

a) In which group did the cholesterol level of the participants **decrease** the most?

....

b) Suggest a **conclusion** that could be drawn from these results.

....

....

c) Which group was the **control** group? ....

Testing Medicinal Drugs

Q1 Write numbers in the boxes below to show the **correct order** in which drugs are tested.

☐ Drug is tested on live animals.

☐ Human volunteers are used to test the drug.

☐ Drug is tested on human cells and tissues.

Q2 **Thalidomide** is a drug that was developed in the 1950s. Fill in the gaps using the words in the box to describe the history of thalidomide.

morning sickness	sleeping pill	unborn
arm	tested	banned	leprosy	leg

Thalidomide was originally developed as a .... It was also found to be good at relieving .... in pregnant women, but it hadn't been .... for this use. So it wasn't known that thalidomide could affect the .... baby and cause problems with .... and .... development. Thalidomide was .... and stricter testing procedures were introduced. More recently, thalidomide has been used in the treatment of .... and other diseases.

Q3 A drug company is doing a **clinical trial**. They are using a **placebo** in the trial and the trials are '**double blind**'.

a) Give **one** reason why clinical trials have to be done before drugs are made freely available.

....

b) What is a placebo?

....

....

c) What is a double-blind trial?

....

....

Recreational Drugs

Q1 Drinking alcohol and smoking tobacco can cause **health problems**.

a) Underline any examples of health problems that are related to **drinking alcohol**.

mumps liver disease addiction lung disease unconsciousness

b) Underline any examples health problems that are related to **smoking tobacco**.

cancer liver disease addiction lung disease unconsciousness

Q2 Recreational drugs include **cannabis**, **ecstasy** and **heroin**.

a) Give **two reasons** why someone might use recreational drugs.

1. ....

2. ....

b) Give **one** negative effect that cannabis, ecstasy and heroin can have on the body.

....

Q3 A study tried to investigate the **link** between the use of **cannabis** and the use of **hard drugs**. 1000 drug users were questioned about which drugs they had used. The results are shown in the graph.

No. of people

Cannabis Hard drug

Tick the boxes next to the conclusions that can be drawn from this study.

☐ Cannabis is less dangerous than hard drugs.

☐ People are more likely to use cannabis than hard drugs.

☐ Cannabis use leads to hard drug use.

Q4 The use of **legal drugs** causes lots of problems in this country.

a) Why do alcohol and smoking have a **bigger impact** than illegal drugs in the UK?

....

b) Give **one** way that alcohol misuse **negatively** affects the **economy** in the UK.

....

Top Tips: You'd think it'd be the hard illegal drugs that cause the most damage to society — but it's the legal drugs, because of the huge numbers of people who take them. That's why it's important to know all about them. Just because they're legal doesn't meant they don't have risks.

Fighting Disease

Q1 Complete the sentence by choosing the correct words from those listed below.

A pathogen is a .... that causes .... disease.

microorganism virus fatal infectious

Q2 Fill in the gaps in the passage below using the words in the box.

small	bursts	cells	damaging	toxins	damage	poisons	copies

Bacteria are .... organisms which can multiply rapidly inside the body.

Some can make you ill by .... your body cells or producing

.... (poisons).

Viruses are tiny particles — they are not .... Viruses replicate by fooling

body cells into making .... of them. The cell then ....

and releases the new virus. This cell .... makes you feel ill.

Q3 **White blood cells** protect the body from infection.
One way they do this is by producing **antibodies**.

a) Give **two other ways** they protect the body.

1. ....

2. ....

b) Circle the **correct word** from the choices given to explain how antibodies **protect** the body.

The **red** / **white** blood cells recognise the foreign **antigen** / **antibody**.
They then make **antigens** / **antibodies** that are specific to that
antigen / **antibody**. The **antigens** / **antibodies** attack the foreign cell.

Q4 How does the body defend itself against pathogens getting into the **blood** through **cuts**?

....

....

Fighting Disease — Vaccination

Q1 **Vaccination** involves injecting dead or inactive microorganisms into the body.

Tick the correct boxes to say whether the statements about vaccinations are **true** or **false**.

		True	False
a)	Vaccinations usually involve injecting large amounts of pathogens into the body.	☐	☐
b)	White blood cells produce antibodies against the antigens on the injected pathogens.	☐	☐
c)	After a vaccination, the white bloods cells can produce antibodies to fight all kinds of diseases.	☐	☐
d)	After a vaccination, memory cells quickly produce antibodies if the body is infected with the same pathogen.	☐	☐

Q2 John is injected with the **MMR vaccine**.

a) Which **three** diseases does the MMR vaccine protect against?

....

b) The statements below explain why John **won't get ill** from any of the MMR diseases. Write numbers in the boxes to show the correct order of events. The first one's been done for you.

☐ The inactive MMR pathogens had antigens on their surface.

☐ If he is later infected with any of the MMR pathogens, John's memory cells will quickly make antibodies specific to the antigens on that pathogen.

[1] When John was vaccinated, he was given some inactive MMR pathogens.

☐ John's white blood cells learnt to make the antibodies specific to these antigens.

☐ The antibodies will kill the pathogen so John won't get ill.

Q3 Answer these questions about **vaccination**.

a) Describe **one advantage** of vaccination.

....

....

b) Describe **two problems** that could occur with vaccines.

....

....

Top Tips: Vaccination is a really effective way of controlling the spread of disease. And if most of the population is vaccinated against a specific disease, this reduces the chances of an epidemic.

Fighting Disease — Drugs

Q1 What is an **antibiotic**?

....

Q2 Fill in the gaps in the passage below using the words in the box.

drugs	mutations	reproduce	killing
natural selection	resistant	antibiotic-resistant	

Viruses .... using your own body cells.

This makes it very difficult to develop ....

that destroy the virus without .... the body's cells.

Bacteria can mutate. Some of these ....

cause the bacteria to become .... to an antibiotic.

Strains of .... bacteria have increased as a

result of ....

Q3 Name **one** type of **bacterium** that has developed **resistance to antibiotics**.

....

Q4 **Microorganisms** can be **grown** in the laboratory in Petri dishes.
Draw lines to match the **start** of each sentence below with its correct **ending**.

A lid should be taped on the Petri dish...

The Petri dish and culture medium should be sterilised...

The inoculating loop should be sterilised...

... to kill any unwanted microorganisms.

... by passing it through a flame.

... to stop any microorganisms in the air getting in.

Fighting Disease — Drugs

Q5 A new medicine called 'Killcold' contains **painkillers** and **decongestants**.

a) Explain why the name 'Killcold' isn't very accurate.

....

....

b) Why don't doctors give antibiotics for colds?

....

....

c) Why is it important for a doctor to prescribe the right type of antibiotic for an infection?

....

....

Q6 A scientist grew some **bacteria** on a nutrient medium in two Petri dishes. He kept the two dishes at different temperatures, 25 °C and 37 °C. The graph shows the **rates of growth** of the bacteria.

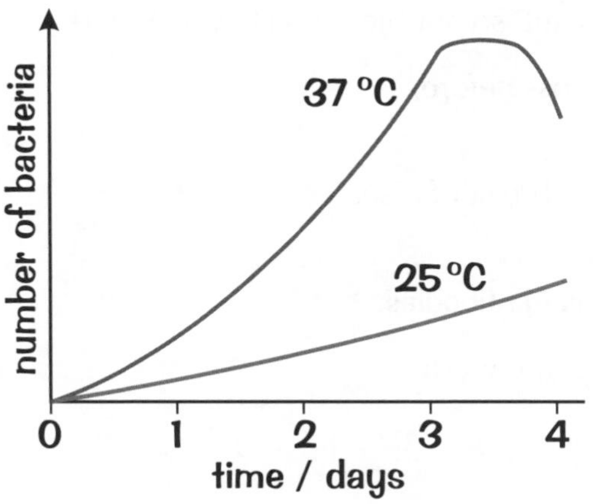

a) What happened to the bacterial colony growing at 37 °C after four days? Circle the correct answer.

It started to increase in number.

It started to decrease in number.

b) i) At which temperature did the bacteria grow faster? Circle the correct answer.

25 °C **37 °C**

ii) Which temperature would be more suitable for growing bacteria in the school lab? Give a reason for your answer.

....

iii) Which temperature would be more suitable for growing bacteria in industrial conditions? Give a reason for your answer.

....

Fighting Disease — Past and Future

Q1 Ignaz Semmelweis worked in a hospital in Vienna in the 1840s. The graph shows the percentage of women dying after childbirth, before and after a **change** that he made.

a) What percentage of women died after childbirth **before** the change?

....

b) **i)** Read the sentences below and circle the one that best describes the **change** that Semmelweis made.

He asked all the doctors to wash their hands using antiseptic solution before seeing patients.

He asked all the doctors to wash their hands with water after seeing patients.

ii) How did this change help to reduce the number of deaths after childbirth?

....

Q2 Some bacteria and viruses **evolve quickly**. Complete the sentences below by circling the correct word from each pair.

a) **Mutations** / **Resistance** can produce new strains of bacteria or viruses.

b) A new strain of bacteria could be antibiotic-resistant, so antibiotics **will** / **won't** work.

c) A new strain could be one we've never come across before, so no-one would be **allergic** / **immune** to it.

d) It's possible that a new strain could cause a big outbreak of disease, called **an epidermis** / **an epidemic**.

e) A new strain of a virus will have different **antigens** / **antibodies**.

f) It's possible that a new virus could spread all over the world — this is called **a pandemic** / **an epidemic**.

Q3 **Antibiotics** were discovered in the 1940s.

a) What has happened to the number of deaths from infectious diseases since the 1940s?

....

b) **Antibiotic-resistant** strains of bacteria are becoming more common.

i) Give **one** example of how humans can slow down the speed at which resistant strains develop.

....

ii) Give **one** way that drug companies are trying to get rid of resistant strains of bacteria.

....

Mixed Questions — Section 2

Q1 Circle the **best word or phrase** from each pair to complete the sentences below.

a) **Carbohydrates** / **Vitamins** are needed in tiny amounts to keep you healthy.

b) **Overeating** / **Undereating** can cause obesity.

c) A farmer is likely to need a lot **more** / **less** energy than someone working in a call centre.

d) Carbohydrates are broken down into sugars to provide **energy** / **materials to build new cells.**

Q2 Tick the boxes below that are next to **true** statements.

Heroin is an example of an addictive, illegal drug. ☐

Alcohol doesn't tend to cause serious problems because it is legal. ☐

You can't get addicted to alcohol. ☐

Some studies have found a link between cannabis use and mental health problems. ☐

It has been proven that the desire to take cannabis and other drugs is genetic. ☐

Q3 Some **drugs** can have a **negative effect** on the body.

a) Some athletes take **steroids**.

i) Why might an athlete use steroids?

....

ii) Give **one** negative health effect of using steroids.

....

b) Some people take **ecstasy**. Give a reason why using ecstasy can increase your risk of **heart disease**.

....

....

Q4 Scientists spend a lot of time **researching** new diets and drugs.

List **three** factors that can help you tell how **reliable** a scientific report is.

1. ....

2. ....

3. ....

Mixed Questions — Section 2

Q5 Draw lines to match each of the **structures** below with its correct **function.**

Structure	Function
valves in veins	cope with the high pressure of blood leaving the heart
thin walls of capillaries	allow the blood to exchange substances with cells
thick, elastic walls of arteries	keep blood flowing in the right direction

Q6 **Protein** is one of six nutrients needed for a **balanced diet**.

a) What condition is likely to develop in people whose diets don't have enough protein?

....

b) Name three other substances needed for a balanced diet.

1. ....

2. ....

3. ....

Q7 Gavin did an experiment to investigate the effectiveness of **three different antibiotics** (1-3). He grew some **bacteria** on a sterile agar plate. Then he placed discs of filter paper, soaked in the three different antibiotics, onto the bacterial culture.

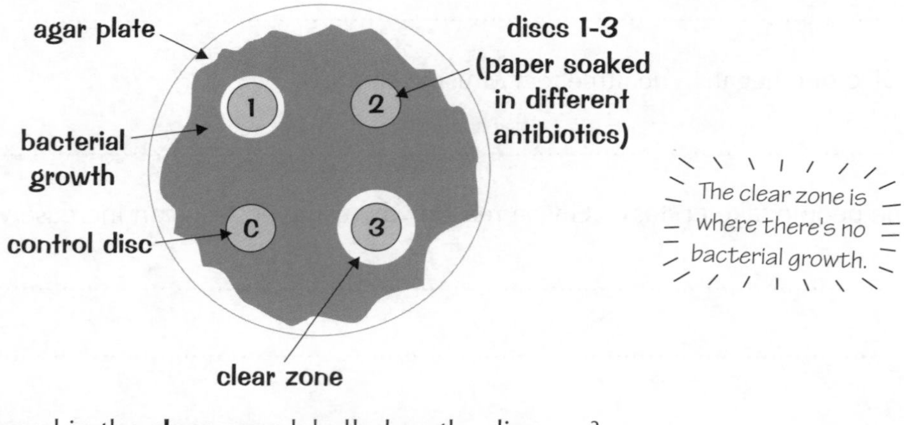

a) What has happened in the **clear zone** labelled on the diagram?

....

b) i) Which of the antibiotics (1, 2 or 3) was the **most effective** against these bacteria?

....

ii) Why **wouldn't** this antibiotic work against the flu, or a common cold?

....

Genes, Chromosomes and DNA

Q1 Complete the passage using the words given below.

nucleus	genes	chromosomes

Most cells in your body have a .... This structure contains .... , which are very long strands of genetic information. Sections of genetic material that control different characteristics are called ....

Q2 Write out these structures in order of size, **starting with the smallest**.

nucleus	gene	chromosome	cell

1. .... 2. .... 3. .... 4. ....

Q3 a) Which of the following is the correct definition of the term '**alleles**'? Underline your choice.

'Alleles' is the collective term for all the genes found on a pair of chromosomes.

'Alleles' are different forms of the same gene.

'Alleles' are identical organisms produced by asexual reproduction.

b) Look at the two statements below and circle the one that is **true**.

Alleles give different versions of a characteristic.

All alleles give identical versions of a characteristic.

Q4 Only one of the following statements is true. Tick the correct one.

- There are two chromosome 7s in a human nucleus, both from the person's mother. ☐
- There are two chromosome 7s in a human nucleus, both from the person's father. ☐
- There are two chromosome 7s in a human nucleus, one from each parent. ☐
- There is only one chromosome 7 in a human nucleus. ☐

Top Tips: If you want to be the next world famous geneticist, you've got to start with the basics. There's some good stuff coming up in this section, like cloning and genetic engineering, but it won't make much sense if you haven't got your head wrapped around the stuff tested here. So if you've got any questions wrong, go back and revise them. Trust me, it'll be worth it.

Genetic Diagrams

Q1 A species of plant has **two alleles** for **flower colour**. The allele for **yellow** flowers **(Y)** is **dominant** over the allele for **white** flowers **(y)**. The possible allele combinations are shown below.

YY   Yy   yy

a) The genetic diagram below shows what happens when a plant with the alleles **Yy** is crossed with a plant with the alleles **yy**. In the spaces below, write what colour the offspring could be. The first one has been done for you.

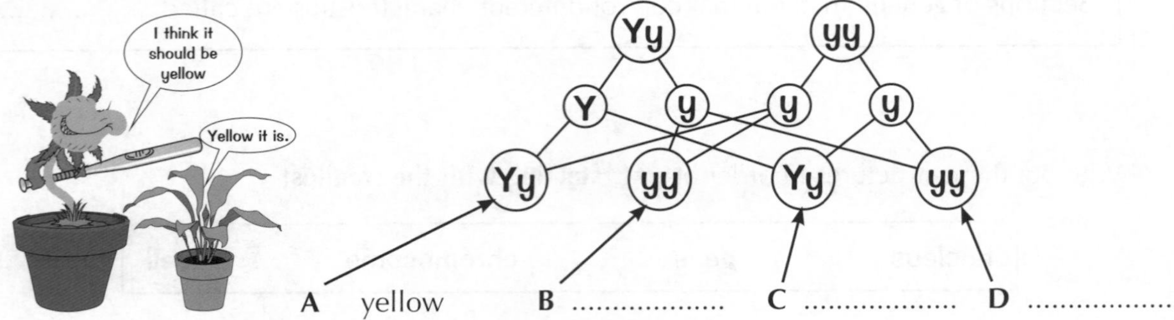

b) What is the chance of the offspring having **yellow** flowers? Circle the correct answer.

0%   25%   50%   75%   100%

Q2 In cats, the allele for black fur **(B)** is **dominant** over the allele for brown fur **(b)**. **Two black cats**, Jasper and Belle, have a litter of kittens. Most are black, but one is **brown**. Tick the boxes to show whether the following statements are **true** or **false**.

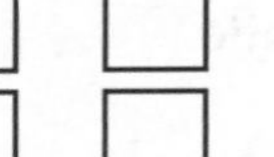

		True	False
a)	The brown kitten has the alleles bb.	☐	☐
b)	Jasper's alleles are BB.	☐	☐
c)	Belle's alleles could be Bb or bb.	☐	☐
d)	All the kittens should be black.	☐	☐

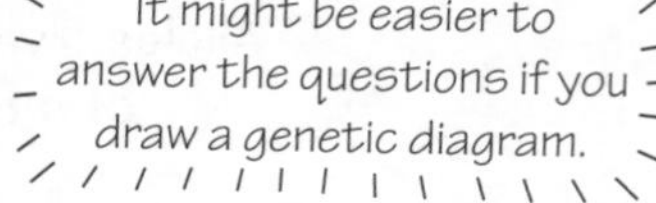

It might be easier to answer the questions if you draw a genetic diagram.

Q3 The ability to roll the tongue is controlled by a **single gene** — rolling **(R)** is **dominant** to non-rolling **(r)**. Use this information to complete the following sentences by circling the correct word(s).

> Sandeep is unable to roll his tongue. This is caused by a **recessive / dominant** allele so it will show up when there **is one copy / are two copies**. This means that Sandeep must have the alleles **rr / Rr / RR**.

Genetic Diagrams

Q4 Use the words below to complete the passage about **alleles**. You may need to use some words more than once.

one	recessive	dominant	two

When the alleles for a certain gene are different, you have instructions for .... different versions of a characteristic. You only develop .... version of the characteristic though. The version of the characteristic that appears is caused by the .... allele. The other allele is called the .... allele — to show a characteristic that's controlled by this allele, you need to have .... copies of it.

Q5 In humans, the allele for cheeks with **dimples** (**D**) is **dominant** over the allele for cheeks with **no dimples** (**d**). Adam's mum has no dimples and his dad has dimples.

a) Complete the Punnett square below to show the genetic cross between Adam's parents.

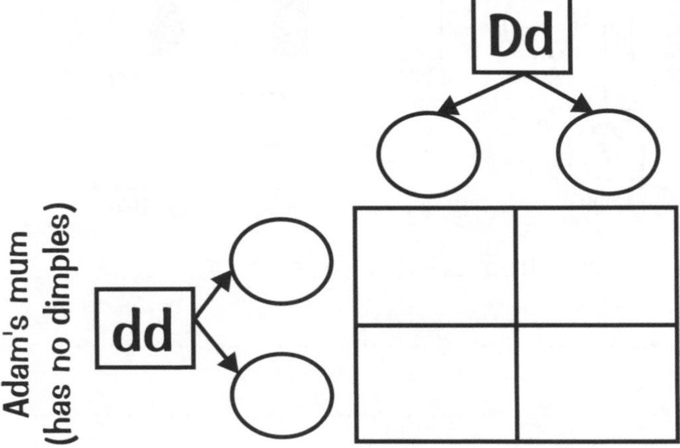

b) **i)** What is the chance of Adam's baby sister having **dimples**? Circle the correct answer.

0%	25%	50%	75%	100%

ii) What is the chance of her having **the recessive allele**? Circle the correct answer.

0%	25%	50%	75%	100%

Genetic Disorders and Sex Chromosomes

Q1 Use the words to fill in the gaps in the passage below about how a person's **sex** is determined.

Everybody has one pair of chromosomes that determine whether they are male or female. These chromosomes are called the .... chromosomes. There are two types, the .... chromosome, which can be found in males and females, and the .... chromosome, which is found in .... only.

Q2 **Cystic fibrosis** is a **recessive** genetic disorder. The family tree below shows a family with a history of cystic fibrosis.

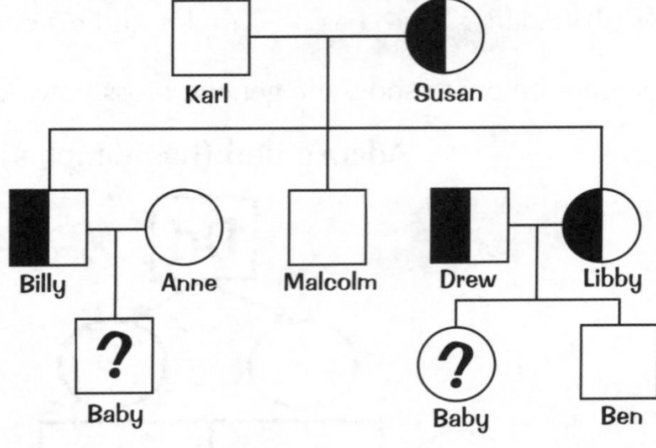

a) Explain why Susan does not suffer from cystic fibrosis.

....

....

....

b) Both Libby and Anne are pregnant. They don't know whether their babies will have the disorder.

i) Is there a chance that Anne's baby will suffer from cystic fibrosis?

....

ii) Is there a chance that Libby's baby will suffer from cystic fibrosis?

....

Reproduction

Q1 Circle the correct words in each statement below to complete the sentences.

a) Sexual reproduction involves **one** / **two** individual(s).

b) The cells that are involved in sexual reproduction are called **parent cells** / **gametes**.

c) Asexual reproduction produces offspring with **identical** / **different** genes to the parent.

d) **Asexual** / **Sexual** reproduction creates offspring with different features to the parent(s).

e) In **asexual** / **sexual** reproduction there is no mixing of genetic information.

Q2 Complete each of the sentences by choosing the correct word from the words listed below them.

a) Offspring that have the same genes as their parent are called ....

twins **clones** **Dave**

b) The human male gamete is a ....

penis **testicle** **sperm**

Billy...?

c) During sexual reproduction the gametes from each parent ....

fuse together **split apart** **swap chromosomes**

Q3 Complete the diagrams by writing the correct number of chromosomes in each empty nucleus.

a) Sexual reproduction

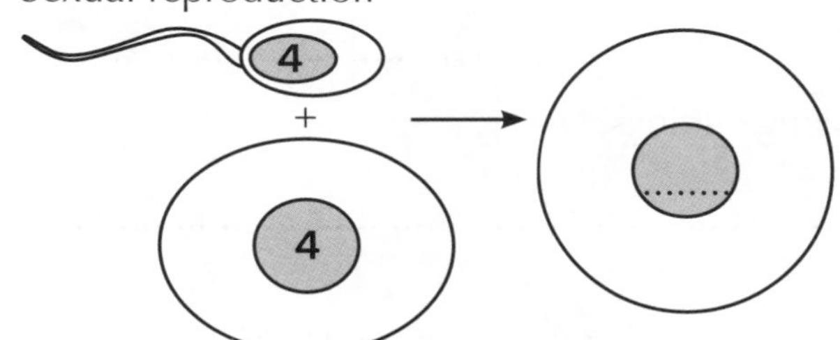

b) Asexual reproduction

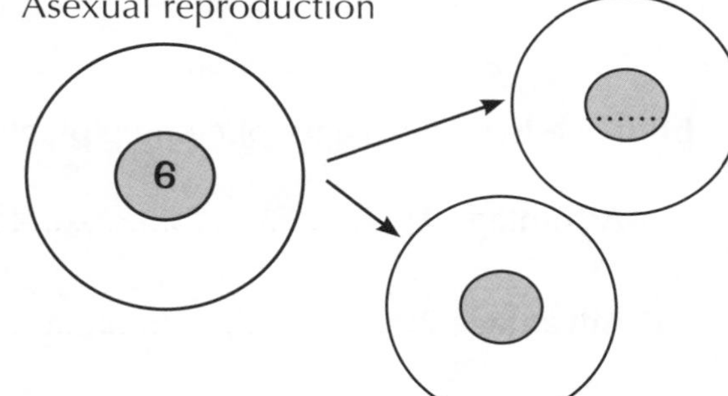

Q4 Lucy cut her hand, but a week later she noticed that the cut had almost disappeared.
The skin covering it looked just the same as the skin on the rest of her hand.
This happened by the same process as **asexual reproduction**.
Suggest why the skin on Lucy's hand looked the same as it had before she had cut herself.

....

....

Cloning

Q1 Animals can be cloned using **embryo transplants**, as shown in the diagram below.

Draw a line from each description below to its correct place on the diagram.
One has been done for you.

- An embryo develops.
- The embryo is then split many times, before any cells become specialised.
- The embryos are put into the wombs of (implanted into) lots of other cows.
- Prize bull and cow are mated.
- The embryos are clones, so all the baby calves will have the same genes.

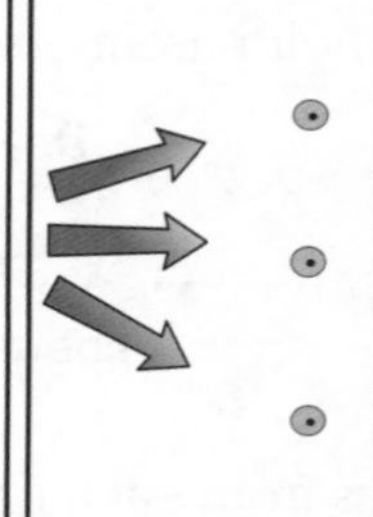
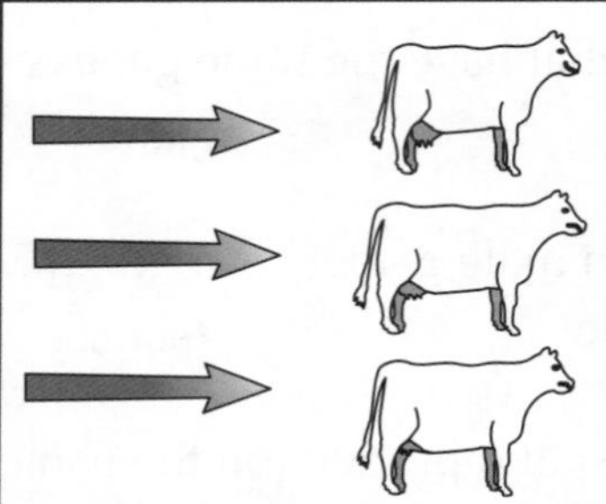
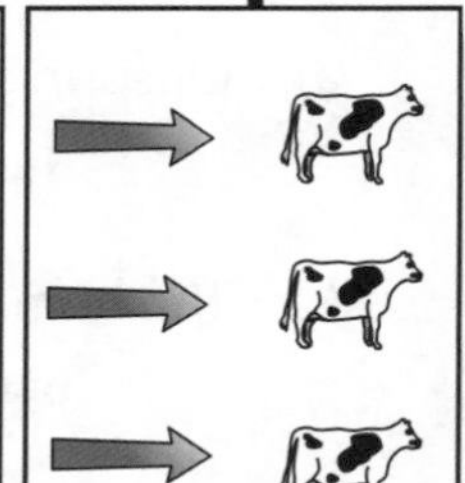

Q2 Plants can also be cloned by using **tissue culture** and taking **cuttings**.

a) Briefly describe how tissue culture works.

....

....

b) Give **two** advantages of cloning plants by taking cuttings.

Advantage 1: ....

Advantage 2: ....

Q3 **Dolly** the sheep was cloned from an adult cell.

Write the correct letter (B, C or D) next to each label below to show where it belongs on the diagram.
The first one (A) has been done for you.

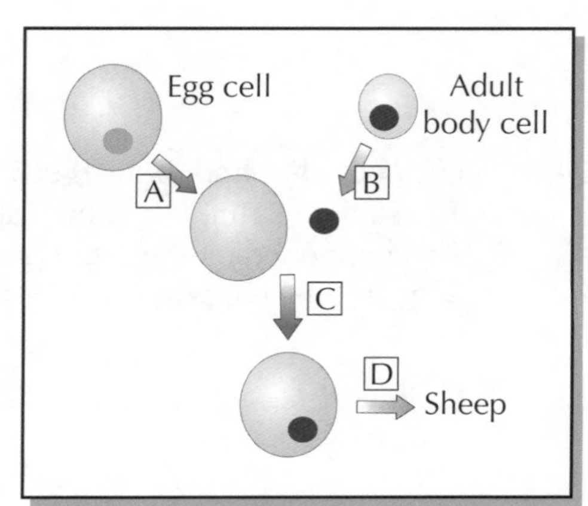

removing and discarding a nucleus .....A.....

implantation in an adult female ....

useful nucleus removed ....

putting the useful nucleus into an empty egg cell ....

Genetic Engineering

Q1 Genetic engineering can be used to **transfer genes** from humans into bacteria.

Draw a line from each description below to its correct place on the diagram.

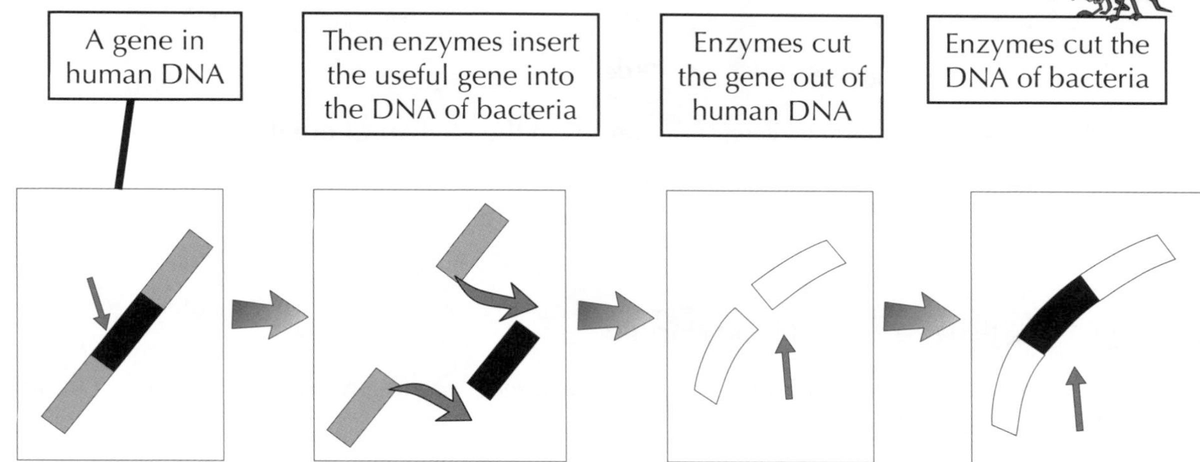
A gene in human DNA
Then enzymes insert the useful gene into the DNA of bacteria
Enzymes cut the gene out of human DNA
Enzymes cut the DNA of bacteria

Q2 Circle the correct word from each pair to complete the passage below.

Useful genes can be transferred into animals and plants at the **very early / very late** stages of their development. This means they'll **develop / inherit** useful characteristics. GM stands for **genetically malleable / genetically modified**. GM crops have had their genes **changed / removed**.

Q3 Circle **three things** below that some GM crops can be made **resistant** to.

crop circles **viruses** **cloning** **insects** **herbicides** **fire**

Q4 GM crops have **pros and cons**. Draw lines to match up the two halves of the sentences below.

Pro: GM crops can increase	safe to eat.
Con: GM crops might decrease	the yield of a crop.
Pro: GM crops can include extra nutrients to	prevent deficiency diseases.
Con: some people worry GM crops aren't	the number of flowers that live by the crops.

Classification

Q1 Organisms can be **classified** into kingdoms and then smaller groups, e.g. species.

a) Complete the subdivision of kingdoms using the words given below.

kingdom ⟶ phylum ⟶ .... ⟶ .... ⟶ .... ⟶ .... ⟶ species

genus   order   class   family

b) What is the main characteristic of organisms in the phylum **Chordata**?

....

Q2 All living things are divided into **kingdoms**.

a) Draw **one** line from each **kingdom** to the **features** of organisms that belong to that kingdom. One has been done for you.

Plants	Are unicellular and have a nucleus
Animals	Are saprophytes
Fungi	Contain chlorophyll
Protoctists	Are unicellular but don't have a nucleus
Prokaryotes	Are heterotrophs

b) Name **one** kingdom that includes organisms **without** a cell wall.

....

c) Explain why viruses cannot be placed in any of the kingdoms listed above.

....

Q3 Some organisms can **interbreed** to produce **fertile** offspring.

a) Circle the correct word from each pair to complete the sentences below.

i) Interbreed means **breed together** / **live together**.

ii) Fertile offspring are children that can **grow fast** / **breed**.

iii) Organisms are of the same species if they **can** / **can't** interbreed to produce fertile offspring.

b) The answer to part **a) iii)** is called the species definition.
Give **two** reasons why the species definition doesn't always work.

1. ....

2. ....

Adaptations

Q1 Complete each of these sentences by choosing the correct word from those listed below.

a) Many animals would find it difficult to survive in the desert because it is very ....

Windy **Hot** **Wet**

b) Many animals would find it difficult to survive in the Arctic because it is very ....

Dark **Hot** **Cold**

c) Many plants would find it difficult to survive in the desert because it is very ....

Sandy **Wet** **Dry**

d) Some microorganisms can survive in extreme conditions such as very .... lakes.

Salty **Wet** **Dry**

Q2 Circle the correct word from each pair to complete the passage below.

> Microorganisms that have adapted to live in extreme conditions are known as **extremophobes / extremophiles**. For example, bacteria living on deep-sea volcanic vents can cope with very high **pressure / light levels** and **temperature / saltiness**.

Q3 The picture shows a **cactus** plant.

a) Where are cactus plants usually found? Underline the correct answer below.

In Arctic regions **In the desert** **In the mountains** **Near the sea**

b) Explain how each of the following parts of the cactus help it to survive in its normal habitat.

i) Spines ....

....

ii) Stem ....

....

iii) Roots ....

....

Adaptations

Q4 Some plants and animals are adapted to **avoid being eaten.**

a) i) The fox on the right lives in the Arctic. State **one** feature of the fox that helps it to avoid predators.

white fur
hairy coat
small ears

....

ii) Explain how the feature described in **i)** helps the fox to avoid predators.

....

b) Wasps are brightly coloured. Explain how this helps protect them against predators.

....

c) State a feature that bees have to help them avoid being eaten.

....

Q5 Pictures of a **polar bear** and a small rodent called a **kangaroo rat** are shown below.

Diagrams are not to scale.

a) Which of these animals do you think has the smallest body surface area? ....

b) Which animal has the smallest body surface area **compared to its volume**?

....

This is a tricky one. Remember, long, thin shapes have a big surface area compared to their volume.

c) Does having a **smaller** body surface area compared to volume mean that more or less **heat** can be lost from an animal's body?

....

d) The kangaroo rat lives in hot desert regions. Would you expect its body surface area compared to volume to be bigger or smaller than the polar bear's? Explain why.

....

....

....

Variation

Q1 Complete this passage by circling the **best** word or phrase from each highlighted pair.

> Usually, organisms of the same species **have differences** / **are identical**.
>
> This is partly because different organisms have different **genes** / **cells**, which are passed on in **gametes** / **body cells** from which the offspring develop. Identical twins are exceptions to this. But even these usually have some different features, such as **hair style** / **eye colour**, and that is due to their **diet** / **environment**. Most characteristics are controlled by **a mixture of genetic and environmental factors** / **either genetic or environmental factors**.
>
> The differences between individual organisms are known as **variation** / **inheritance**.

Q2 Tick the box to show whether these statements are **true** or **false**.

		True	False
a)	Quite a lot of plants get some genes from their mother and some from their father.	☐	☐
b)	The mixing of genes from two parents doesn't cause genetic variation.	☐	☐
c)	The height of a plant is controlled by its genes and the environment.	☐	☐

Q3 Helen and Stephanie have identical genes because they are identical twins.
Helen has the blood group B.

a) Do you think that Stephanie will have blood group B too? Explain your answer.

....

....

b) Stephanie has a birthmark on her shoulder shaped like a monkey. Helen doesn't.
Do you think birthmarks are caused by your genes? Explain why.

....

....

....

c) Helen thinks that her **intelligence** is determined only by her **genes**.
Is she right? Explain your answer.

....

Evolution

Q1 **Evolution** can occur as a result of **mutations**.
Tick the sentences below that correctly describe how this can happen.

- ☐ A mutation is a change in an organism's DNA.
- ☐ Most mutations are helpful by producing a useful characteristic.
- ☐ Useful characteristics may give an organism a better chance of surviving and reproducing.
- ☐ A helpful mutation is more likely to be passed on to future generations by natural selection.
- ☐ Over time, the helpful mutation will become less common in a population.

Q2 The diagram below shows the **evolutionary relationships** of four different species.

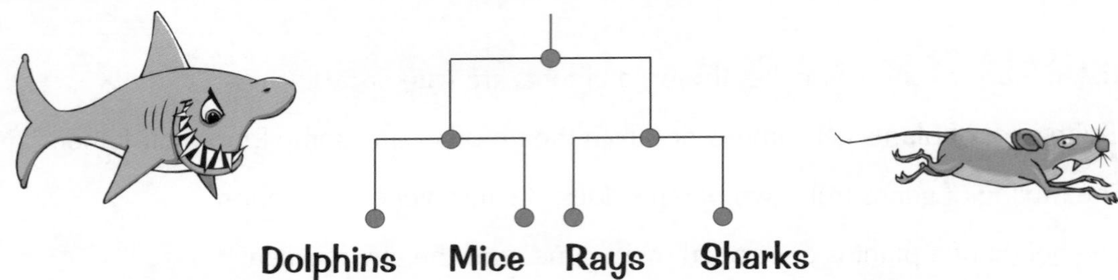

a) Tick the box next to the pair of species below that has the most recent common ancestor.

☐ Mice and Rays ☐ Rays and Sharks ☐ Mice and Sharks

b) Sharks and dolphins share **similar characteristics** even though they are **not** closely related.
Tick the box next to **one** thing that this could tell us about their ecological relationship.

☐ They could be in competition. ☐ They aren't in competition. ☐ They haven't evolved.

Q3 The buff tip moth's appearance **mimics a broken stick**, making it well-camouflaged.
The statements below describe how this feature might have evolved. Write numbers in the boxes to show the order the statements should be in. The first one has been done for you.

- [1] Ancestors to the buff tip moth showed variation in their appearance. Some had genes that made them look a bit like a stick.
- ☐ So the stick-like moths were more likely to survive and reproduce.
- ☐ Genes that made the moths look like sticks were more likely to be passed on to the next generation.
- ☐ Short-sighted birds in poor light didn't spot the stick-like moths.

More About Evolution

Q1 Which of the statements below give a reason why some scientists did **not** at first agree with Darwin's idea of **natural selection**? Circle the letters next to the correct statements.

- **A** He could not explain how new characteristics appeared or were passed on to offspring.
- **B** Characteristics that are caused by the environment can be inherited.
- **C** They thought he was making up the evidence.
- **D** His ideas went against common religious beliefs.
- **E** There wasn't enough evidence to convince many scientists.
- **F** They didn't trust men with beards.

Q2 Complete this passage by circling the **best** word or phrase from each highlighted pair.

> **Bismarck / Lamarck** argued that if a characteristic was used a lot by an organism then it would become **more developed / stunted** during its lifetime. For example if an anteater used its tongue a lot to reach ants in anthills, its tongue would get **longer / shorter**. He believed this acquired characteristic would be passed on to **the next generation / animals living nearby**.

Q3 Tick the boxes to show whether the following statements are **true** or **false**.

		True	False
a)	Scientists have found evidence for evolution by looking at fossils.	☐	☐
b)	Fossils show that species have become simpler as time has gone on.	☐	☐
c)	Similarities and differences in DNA can be used to work out how life has evolved.	☐	☐
d)	The more distantly related two species are, the more different their DNA is.	☐	☐

Q4 Lamarck and Darwin came up with **different ideas** to explain how evolution works.

Give **two** reasons why scientists may come up with different ideas to explain similar observations.

....

....

Top Tips: Darwin might seem like a boring old dead guy, but don't be fooled. His theory on evolution had a huge effect on the way we think about ourselves and where we come from.

Competition and Environmental Change

Q1 The resources below are **essential** for life.

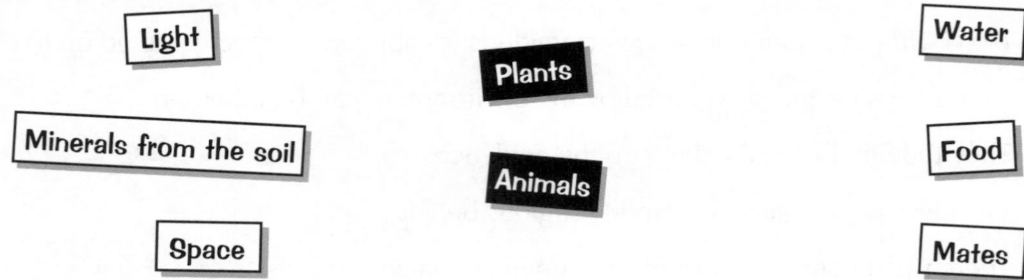

a) Draw lines to connect the boxes to show which resources are essential for plants, essential for animals and essential for both.

b) What would happen if two species in a habitat need the same resource?

....

c) Give one way that organisms rely on other species for their survival.

....

Q2 **Algae** are tiny organisms that are eaten by **fish**. The graph shows how the size of a population of algae in a pond varied throughout one year.

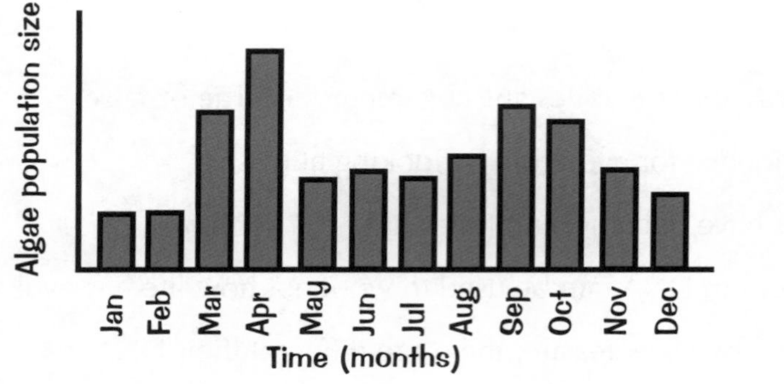

a) In which month was there the most algae in the pond?

....

b) Tick the boxes next to any factors that **could** explain why there were **more** algae in the pond this month.

Factor	
Water temperature	
Higher number of predator fish	
More diseases of algae	
Lower number of predator fish	

Competition and Environmental Change

Q3 The table shows how the UK's barn owl population has changed over a period of 20 years.

Year	No. of barn owl pairs (thousands)
1970	7
1980	4.5
1990	1.7

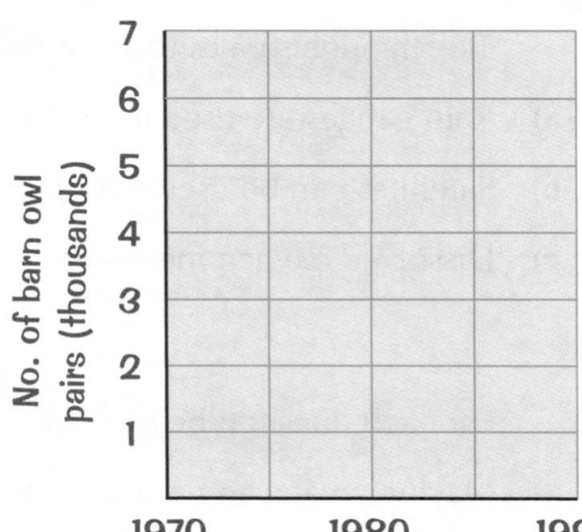

a) Use the table to plot a line graph showing the change in the size of the barn owl population over time. Use the grid provided.

b) Describe the trend shown by the graph.

....

....

c) Suggest one **living factor** that could have caused this trend.

....

Q4 The graph shows the **maximum height** up a mountain at which a **snail** species was found between 1916 and 2008.

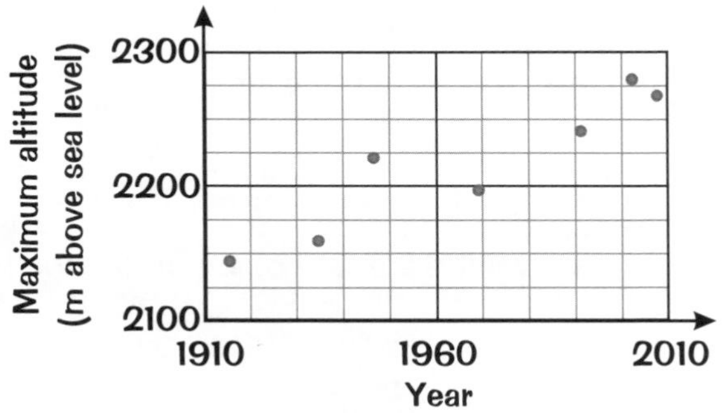

a) What does a **change in the distribution** of an organism mean?

....

b) From the graph, briefly describe the change in the distribution of the **snail species** over the last 100 years.

....

....

c) Other than temperature, name a **non-living factor** that can affect the distribution of a species.

....

Measuring Environmental Change

Q1 Tick the right boxes to say whether the sentences below are **true** or **false**.

	True	False
a) Rain gauges are used to measure the amount of rainfall in an area.	☐	☐
b) Satellites can be used to measure sea surface temperature.	☐	☐
c) Dissolved oxygen meters measure the concentration of dissolved carbon in water.	☐	☐

Q2 For each question below, tick the box that gives the right answer.

a) Mayfly larvae can be studied to see how much **sewage** is in water. What is the name for an organism used in this way?

☐ Indicator species. ☐ Sewage species.

Juanita recorded the number of mayfly larvae in water samples taken at three different distances away from a sewage outlet. Her results are shown on the right.

Distance (km)	No. of mayfly larvae
1	3
2	11
3	23

b) Give one thing that she would have to do to make this experiment a fair test.

☐ Put the animals back after the test. ☐ Collect the samples in the same way.

c) What can you conclude from these results?

☐ Mayfly larvae prefer clean water. ☐ Mayfly larvae prefer water containing sewage.

d) Suggest why sewage may decrease the number of mayfly larvae.

☐ It leads to less oxygen in the water. ☐ It leads to more oxygen in the water.

Q3 The graph below shows the amount of sulfur dioxide released in the UK between 1970 and 2003.

Sulfur dioxide emissions (million tonnes)
0 1 2 3 4 5 6
1970 1975 1980 1985 1990 1995 2000
Year

a) In which year shown on the graph were sulfur dioxide emissions highest? ....

b) Approximately how much sulfur dioxide was emitted in 2003? ....

c) What type of living organism is a good indicator of the concentration of sulfur dioxide in the air?

....

Pyramids of Biomass and Energy Transfer

Q1 The **pyramid of biomass** below describes a seashore food chain.

crab

winkle

algae

a) Which organism is feeding on the winkles?

....

b) Which organism has the greatest biomass?

....

c) How does the biomass change each time you go up a level in the pyramid?

....

Q2 Tick the boxes to show whether these statements are **true** or **false**.

		True	False
a)	Without sunlight, nearly all life on Earth would die.	☐	☐
b)	Green plants and algae use light energy to make food — this is called photosynthesis.	☐	☐
c)	This energy cannot be stored in the cells of plants and algae.	☐	☐
d)	Animals and plants release energy through the process of photosynthesis.	☐	☐
e)	Energy cannot be lost from food chains as heat.	☐	☐

Q3 A single **robin** has a mass of 15 g and eats caterpillars. Each robin eats 25 **caterpillars** that each have a mass of 2 g. The caterpillars feed on 10 **stinging nettles** that together have a mass of 500 g.

a) Work out the total mass of caterpillars eaten by a robin.

....

Now study the pyramid diagrams shown and answer the questions that follow.

A B C D

b) i) Which is most likely to represent a pyramid of **biomass** for these organisms? ....

ii) Label the correct pyramid with the names of the three organisms.

c) Explain how you decided on your answer to part **b) i)** above.

....

d) Work out the mass of stinging nettles that **each caterpillar** eats.

....

Energy Efficiency and Decay

Q1 A **food chain** is shown in the diagram.

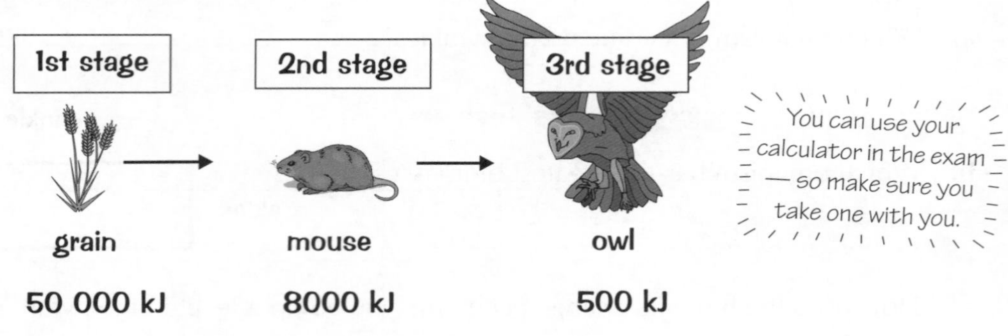

a) Calculate the **amount** of energy lost between the:

i) 1st and 2nd stages.

....

ii) 2nd and 3rd stages.

....

b) Calculate the **efficiency** of energy transfer from the:

i) 1st to 2nd stages.

....

ii) 2nd to 3rd stages.

....

Q2 Complete the passage by inserting the most appropriate words from the list below.

plants	take	microorganisms	soil
dead organisms	waste products	decay	

Living things are made of materials they .... from the world around them. Materials are returned to the environment in .... or when .... decay. Materials .... because they're broken down by .... So all the important materials return to the ...., ready to be used by ....

Energy Efficiency and Decay

Q3 Look at the picture of the **compost bin** below. Then choose **two more** of the features shown and explain how each feature aids the process of decomposition. (The first one has been done for you.)

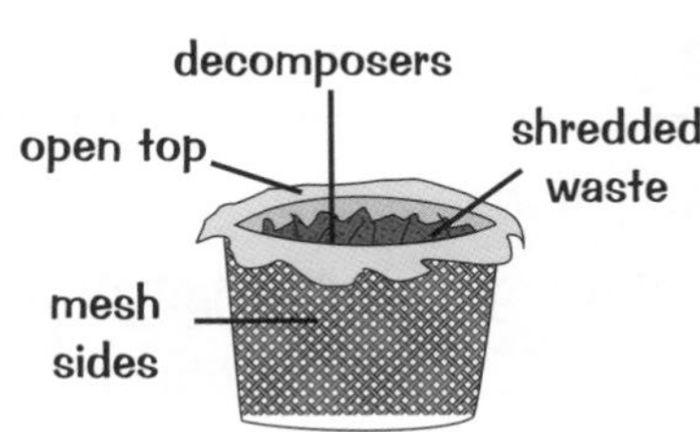

Feature	How it aids decomposition
Decomposers	Adding more decomposers will speed up decay.

Q4 Study the **energy transfer** diagram shown.

Using the figures on the diagram, calculate the **efficiency** of energy transfer from the **Sun** to the **grass**.

....

....

....

....

Sun 103 500 kJ
Grass 2070 kJ
Rabbits 100 kJ
Cows 90 kJ

Q5 In a **stable community**, the materials that are taken out of the soil and used are balanced by those that are put back in. Decide whether each of the following examples describes a stable community or not — write **stable** or **not stable** in the spaces provided.

a) A farmer plants a field of wheat. In Autumn he harvests the crop.

....

b) In Autumn leaves fall from trees to the grass below where they decay.

....

c) James rakes up the leaves on the ground of his orchard.

....

d) When Julie mows the lawn she leaves the cuttings on the lawn's surface.

....

The Carbon Cycle

Q1 Complete the passage by inserting the most appropriate words from the list below.

respire **carbohydrates** **microorganisms** **carbon dioxide**
detritus **photosynthesis** **eating** **waste**

Green plants and algae remove .... from the air and use it in .... Plants return this gas to the air when they .... — this process occurs at all times in all living organisms including animals and .... Animals obtain a supply of carbon by .... plants. Through digestion, carbon is made available from fats, proteins and .... that are stored in plant tissues. Carbon is released from dead tissues and animal .... by .... feeders.

Q2 Draw lines to match the statements below with their correct endings.

Plants use...	respiration whilst decaying waste and dead tissue.
Microorganisms release carbon dioxide by...	photosynthesis.
Animals and plants release...	carbon through feeding.
Animals take in...	carbon dioxide to build complex molecules.
Plants take in carbon by...	carbon dioxide through respiration.

Q3 The diagram below shows a version of the **carbon cycle**.

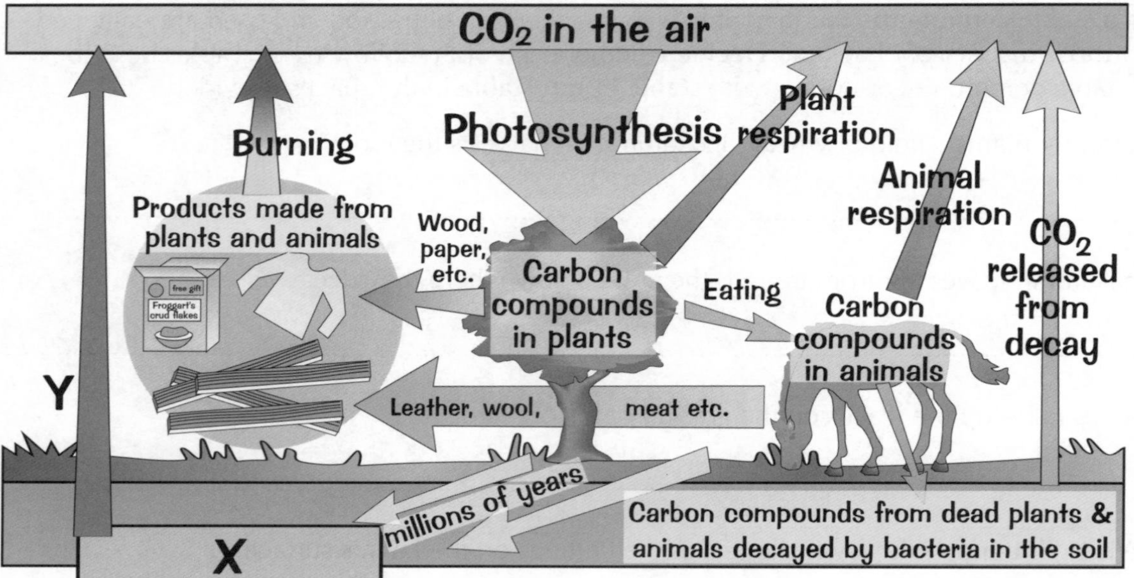

a) Name substance **X** shown on the diagram above. ....

b) Name the process labelled **Y** on the diagram above. ....

The Nitrogen Cycle

Q1 Match up each type of **organism** below with the way it obtains **nitrogen**.

Plants	By eating other organisms
Animals	By absorbing nitrates from the soil

Q2 The diagram below shows the nitrogen cycle.

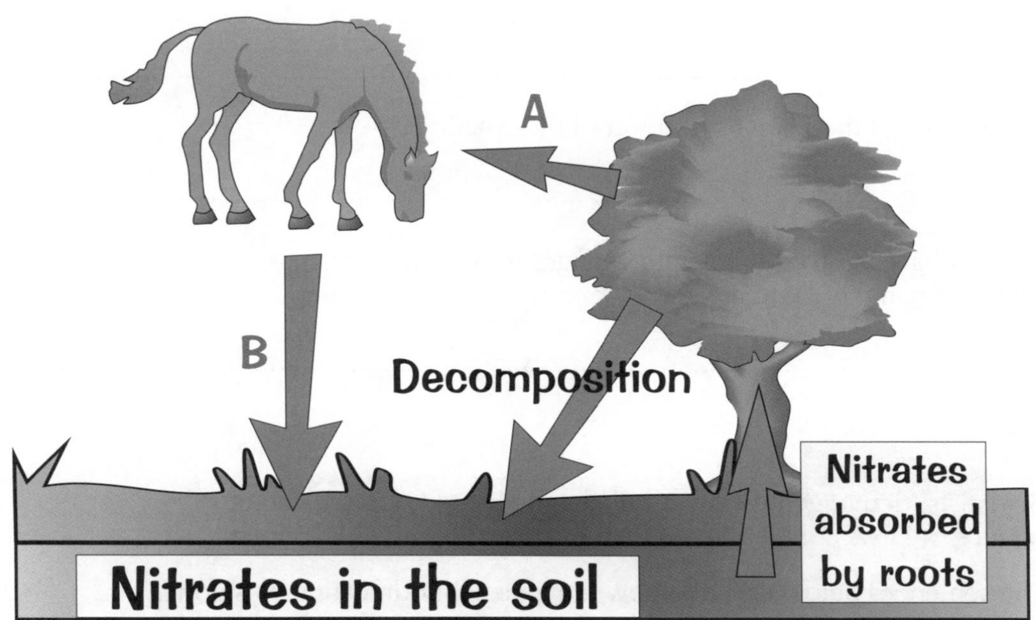

a) Underline the name of the process labelled **A** in the list below.

decomposition   photosynthesis   eating   respiration

b) What do plants make from **nitrates**? Underline the correct answer below.

fats   carbohydrates   proteins   sugar

c) i) Name the process labelled **B** on the diagram.

....

ii) What type of organisms are responsible for process **B** on the diagram?

....

Top Tips: Don't get stressed out if there's a nitrogen cycle question in your exam paper and the cycle doesn't look like the one above — there are a few different ways to draw it. But if you know what's going on in one version of a nitrogen cycle, you know what's going on in all of them. Phew.

Mixed Questions — Section 3

Q1 The graph shows how the **body temperatures** of a camel and a goat change throughout the day in a hot desert.

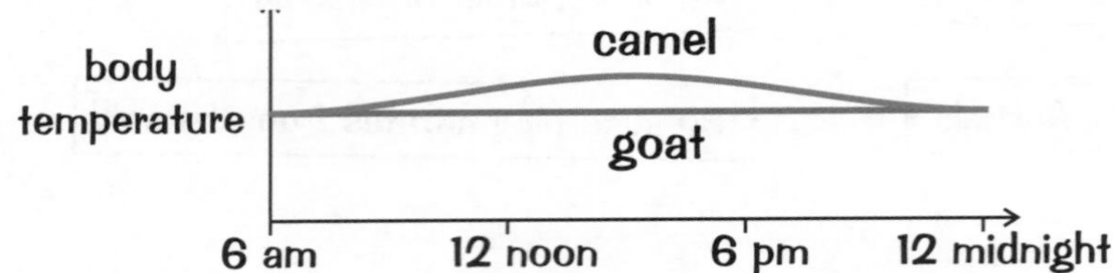

a) Between 6 am and 12 noon, what happened to the body temperature:

i) of the camel? ....

ii) of the goat? ....

b) Which one of the animals keeps cool by sweating?

....

c) Camels have evolved to tolerate changes in body temperature.
State the name of Darwin's theory of how evolution occurs.

....

Q2 Scientists tried to **genetically modify** some bacteria. They inserted a piece of DNA containing the human gene for **growth hormone**.

a) The sentences below describe how the genetic modification was done.
Complete each of the sentences by choosing the correct word from those listed below.

i) Genes were cut from the human .... using enzymes.

bacteria

ii) The DNA of the bacteria was .... using enzymes.

cut | modified | transferred

iii) The gene for growth hormone was inserted into the bacterial DNA using ....

enzymes | genes | DNA

Afterwards, the bacteria were grown on agar plates.

b) The bacteria produced all had exactly the same genes.
What type of reproduction do you think took place?

....

Mixed Questions — Section 3

Q3 An experiment was done with two **fertilised natterjack toad eggs**. The eggs came from completely different parents. The nucleus of **egg A** was put into **egg B**, and the nucleus of egg B was **removed** (see the diagram on the right).

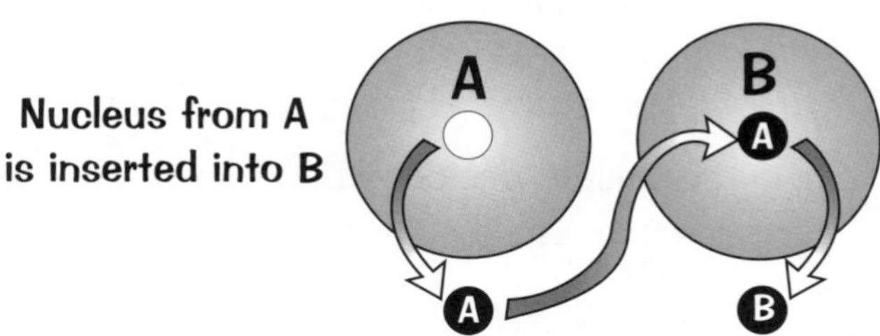
Nucleus from A
is inserted into B
A
B
A
A
B
Nucleus from B
is discarded

a) Egg **B** grew into a toad. Would you expect it to look more like the parents of egg **A** or the parents of egg **B**?

....

b) Explain your answer to part **a)**.

....

....

c) **Competition** with other amphibians has had an effect on the number of natterjack toads. Suggest **two** things that the toads may have been competing for.

....

d) Because of their permeable skin, amphibians are '**indicator species**'.

Explain what this term means.

....

....

Q4 Give **three issues** involved in cloning.

1. ....

....

2. ....

....

3. ....

....

Atoms and Elements

Q1 **Complete** the following sentences with the words in the box.

zero electrons protons protons element

a) Atoms always have a charge of ....

b) A substance that is only made up of one type of atom is called an ....

c) An atom has the same number of .... and ....

d) The number of .... in the nucleus decides what element an atom is.

Q2 **Complete** this table.

Particle	Charge
Proton	
	0
Electron	

Q3 **What am I?**

Choose from: **nucleus** **proton** **electron** **neutron**

a) I am in the centre of the atom. I contain protons and neutrons. ....

b) I move around the nucleus in a shell. ....

c) I am positively charged. ....

d) I have no charge. ....

e) In a neutral atom there are as many of me as there are electrons. ....

Q4 A helium atom is shown below. Label the diagram. One label has been done for you.

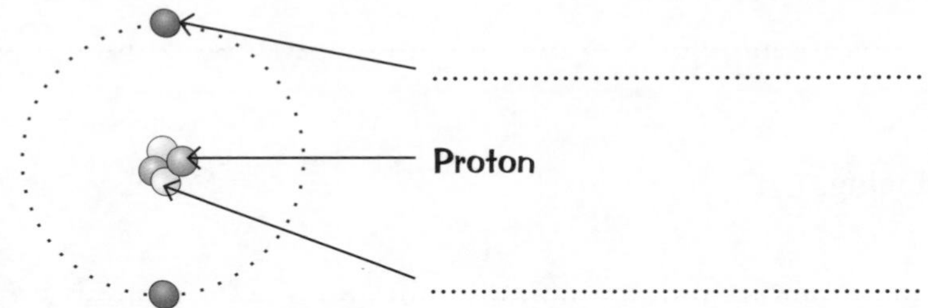

Q5 Look at these diagrams of substances. Circle the ones that contain only **one element**.

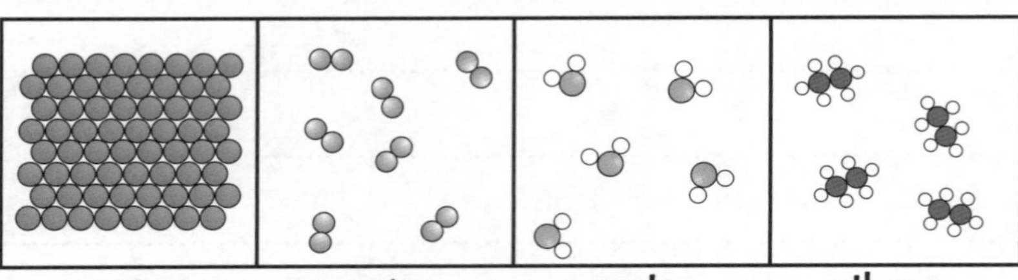

The Periodic Table

Q1 Choose from these words and symbols to fill in the blanks.

left **similar** **elements** **Cu** **Ca** **vertical** **symbol**

a) A group in the periodic table is a .... column of elements.

b) Metals are on the .... side of the periodic table.

c) There are about 100 different .... in the periodic table.

d) Each element has a different ....

e) Elements in the same group have .... properties.

f) The symbol for copper is .... and the symbol for calcium is ....

Q2 **Sodium** appears in the periodic table as shown below.

23 Na 11

a) Circle the atomic number on the diagram to the left.

b) How many protons does Na have? ....

c) How many electrons does Na have? ....

d) How many neutrons does Na have? ....

Q3 Elements in the same group **react in a similar way**.

Look at the periodic table on the inside front cover of this book to help you.

a) Tick the pairs of elements that would react in a similar way.

A potassium and rubidium ☐ **C** calcium and oxygen ☐

B helium and fluorine ☐ **D** calcium and magnesium ☐

b) Fill in the gaps to explain why sodium and potassium react in a similar way with water.

properties	**Group 1**	**outer electrons**

Sodium and potassium are both in ....

This means that they both have the same number of ....

This gives them similar ....

Q4 Tick the boxes to show whether the sentences are **true** or **false**.

	True	**False**
a) Group 7 elements are known as the noble gases.	☐	☐
b) Helium is a noble gas.	☐	☐
c) Noble gases have a full outer shell of electrons.	☐	☐
d) All noble gases are unreactive.	☐	☐

Electron Shells

Q1 Tick the boxes to show whether each statement is **true** or **false**.

		True	False
a)	Electrons occupy shells in atoms.	☐	☐
b)	The outer shells are always filled first.	☐	☐
c)	Atoms are unreactive when they don't have full shells.	☐	☐
d)	Reactive elements have full outer shells.	☐	☐

Q2 Only a certain number of electrons are allowed in each shell.

Look at the diagram below. Describe two things that are **wrong** with it.

1. ....

....

2. ....

....

Q3 Write out the **electronic structure** for the elements below. Their atomic numbers are given in brackets.

a) Beryllium (atomic number = 4) ....

b) Oxygen (atomic number = 8) ....

c) Silicon (atomic number = 14) ....

Q4 Use the words below to fill in the blanks in the passage. You will need to use some words more than once.

outer shell	reactive	unreactive

The reactivity of an element depends on how many electrons it has in its .... Elements with full outer shells are .... Elements with outer shells that aren't full are .... So, noble gases are .... and Group 1 elements are ....

Electron Shells

Q5 **Chlorine** has an atomic number of 17.

a) What is its electronic structure? ....

b) Draw the electrons on the shells in the diagram. 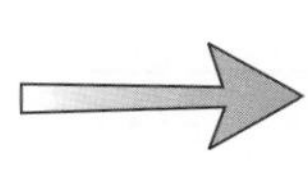

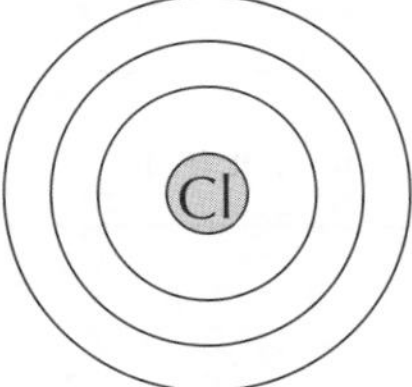

c) Why is chlorine reactive?

....

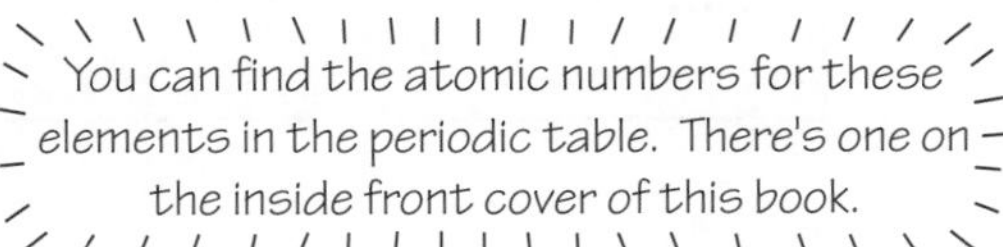

You can find the atomic numbers for these elements in the periodic table. There's one on the inside front cover of this book.

Q6 Draw the **full electronic structures** for these elements. (The first three have been done for you.)

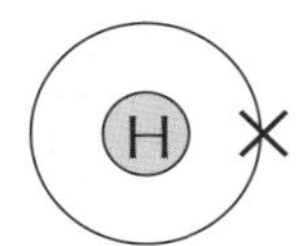

Hydrogen

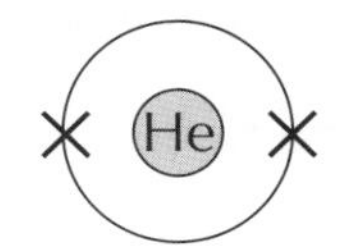

Helium

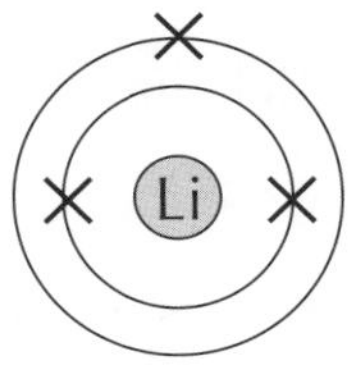

Lithium

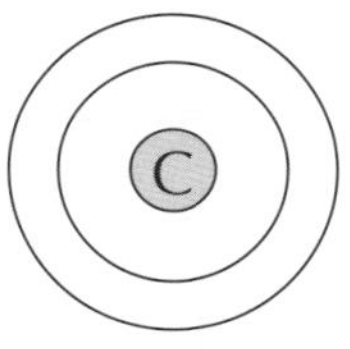

a) Carbon

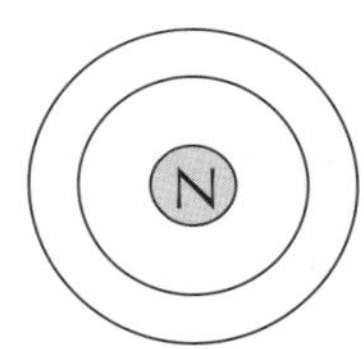

b) Nitrogen

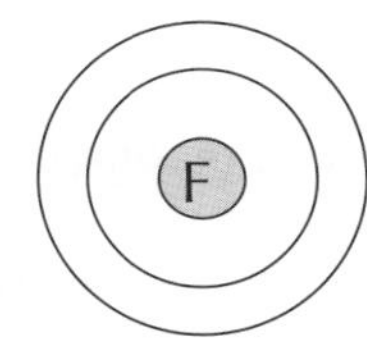

c) Fluorine

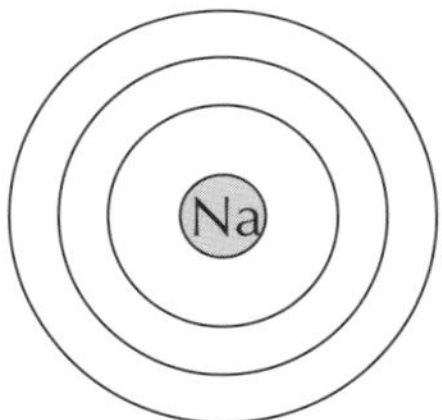

d) Sodium

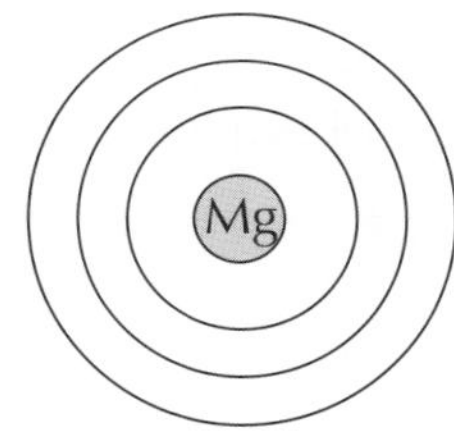

e) Magnesium

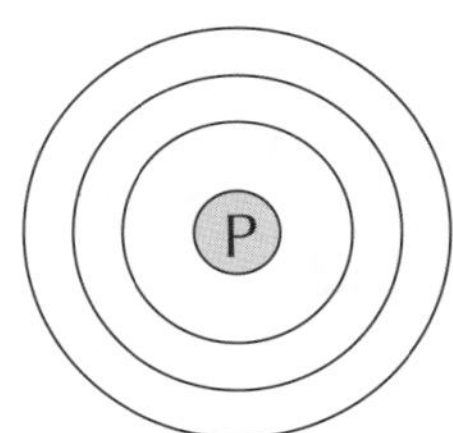

f) Phosphorus

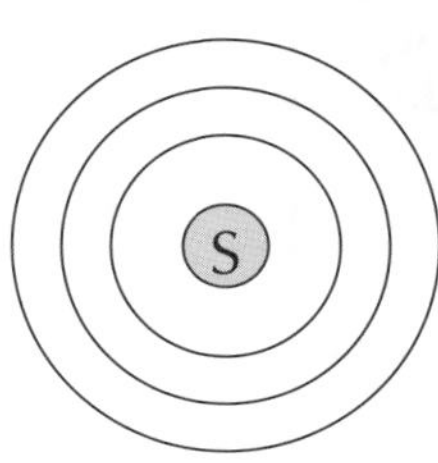

g) Sulfur

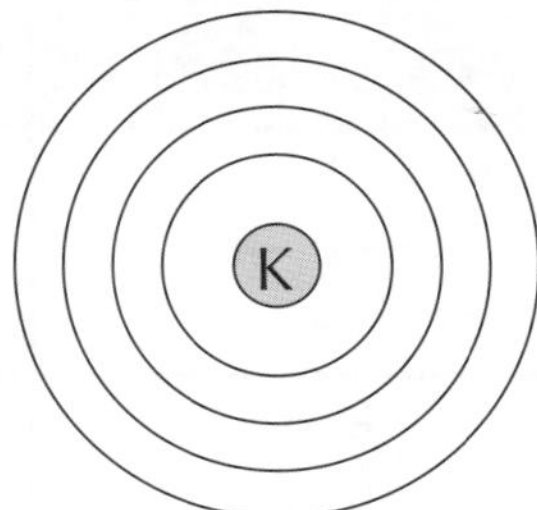

h) Potassium

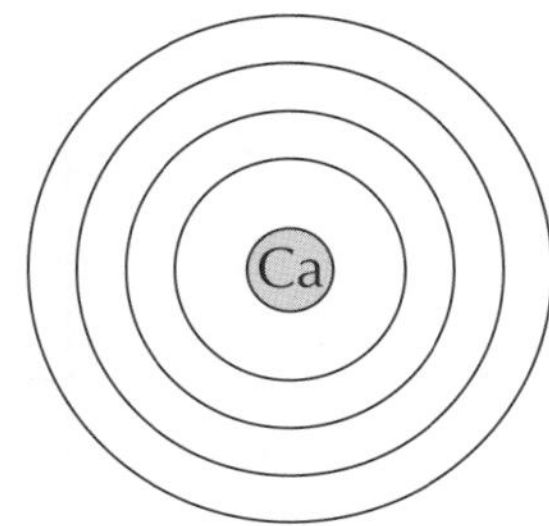

i) Calcium

Top Tips: Once you've learnt the 'electron shell rules' these are pretty easy — the first shell can only take 2 electrons, and the second and third shells a maximum of 8 each. Don't forget it.

Compounds and Formulas

Q1 Use the words below to fill in the blanks in the passage.

molecules	electrons	covalent

Atoms react to gain a full outer shell of .... A compound formed from non-metals is made up of .... Each atom shares an electron with another atom — called a .... bond.

Q2 Tick the boxes to show whether the sentences are **true** or **false**.

		True	False
a)	Compounds formed from metals and non-metals are made up of ions.	☐	☐
b)	Metals lose electrons to form negative ions.	☐	☐
c)	Compounds formed from non-metals involve sharing electrons.	☐	☐

Q3 The **displayed** formula for **ethanol** is shown on the right.

```
  H H
  | |
H-C-C-O-H
  | |
  H H
```

a) What is the **molecular** formula of ethanol? ....

b) How many **carbon** atoms does a molecule of ethanol contain?

....

c) How many atoms does a molecule of ethanol contain **in total**?

....

Q4 Complete the table to show the **molecular formulas** of methane, ethane and propane.

NAME	DISPLAYED FORMULA	MOLECULAR FORMULA
METHANE	H above, H–C–H, H below (C bonded to four H)	a)
ETHANE	H H above, H–C–C–H, H H below	b)
PROPANE	H H H above, H–C–C–C–H, H H H below	c)

Chemical Reactions

Q1 Complete the table below to show the **reactants** and the **products** in each of the equations.

Equation	Reactants	Products
$C + O_2 \rightarrow CO_2$		
nitrogen + hydrogen → ammonia		
$2Na + Cl_2 \rightarrow 2NaCl$		

Q2 This is the **equation** for burning hydrogen in air:

$$2H_2 + O_2 \rightarrow 2H_2O$$

a) How many H and O atoms are shown on the **left-hand** side of the equation?

H .... O ....

b) How many H and O atoms are shown on the **right-hand** side of the equation?

H .... O ....

c) Is this equation balanced? Explain your answer.

....

Q3 Tick the correct boxes to show which of the following equations are **balanced** correctly.

	Correctly balanced	Incorrectly balanced
a) $H_2 + Cl_2 \rightarrow 2HCl$	☐	☐
b) $CuO + HCl \rightarrow CuCl_2 + H_2O$	☐	☐
c) $N_2 + H_2 \rightarrow NH_3$	☐	☐
d) $CuO + H_2 \rightarrow Cu + H_2O$	☐	☐
e) $CaCO_3 \rightarrow CaO + CO_2$	☐	☐

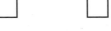

$Fe_2O_3 + 3CO \rightarrow 2Fe + 3CO_2$

Top Tip: To find out if an equation is balanced or not, just take one type of atom at a time. Count them up on both sides, see if they match, then move on to the next type of atom. Easy as pie.

Chemical Reactions

Q4 Here is the equation for how carbon **monoxide** is produced. It is **not** balanced correctly.

$$C + O_2 \rightarrow CO$$

Circle the **correctly balanced** version of this equation.

$C + O_2 \rightarrow CO_2$ $C + O_2 \rightarrow 2CO$ $2C + O_2 \rightarrow 2CO$

Q5 In a chemical reaction, **reactants** are changed into **products**.

Magnesium (Mg) can be burnt in **oxygen** (O_2) to form **magnesium oxide** (MgO).

a) What are the reactants and the products in this reaction?

Reactants: .... Products: ....

b) Write the **word** equation for this reaction.

....

c) Write the balanced **symbol** equation for the reaction.

....

Q6 **18 g** of **calcium oxide** were reacted with some **water**. **Calcium hydroxide** was formed.

a) Write down the word equation for this reaction.

....

b) Circle the correct words in the sentences below.

Atoms are / aren't made or lost during a reaction.

So, the mass of the reactants is the same as / different from the mass of the products.

c) The mass of the product, calcium hydroxide, at the end of the reaction was 29 g.
What mass of water was used?

....

....

Q7 **Balance** the following symbol equations by writing numbers in the spaces.

a) CO_2 + ... H_2 → CH_4 + ... H_2O

b) K_2O + H_2O → .... KOH

c) $MgCO_3$ + ... HCl → $MgCl_2$ + H_2O + CO_2

d) .... Li + ... H_2O → .... LiOH + H_2

Materials and Properties

Q1 Complete the statements below by circling the correct words.

a) A **weak** / **strong** material is good at resisting forces.

b) You can test how strong something is by seeing how much force is needed to **break** / **move** it.

c) A material that has good tension strength can resist **pulling** / **pushing** forces.

d) A material with poor compressive strength has low resistance to **pulling** / **pushing** forces.

e) Climbing ropes need a **low** / **high** tension strength.

Q2 Complete the table by stating if each substance is a **liquid** or a **solid** at room temperature (20 °C).

Substance	Water	Sulfur	Propanone	Sodium chloride
Melting point (°C)	0	115	-95	801
Boiling point (°C)	100	444	56	1413
State at room temperature				

Q3 Tick the boxes to show whether the statements are **true** or **false**.

	True	False
a) Density is how much mass there is in a certain volume.	☐	☐
b) In a very dense material the particles are very spread out.	☐	☐
c) In a very dense material the particles are packed close together.	☐	☐

Q4 Answer the following questions about the properties of materials.

a) What is the most important type of **strength** for building materials like bricks to have?
Tick the box next to the correct answer.

Tension strength ☐

Compressive strength ☐

b) Why are **diamonds** used to make the tips of **industrial drills**?
Circle the best answer below.

A Diamond has a high melting point.

B Diamond is very hard

C Diamond is very soft

D Diamond is very dense

Materials, Properties and Uses

Q1 Match each of the items, A–D, with the material you would use to make it.

A diving suit B child's toy plane C window pane D washing line

a) A plastic that is strong, easy to mould, and brightly coloured. ....

b) Nylon fibres, which are flexible and have high tension strength. ....

c) A material that's waterproof, soft and flexible. ....

d) A plastic that's hard and strong, and you can see through it. ....

Q2 Draw lines to match the following sentences with their correct endings.

Slate is used for making roof tiles because...

Stainless steel is used for making knives and forks because...

Rubber is used for making car tyres because...

...it lasts a long time.

...it is strong but flexible.

...it is non-toxic.

Q3 Different materials are suitable for different uses.

a) Give **one** reason why **metal** is a good material for making a **saucepan**.

....

....

b) Give **one** reason why **wood** is a good material for making a **saucepan handle**.

....

....

Q4 A new type of material has been discovered. It is **strong** and **flexible**, but **not waterproof**.

a) Circle the product that this material would be **most suitable** for making.

rain coat pyjamas shirt buttons

b) Name **one** other property the material needs to have to be suitable for making this product.

....

c) Give **one** reason why the new material is not suitable for making tents.

....

....

Properties of Metals

Q1 This table shows some of the **properties** of three different **metals**.

Metal	Heat conduction	Cost	Resistance to corrosion	Strength
1	average	high	excellent	good
2	average	medium	good	excellent
3	excellent	low	good	good

Use the information in the table to choose which metal would be **best** for making each of the following:

a) Saucepan bases ....

b) Car bodies ....

c) A statue to be placed in a town centre ....

Think about how long a statue would have to last for.

Q2 **Copper** has lots of uses.

a) Give two properties of copper that make it suitable for use in **plumbing**.

1. ....

2. ....

b) Give one property of copper that makes it useful for **electrical wiring**.

....

Q3 **Aluminium** and **titanium** are similar in some ways but different in others.

a) Complete this table to compare the properties of **aluminium** with those of **titanium**.

Property	Aluminium	Titanium
Density		
Strength	low	high
Corrosion resistance		

b) Titanium is an element found in the central block of the periodic table. What are elements in this central block called?

....

Alloys

Q1 Fill in the gaps in the text below with the words provided.

alloys	pure	properties

.... metals often aren't quite right for certain uses.
Because we know about the .... of different metals,
we can design .... to fit these uses.

Q2 Most iron is made into the alloy **steel**.

Tick the boxes to show whether the following statements are true or false.

		True	False
a)	An alloy can be a mixture of two metals.	☐	☐
b)	An alloy can't be a mixture of a metal and a non-metal.	☐	☐
c)	Steel is made by adding a small amount of carbon to iron.	☐	☐
d)	Iron straight from the blast furnace has lots of uses.	☐	☐
e)	Iron straight from the blast furnace is used as cast iron.	☐	☐

Q3 Draw lines to connect the correct phrases in each column. One has been done for you.

Metal / Alloy	**Property**
low-carbon steel	brittle
iron from a blast furnace	doesn't corrode
high-carbon steel	easily shaped
stainless steel	very hard

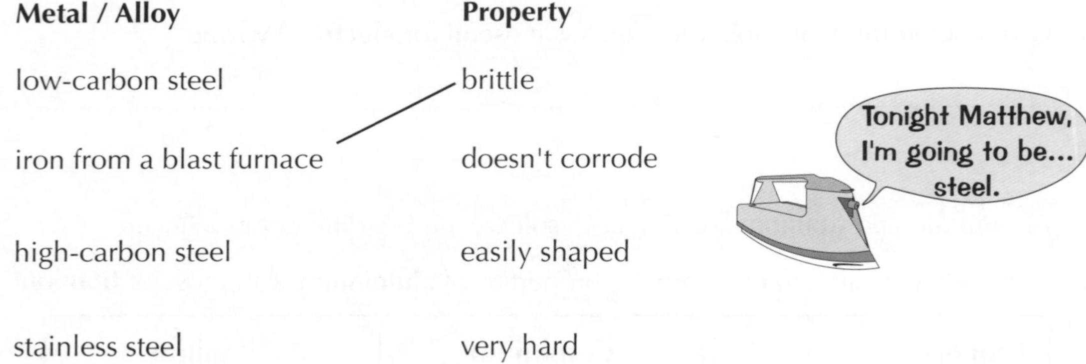
Tonight Matthew, I'm going to be... steel.

Q4 Metals such as copper, silver and nickel are sometimes added to the gold used in **jewellery**. This makes the jewellery **cheaper**.

Give **another reason** why other metals are added to gold when making jewellery.

....

Top Tips: Alloys are all about bending metals to your will and getting them to do what you want. Do the same with the examiner. Learn all about iron and its alloys, and then if you get a question on it in the exam, you'll be able to impress him. You'll be a step closer to the mark you want.

Getting Metals from Rocks

Q1 Use the words below to fill the gaps in the passage.

compounds	unreactive	ores

Some .... elements like gold are found in the Earth as the metal itself. But most metals are found as .... from which they need to be extracted. Rocks that contain enough metal to make extraction worthwhile are called ....

Q2 **Carbon** can be used to extract metals that are **below** it in the reactivity series.

a) Oxygen is removed during this process. What is this called? Circle the correct word.

oxidation **reduction** **decomposition**

b) Iron can be extracted from iron oxide using carbon in a blast furnace.
Complete the word equation for the reaction.

iron oxide + ... → .... + carbon dioxide

c) What method is used to extract metals that are above carbon in the reactivity series?

....

Q3 Imagine that three new metals, **antium**, **bodium**, and **candium** have been discovered.

Read each of the following statements about the metals.

- **Antium is the only one of the three found in the Earth as pure metal and not as a compound.**
- **Bodium cannot be extracted from its oxide by reduction with carbon.**
- **Candium can be extracted from its oxide by reduction with carbon.**

Use the information above to put the new metals in order of reactivity relative to carbon.

Getting Metals from Rocks

Q4 Use the words below to fill in the blanks to complete the paragraph.

negative	electricity	liquid

Electrolysis is used to extract metals like aluminium from their ores.

Electrolysis is breaking down a substance using ....

It requires a .... to conduct the electricity.

During electrolysis, positive ions move towards the

.... electrode.

Q5 Aluminium is extracted from aluminium oxide using electrolysis.
Why is this an **expensive** process?

....

....

Q6 The graph shows the average **cost** of extracting aluminium over a ten year period.

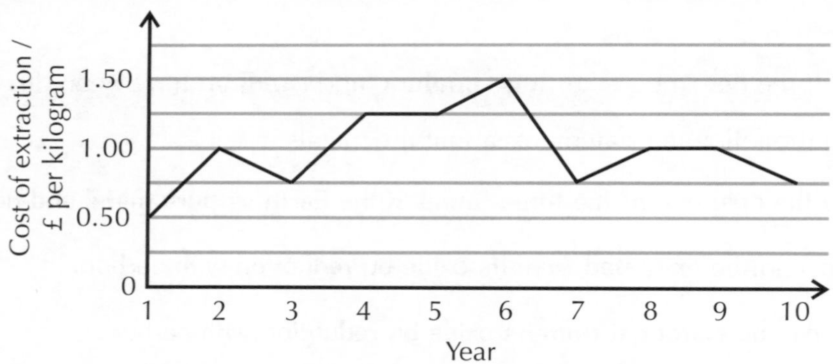

a) In which year was the cost of extracting aluminium **lowest**?

....

b) The cost of mineral extraction per kilogram is 75% of its market value.
In which year was aluminium's market value £2.00 per kilogram?

....

Top Tips: Remember that electrolysis isn't just used to extract metals like aluminium. It can also be used to purify metals. For example, copper can be extracted cheaply using carbon, but you end up with quite impure copper — so it gets purified using electrolysis. Problem sorted.

Getting Metals from Rocks

Q7 Copper can be **extracted** from a solution by **displacement**.

For example, if scrap iron is put into copper sulfate solution, you get copper and iron sulfate.

iron + copper sulfate → copper + iron sulfate

a) Why does this reaction take place?

....

b) Why would it **not** be possible to extract aluminium by reacting iron with aluminium sulfate?

....

....

The Reactivity Series	
Aluminium	Al
CARBON	C
Zinc	Zn
Iron	Fe
Tin	Sn
Copper	Cu

Q8 Copper-rich ores are in short supply.
Phytomining can be used to extract copper from the soil.

Fill in the gaps in the passage.

ash	leaves	copper

Phytomining involves growing plants in soil that contains ....

The plants can't use it so it builds up in their ....

When the plants are harvested, dried and burnt, it can be collected from the

....

Q9 Scientists are researching **alternative** methods of extracting copper.
Bioleaching is one alternative method which can be used.

a) **Explain** how bioleaching can be used to extract **copper** from copper sulfide.

....

....

....

b) Explain why alternative extraction methods, like bioleaching, are so important.

....

....

Impacts of Extracting Metals

Q1 New mines always have **social**, **economic** and **environmental** effects. Complete this table with **three** more effects that a new mine can have.

EFFECTS OF MINES
1) Services, e.g. health care may be improved because more people come to live in the area. 2) Pollution from extra traffic.

Try to include both positive and negative effects.

Q2 **Recycling** metals is important.

Explain why it's important to recycle metals rather than mining and extracting new metals.

....

....

....

....

....

....

....

Top Tips:

Mmm, baked beans on toast. Lovely. And it's one of your five a day — fancy that. You've got to wash out the tins and recycle them though. Even if it seems like a right pain, it's definitely worth the effort. In some countries it's illegal not to sort out your rubbish for recycling.

Nanotechnology

Q1 **Nanotechnology** is a branch of science that deals with **very small particles**.

a) How big are nanoparticles? Circle the correct answer.

1 – 100 nanometres **1 nanometre** **100 – 1000 nanometres**

b) Give an example of a nanoparticle that is made **naturally**.

....

c) Nanoparticles are added to the plastic that's used to make the frames of some tennis rackets. Give **two** ways that the nanoparticles improve the properties of the plastic.

1. ....

2. ....

Q2 Many people are **worried** about using products that contain **nanoparticles**.

Why might people be worried about using products that have nanoparticles in? Tick the box next to the best explanation.

- ☐ **We know that all nanoparticles are harmful to human health.**
- ☐ **We don't know what long-term effects nanoparticles might have on human health.**
- ☐ **We don't know what short-term effects nanoparticles have on human health.**

Q3 Circle the letters of the **two** statements about nanotechnology that are **true**.

A Nanoparticles have the same properties as larger particles of the same material.

B Nanoparticles have a large surface area to volume ratio. This can affect the properties of the material.

C Nanoparticles show different properties to larger particles of the same material.

D Nanoparticles have a very small surface area to volume ratio because of their small size.

Q4 Complete the statements below by circling the correct words.

a) Nanoparticles are about the same size as **grains of sand** / **molecules**.

b) Some nanoparticles are made by accident — for example, when fuels are burnt, nanoscale particles of **silver** / **soot** are produced.

c) Silver nanoparticles **can** / **can't** kill bacteria. Normal silver particles **can** / **can't** kill bacteria.

d) Silver nanoparticles are used to help make **bandages** / **golf clubs**.

Mixed Questions — Section 4

Q1 All metals have some things in common.

a) Put a tick in the correct box to show where **metals** are found on the periodic table.

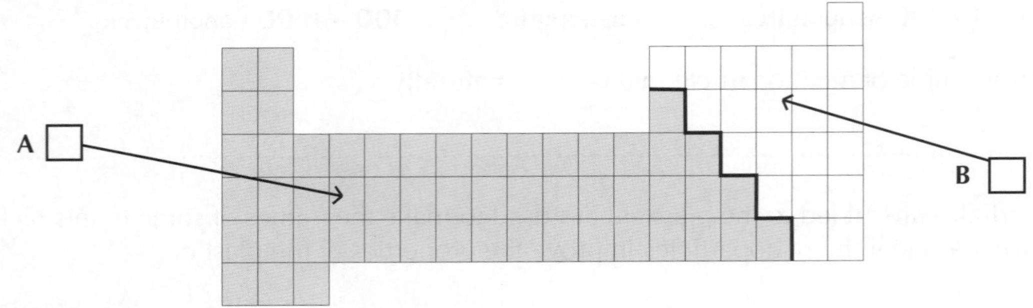

b) Read each of the following statements about metals. If the statement is **true**, tick the box.

- ☐ Metals are generally strong but also malleable.
- ☐ All metals are corrosion-resistant.
- ☐ Metals conduct electricity well.
- ☐ Generally, metals are poor conductors of heat.
- ☐ Properties of a metal can be altered by mixing it with another metal to form an alloy.

c) Look at the information in the table below. R, S, T and U are all metals.

Material	Strength	Cost/kg (£)	Density (g/cm^3)	Melting Point (°C)
R	High	100	3	1000
S	Medium	90	5	150
T	High	450	8	1200
U	Low	200	11	1070

i) Which material would be most suitable to build an **aeroplane body**? ....

ii) Explain your answer.

....

....

Q2 Calcium has an **atomic number** of 20.

a) How many electrons does calcium have? ....

b) Complete the diagram on the right to show the electronic structure of calcium.

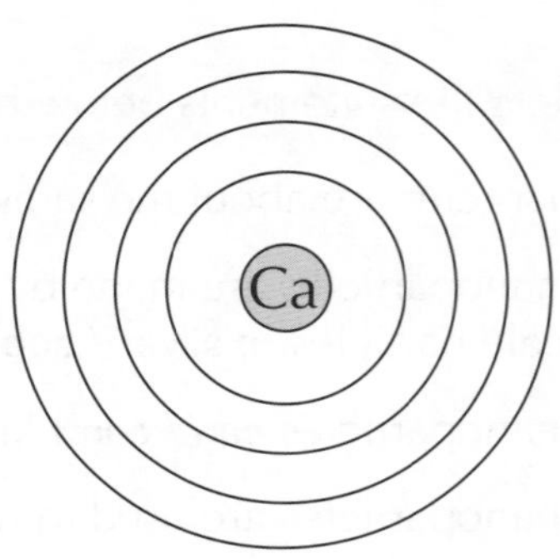

Mixed Questions — Section 4

Q3 The metals **aluminium** and **copper** can be extracted from their ores.

a) Circle the correct word in the sentence below.

There is a **limited / unlimited** amount of metals in the Earth.

b) Copper metal can be extracted from its ore by **reduction** using carbon.

i) What is done to this copper to make it pure enough to use for **electrical wiring**?

....

ii) Name **one other** metal that can be extracted from its ore by **reduction** using carbon.

....

c) **i)** One of the most common elements present in the Earth's crust is aluminium. Explain why aluminium metal can only be extracted using **electrolysis**.

....

....

ii) Name **one other** metal that can only be extracted using **electrolysis**.

....

Q4 Materials are chosen for products based on their **properties**.

a) Complete the table by picking a **material** from the list below to use in each product. Give **one property** of the material that makes it suitable for use in the product. You should only use each material **once**.

stainless steel	cotton	oak	glass	silver nanoparticles

Product	Material	Property
Frying pan		
Window		
Surgical masks		
Cushion cover		
Bookcase		

b) Tick the boxes to show whether the statements below are **true** or **false**.

	True	False
i) Tension strength is how much a material can resist a pushing force.	☐	☐
ii) Ropes need a lot of tension strength so that they don't snap.	☐	☐
iii) Nylon is good for making ropes because it has good compressive strength.	☐	☐

The Earth's Structure

Q1 The diagram shows the Earth's structure. Label the **crust**, **mantle** and **core**.

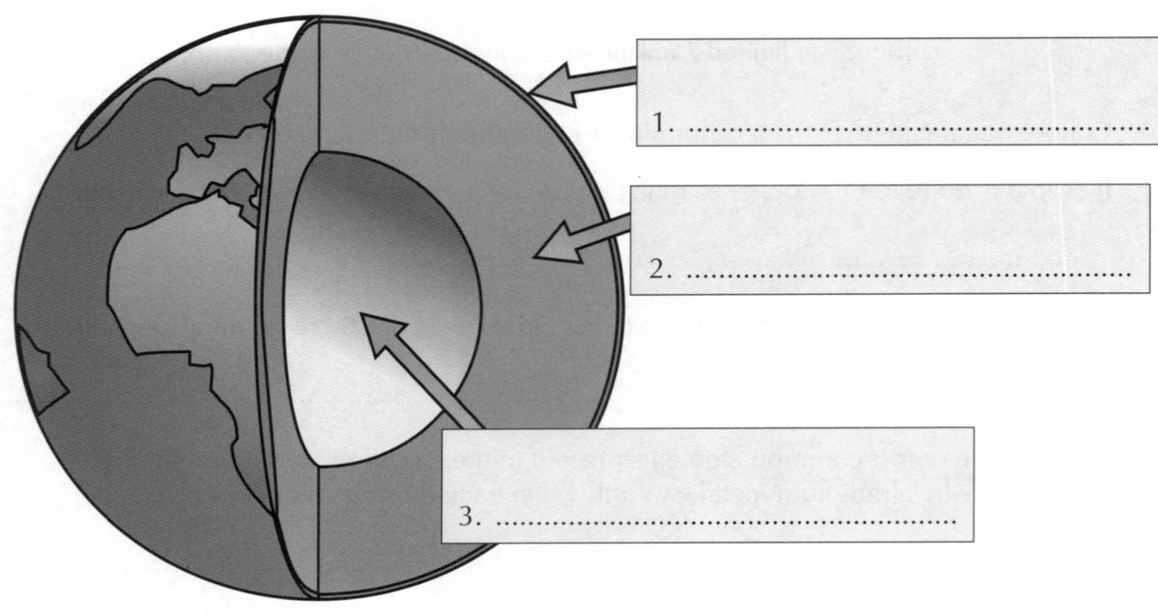

Q2 The map on the left shows where most of the world's **earthquakes** take place. The map on the right shows the **tectonic plates**.

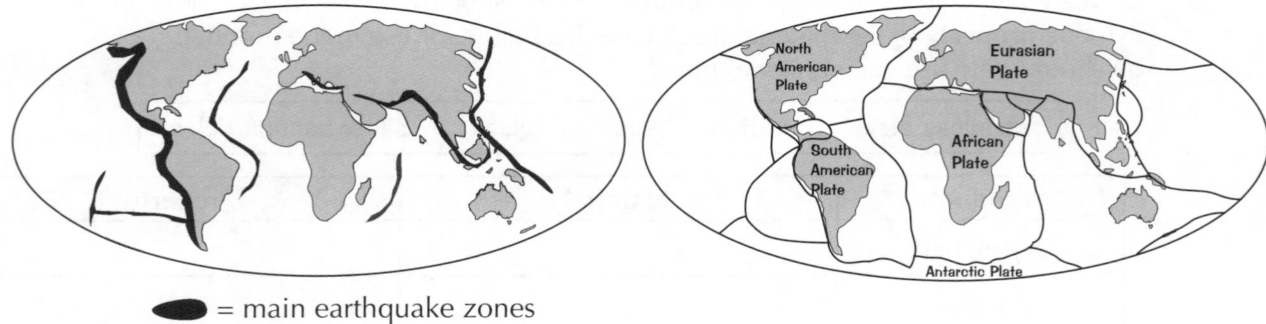

= main earthquake zones

Compare the earthquake map to the one showing the tectonic plates.
What do you notice about the main earthquake zones?

....

....

The Earth's Structure

Q3 Look at the diagram showing the boundary between two tectonic plates.

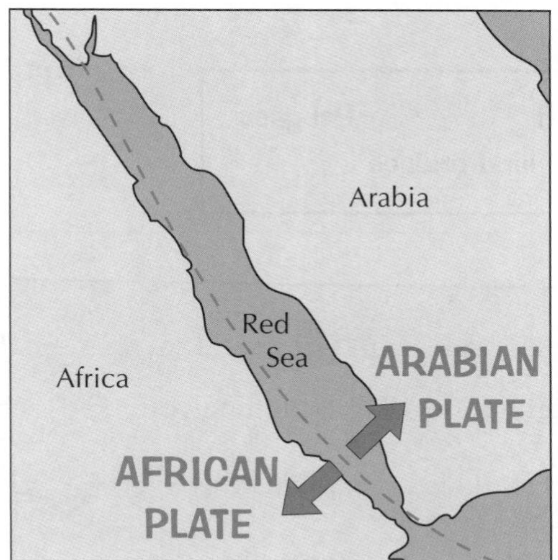

The Red Sea is widening at a speed of 1.6 cm per year.

If the sea level remains the same, how much will the Red Sea widen in 10 000 years?

....

....

Remember to include a unit in your answer.

Q4 Match up the words to their description. One has been done for you.

Crust	Hot spots that often sit on plate boundaries
Mantle	Caused by sudden movements of plates
Convection current	Caused by heat from radioactive decay in the mantle
Tectonic plates	Thinnest of the Earth's layers
Earthquakes	Large pieces of crust and upper mantle
Volcanoes	Slowly flowing, mostly solid layer that plates float on

Q5 Why is it difficult to **predict** when earthquakes are going to happen?

....

....

Top Tips: The problem with predicting earthquakes and volcanic eruptions is that it's nowhere near 100% reliable. There are likely to be shed-loads of people living near a volcano or on the boundary between two plates. It'd be impossible to evacuate them all every time scientists thought there might possibly be an eruption or an earthquake some time soon. It just wouldn't work.

Plate Tectonics

Q1 Below is a letter that Alfred Wegener might have written to a newspaper explaining his ideas. Use the words in the box below to fill in the gaps.

fossils	continental drift	Pangaea
spinning	land bridges	

Dear Mr Schmidt,

I must reply to your very incorrect article of March 23rd 1915 by telling you about my theory of .... Finally I can explain why the .... of plants and animals found on opposite sides of the Atlantic Ocean are almost the same. The idea that there were once .... between these continents is complete rubbish.

I propose that South America and Africa were once part of a much larger land mass. I have named this .... This supercontinent has slowly been drifting apart over millions of years. The pieces are being pushed by tidal forces and by the Earth ....

I will soon be writing a full report of my scientific findings.

Yours faithfully,

A Wegener

Q2 Tick the boxes to show whether the following statements are true or false.

	True	False
The Earth's continents seem to fit together like a big jigsaw.	☐	☐
Some rock layers are the same on different continents.	☐	☐
Most scientists immediately agreed with Wegener's ideas.	☐	☐
Investigations of the ocean floor showed that although Wegener wasn't absolutely right, his ideas were pretty close.	☐	☐

The Three Different Types of Rock

Q1 Join up each **rock type** with how they're **formed** and an **example**.

ROCK TYPE	HOW IT'S FORMED	EXAMPLE
igneous rocks	formed from layers of sediment	granite
metamorphic rocks	formed when magma cools	limestone
sedimentary rocks	formed under intense heat and pressure	marble

Q2 Circle the correct words to complete the passage below.

Igneous rock is formed when magma pushes up into (or through) the **crust / mantle** and **heats up / cools**. Igneous rocks are made of crystals. The **size / colour** of these crystals depends on how quickly the magma has **cooled / heated up**.

Q3 Erica notices that the walls of her local church contain a few **fossils**.

a) Which of the following rocks is it likely that the church is built from? Circle your answer.

Limestone **Marble** **Granite**

b) Explain your answer.

....

Q4 True or false? Tick the correct box.

	True	False
a) Sedimentary rocks only take ten years to form.	☐	☐
b) Chalk is an igneous rock.	☐	☐
c) Limestone can be turned into a different type of rock in a natural process.	☐	☐
d) Sedimentary rocks are not eroded easily compared to other rocks.	☐	☐
e) The shape of our landscape is changing because of erosion.	☐	☐

Top Tips: You might think that rocks are just boring lumps of... rock. But you'd be wrong — rocks are actually boring lumps of different kinds of rock. And the kind of rock they are depends on how they're formed — and this is the stuff you need to make sure you know.

Using Limestone

Q1 What compound is **limestone** mainly made of?

....

Q2 **Carbonates** break down when heated to form two products.

a) i) Name the two products formed when limestone is heated.

1. ....

2. ....

ii) What type of reaction is this? Circle the correct answer.

neutralisation **thermal decomposition** **cracking**

b) True or false? Tick the boxes to show your answers.

	True	False
i) Magnesium carbonate doesn't break down when heated.	☐	☐
ii) A Bunsen burner isn't hot enough to make all of the Group 1 carbonates break down.	☐	☐

Q3 The hills of Northern England are dotted with the remains of **lime kilns**. Farmers used these kilns to heat **limestone** to make calcium oxide.

a) Write a word equation for the reaction that takes place in a lime kiln.

....

b) Calcium oxide reacts with water to make calcium hydroxide. Calcium hydroxide is an **alkali**. Suggest what farmers use calcium hydroxide for.

....

c) When calcium hydroxide is added to water, it makes a solution called limewater.

i) What gas do chemists use limewater to test for?

....

ii) What happens to the limewater if this gas is present?

....

Top Tips: If you're asked for a word equation, make sure you use the correct chemical names of the reactant and products. And remember — the reactants (what you start off with) come before the arrow. The products (what you end up with) come after the arrow.

Using Limestone

Q4 Use the words below to fill the gaps in the passage.

mortar	limestone	concrete

Heating .... with clay in a kiln makes cement. Cement can be mixed with sand and water to make .... which is used to stick bricks together. When cement is mixed with aggregate and sand it makes .... which is a very common building material.

Q5 When a carbonate reacts with an acid a **salt** is formed.

a) Complete the **word equation** below to show all the products formed when a metal carbonate reacts with an acid.

metal carbonate + **acid** → **salt** + ... + ...

b) Write the **word equation** for the reaction between **magnesium carbonate** and **sulfuric acid**.

....

c) Name **two other** carbonates which will react with an acid.

1. ....

2. ....

d) Explain why **limestone buildings** are damaged by acid rain.

Think about what limestone is made of.

....

....

Q6 Limestone quarries can cause some **problems** but they have **advantages** too.

a) Give **two problems** that are caused by quarrying limestone.

1. ....

2. ....

b) Give two ways that quarries can benefit local communities.

1. ....

2. ....

Salt

Q1 Tick the boxes to show whether the following statements are **true** or **false**.

		True	False
a)	Salt is only found underground.	☐	☐
b)	There are no deposits of rock salt in Cheshire.	☐	☐
c)	Salt can be mined by pumping hot water underground.	☐	☐
d)	The holes left by mining salt must be filled in, or they could cause subsidence.	☐	☐
e)	Salt is used as a preservative and a flavouring.	☐	☐

Q2 **Circle** the correct answer for the question below.

What two products of the electrolysis of brine are used to make bleach?

Chlorine and hydrogen. **Hydrogen and sodium hydroxide.** **Chlorine and sodium hydroxide.**

Q3 The diagram shows the **industrial set-up** used to electrolyse concentrated brine.

a) i) Which electrode is hydrogen formed at: **positive** or **negative**? ....

ii) Which electrode is chlorine formed at: **positive** or **negative**? ....

b) Why are inert electrodes used?

....

....

c) Identify the substances labelled A, B and C on the diagram. Choose from the options in the box below.

Cl_2	H_2	brine

A .... B .... C ....

Q4 Salt is a source of **chlorine**, **hydrogen** and **sodium hydroxide**. Match up these chemicals with the products they are used to make.

margarine

soap

used to sterilise water

Chlorine

Sodium hydroxide

Hydrogen

plastics such as PVC

solvents

Salt in the Food Industry

Q1 Salt is used a lot in the food industry.
Why might salt be added to food? Tick **two** correct statements.

- It's used as a preservative. ☐
- It's used to add colour. ☐
- It's used to improve the flavour. ☐
- It's used to help mix foods. ☐

A preservative helps food to last longer.

Q2 It is recommended that adults should eat no more than **6 g** of salt each day.

a) Your friend thinks that there is no way that she can be eating too much salt as she never sprinkles any on her food. Explain why she is wrong.

....

b) She eats a sandwich that contains 1.2 g of salt and a pizza that has 4.4 g.
How much more salt could she eat without going over the recommended amount?

....

....

Q3 Eating too much salt can affect your **health**.

a) Eating too much salt could increase the chance of getting which **three** health problems?
Circle the correct answers.

high blood pressure **Parkinson's disease** **mouth cancer**

osteoporosis **strokes** **glandular fever**

b) Give one reason why food manufacturers may still put lots of salt in their products even though it may be unhealthy.

....

....

Q4 The Department of Health and the Department for Environment, Food and Rural Affairs play a role in public health. State **two** of their jobs.

1. ....

2. ....

Top Tips: Salted peanuts are my favourite. Mmmmmmmm, once I have one I can't stop. But too much salt is bad for you so I always eat peanuts with chopsticks. Then I can't eat whole handfuls in one go. I think the Department of Health said about it once in a pamphlet.

Chlorination

Q1 Complete the passage below using the following words.

algae drinking water kills microorganisms chlorine chlorination smells

In the UK .... is used to treat the ....

This process is called .... This has benefited public health

because it .... disease-causing .... It also stops

.... growing and gets rid of bad tastes and ....

Q2 **Chlorine** can be produced by **electrolysing brine** (sodium chloride solution).

a) Suggest **one** other way of producing chlorine.

....

b) Explain why adding sodium chloride to water does not kill microorganisms.

....

....

Q3 The graph below shows how the number of cases of the disease typhoid has changed over the last 100 years in Unwelland.

a) Describe what happened when chlorination was introduced.

....

....

....

b) Explain your answer to part **a)**.

....

....

....

c) Give **one** possible health problem caused by using chlorine to treat water.

....

....

Impacts of Chemical Production

Q1 **PVC** is a material that is used in lots of different products.

a) Circle the **three** elements that PVC is made of from the list below.

carbon   phosphorus   hydrogen   chlorine   vanadium   oxygen

b) Plasticisers are often added to PVC to improve its properties.

Describe **one problem** caused by using plasticisers.

....

....

Q2 Pollutants from the chemical industry can get into **food chains** like the one shown below.

Algae → Water louse → Dragonfly nymph → Water shrew → Kestrel

a) If the stream is polluted by a chemical the kestrels are likely to suffer the most.
Why is this? Circle the correct answer below.

The kestrels live longer.

The kestrels can feed from lots of different areas.

The amount of chemical in each animal increases as you go along the food chain.

b) Which other organism(s) in the food chain could suffer?

....

Q3 Mark is investigating the safety of the plastics and components used to make computer monitors. His friend Emma tells him that there's **no risk** to the environment or human health from any of the components in the monitors because they will have all been tested.

Do you think Emma is correct? Explain your answer.

....

....

....

Hazard Symbols, Acids and Alkalis

Q1 Draw lines to match the **symbols** below with their **meanings** and **hazards**.

	Symbol	Meaning	Hazard
a)		toxic	can cause death if swallowed, breathed in, or if it seeps through the skin
b)	Xi	corrosive	causes reddening or blistering of the skin
c)		irritant	provides oxygen which allows other materials to burn more strongly
d)		harmful	damages living tissue, like eyes and skin
e)	Xh	oxidising	like toxic, but not quite as dangerous

Q2 Use the words in the box below to complete the following sentences about **acids** and **alkalis**.

7	base	acid	water	acidic

a) Solutions which are not alkaline or neutral are said to be ....

b) A substance with a pH less than 7 is called an ....

c) A substance with a pH more than 7 is called a ....

d) An alkali is a base that dissolves in ....

e) The pH of pure water is ....

Q3 Draw lines to match the **pH** value to the **acid/alkali strength**.

pH	5/6	8/9	14	7	1
ACID/ALKALI STRENGTH	strong alkali	weak alkali	weak acid	neutral	strong acid

Reactions of Acids

Q1 **Acids** react with **metal oxides** and **metal hydroxides** to form a salt and water. Use the words below each reaction to complete the word equations.

a) hydrochloric acid + lead oxide → .... chloride + water

oxygen lead hydrogen

b) hydrochloric acid + ... oxide → nickel .... + water

nickel chloride hydride

ACID

Q2 a) Put a tick in the box next to any of the sentences below that are **true**.

i) Metal oxides and metal hydroxides neutralise bases. ☐

ii) Acids react with metal oxides to form a salt and water. ☐

iii) Hydrogen gas is formed when an acid reacts with an alkali. ☐

iv) Salts and water are formed when acids react with metal hydroxides. ☐

v) Sodium hydroxide is an acid that dissolves in water. ☐

b) Use the chemicals below to write **word equations** for the following reactions.

sulfuric acid | water | sodium chloride | hydrochloric acid | copper oxide | copper sulfate | water | sodium hydroxide

i) The reaction between hydrochloric acid and sodium hydroxide.

....

ii) The reaction between sulfuric acid and copper oxide.

....

Q3 Ant stings hurt because of the **acid** they release. The pH values of some household substances are given in the table.

Substance	pH
lemon juice	4
baking soda	9
caustic soda	14
soap powder	11

a) Simon has been stung by an ant. Suggest a substance from the list that he could use to make it less painful.

....

It's dangerous to put a strong acid or alkali onto the skin.

b) Explain your answer.

....

....

....

Reactions of Acids

Q4 One type of **neutralisation** reaction is the reaction between an **acid** and a **metal oxide**.

a) Complete the general equation for the reaction between a metal oxide and an acid.

ACID + METAL OXIDE → .... + ...

b) Which combination of substances would react in this way?
Choose the correct answer from the options below. Tick **one** box.

Magnesium and sulfuric acid. ☐

Sodium hydroxide and water. ☐

Copper oxide and hydrochloric acid. ☐

Q5 Metal oxides and metal hydroxides are bases. Circle the **bases** in the list of compounds below.

copper sulfate

copper oxide

lead hydroxide

sodium chloride

hydrogen chloride

tin oxide

lead sulfide

potassium hydroxide

carbon dioxide

Q6 **Acids** react with **metal carbonates** in neutralisation reactions.

a) Use the words below each reaction to complete the word equations.

i) sulfuric acid + ... carbonate →

copper .... + water + ...

copper sulfate carbon dioxide

ii) .... acid + potassium .... →

.... chloride + ... + carbon dioxide

potassium hydrochloric carbonate water

b) Complete this word equation for the reaction of sulfuric acid with lithium carbonate:

sulfuric acid + lithium carbonate → .... + ...+ ....

Top Tips: Well take my socks off and paint me blue — that's a lot of equations.
But don't forget, if you can remember the different products of neutralisation reactions you can work 'em all out. Just take the name of the metal and add it to the first bit of the acid. The clues are all there...

The Evolution of the Atmosphere

Q1 Tick the boxes to show whether these sentences are **true** or **false**.

		True	False
a)	During the first billion years, lots of volcanoes were erupting.	☐	☐
b)	The Earth's early atmosphere is thought to have been mostly oxygen.	☐	☐
c)	The Earth's early atmosphere was like the atmospheres of Mars and Venus today.	☐	☐
d)	When plants died and were buried, the carbon they had removed from the atmosphere became locked up as fossil fuels.	☐	☐

Q2 Draw lines to put the statements in the **right order** on the timeline. One is done for you.

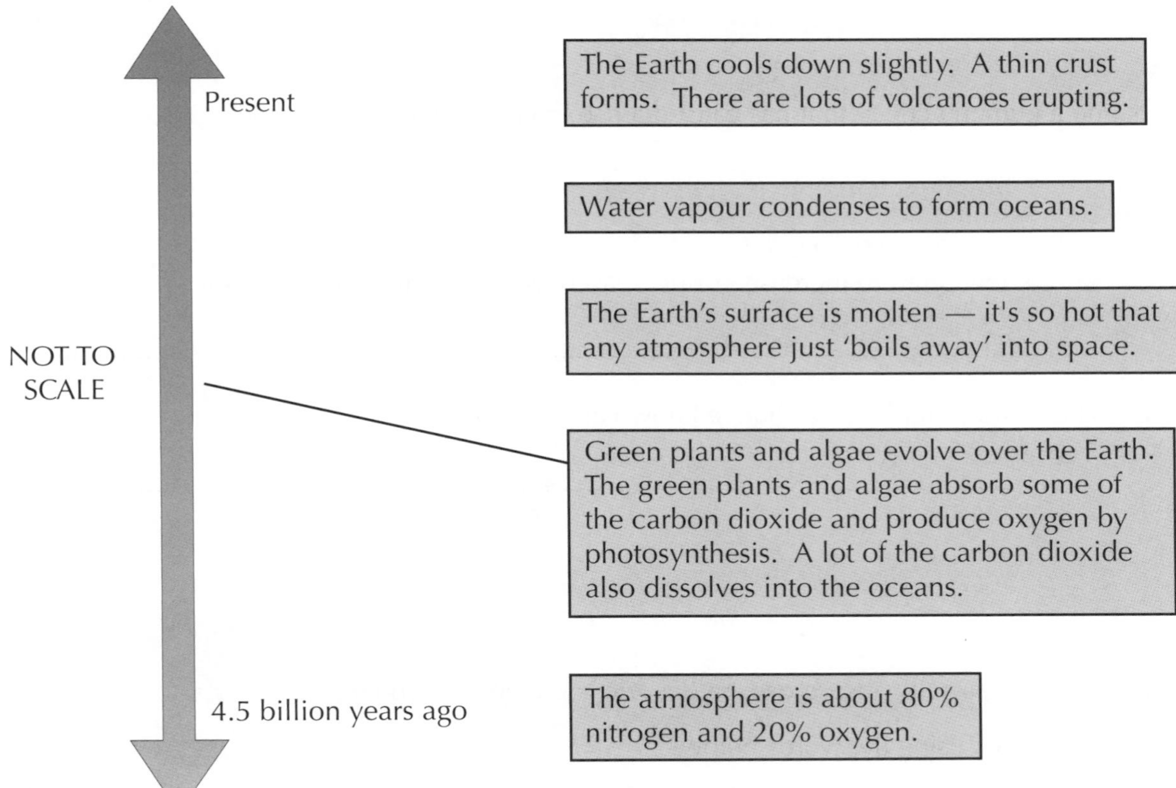

Present
NOT TO SCALE
4.5 billion years ago
The Earth cools down slightly. A thin crust forms. There are lots of volcanoes erupting.
Water vapour condenses to form oceans.
The Earth's surface is molten — it's so hot that any atmosphere just 'boils away' into space.
Green plants and algae evolve over the Earth. The green plants and algae absorb some of the carbon dioxide and produce oxygen by photosynthesis. A lot of the carbon dioxide also dissolves into the oceans.
The atmosphere is about 80% nitrogen and 20% oxygen.

Q3 This pie chart shows the proportions of different gases in the **Earth's atmosphere today**.

Add the labels:

Nitrogen

Oxygen

Carbon dioxide and other gases

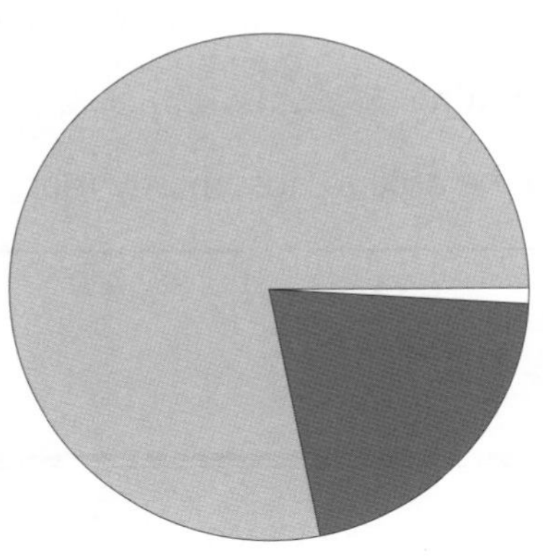

The Evolution of the Atmosphere

Q4 The graphs below show the changes in the atmospheric carbon dioxide level and temperature since 1850.

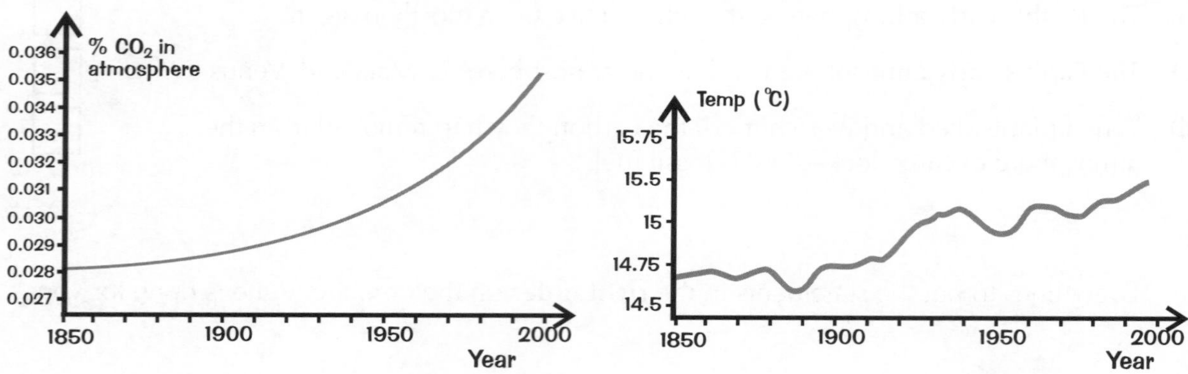

a) Name a human activity that has caused a rise in carbon dioxide over the last 150 years.

....

b) **i)** Look at the temperature graph.
Has the temperature increased or decreased as carbon dioxide has risen?

....

ii) What is this temperature change known as?

....

Q5 The **oceans** naturally absorb carbon dioxide from the atmosphere.

Fill in the gaps using the words below.

acidic	coral	carbon dioxide

The extra carbon dioxide we're releasing is making the oceans too ....
This is putting .... and shellfish in danger. It also means that the oceans may not be able to absorb any more .... in the future.

Top Tips: Like your teacher's fashion sense, the atmosphere took its time over evolving. You can't rush these things. What a result though. We don't want to go messing it up, so it's worth thinking carefully about how our actions might change the atmosphere in the future.

Mixed Questions — Section 5

Q1 **Calcium carbonate** in the form of the rock **limestone**, is one of the most important raw materials for the chemical and construction industries.

a) Calcium carbonate can be processed to make calcium hydroxide.

i) Complete the flow diagram to show how calcium carbonate can be processed.

ii) Give one use of calcium hydroxide.

....

b) Limestone can be processed to form useful building materials. Complete the flow diagram.

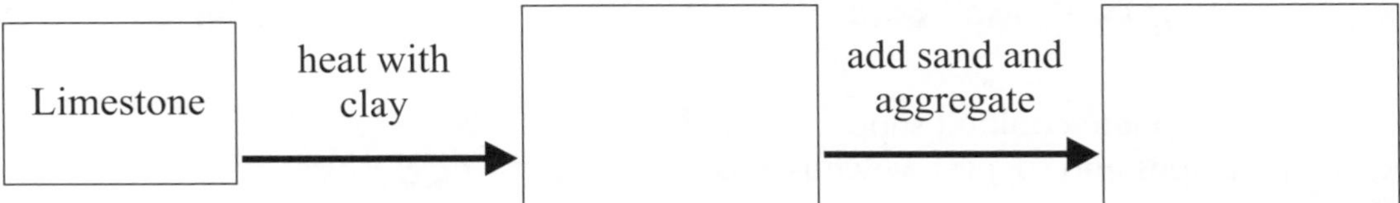

c) Limestone is also used in the manufacture of mortar.
Name the other main ingredients of mortar.

1. ....

2. ....

Q2 People used to think that the Earth's surface was all one piece.
Today, we think it's made up of **separate plates** of rock.

a) Fill in the gaps with the words below.

tectonic plates	surface	tidal forces	convection currents	evidence

Wegener challenged what people believed about the Earth's ....
He had discovered .... that showed the Earth's surface is made up of .... He thought that these were moving around because of .... and the Earth's spinning. We now think that they move around because of ....

b) Name **two** kinds of natural disasters that can occur where plates meet.

.... and ....

Mixed Questions — Section 5

Q3 The graphs below give information about the Earth's atmosphere millions of years ago and today.

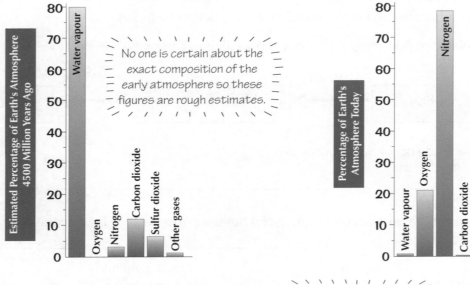

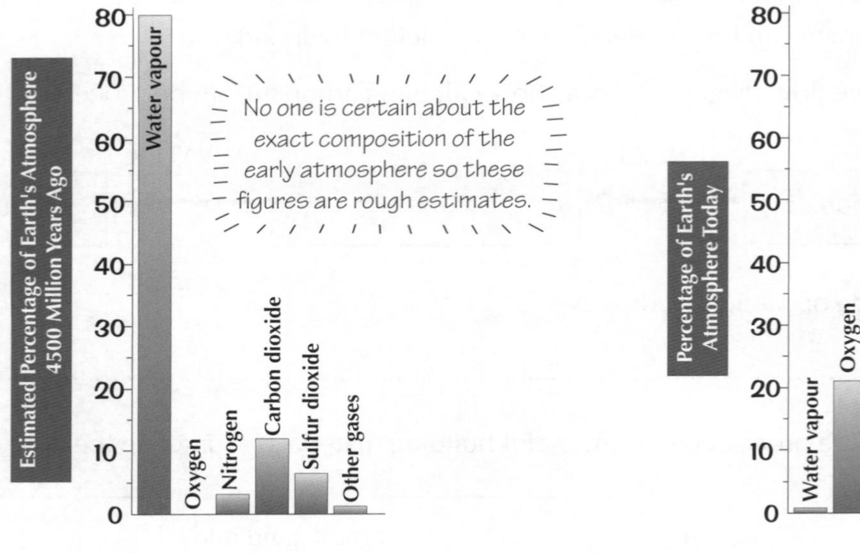

a) The early atmosphere couldn't support animal life. Look at the graphs and suggest why this was.

Think about which gas animals need to survive.

....

b) **i)** Which **organisms** caused an increase in oxygen and a decrease in carbon dioxide?

....

ii) What else caused a decrease in carbon dioxide?

....

Q4 Chlorine, hydrogen and sodium hydroxide are produced by **electrolysing brine**.

a) Place each of the uses listed below into the correct box to show whether it is a use of chlorine, hydrogen or sodium hydroxide. Some uses may belong in more than one box.

PVC soap solvents margarine disinfecting water bleach

CHLORINE
HYDROGEN
SODIUM HYDROXIDE

b) Use the words below to answer the following questions.

nitrogen chlorine hydrogen potassium

i) What is produced at the positive electrode during the electrolysis of brine? ....

ii) What is produced at the negative electrode during the electrolysis of brine? ....

Fractional Distillation of Crude Oil

Q1 Circle the correct words to complete these sentences.

a) Crude oil is a **mixture / compound** of different molecules.

b) Most of the compounds in crude oil are **carbohydrate / hydrocarbon** molecules.

c) The molecules in crude oil **are / aren't** chemically bonded to each other.

d) Physical methods **can / can't** be used to separate out the molecules in crude oil.

Q2 **Fractional distillation** is used to separate crude oil into fractions.

Labels A-C in the box below describe how crude oil is split up by fractional distillation.
Put the letters in the correct boxes on the diagram.

A the different fractions condense and are collected

B crude oil is piped into the column

C the oil evaporates and rises up the column

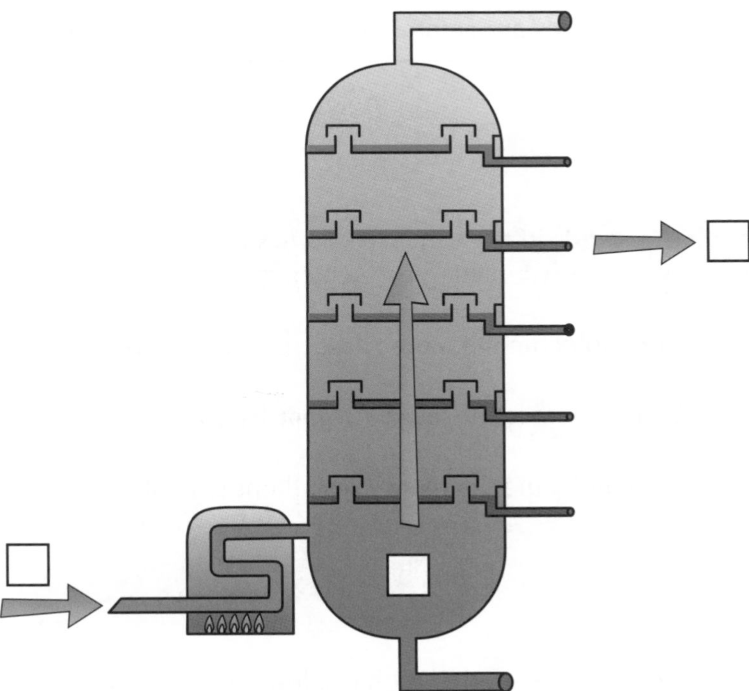

Q3 Each crude oil **fraction** contains molecules with **similar condensing** (or boiling) points.

What else is similar about molecules in the same fraction?

....

Properties and Uses of Crude Oil

Q1 **Crude oil** is a mixture of **hydrocarbons**. These **hydrocarbons** are mostly **alkanes**.

a) Alkanes have a **general formula**. Tick the box next to the correct formula below.

☐ C_nH_{2n} ☐ C_nH_{2n+2} ☐ C_nH_{2n+4}

b) Below is the structure of the first alkane, methane.
Draw the structures of the next two alkanes and name them.

1.

```
    H
    |
H — C — H
    |
    H
```

methane

2. ....

3. ....

c) Circle the correct word in the sentence below.

Alkanes are **saturated / unsaturated** hydrocarbons.

Q2 There are some basic **trends** in the way that **alkanes** behave.
Circle the correct words to complete these sentences.

a) The longer the alkane molecule the **more / less** viscous (gloopy) it is.

b) The shorter the alkane molecule the **lower / higher** its boiling point.

c) The shorter the alkane molecule the **more / less** flammable it is.

Q3 Each hydrocarbon molecule in engine oil has a **long** string of carbon atoms.

Engines get very **hot** when they are in use. Why would hydrocarbon molecules with short carbon chains be unsuitable for use in engine oil?

....

....

Cracking Crude Oil

Q1 Fill in the gaps with the words below.

high	shorter	long	catalyst	cracking	diesel	molecules	petrol

There is more need for .... chain fractions of crude oil such as .... than for longer chains such as ....

Heating .... hydrocarbon molecules to .... temperatures with a .... breaks them down into smaller .... This is called ....

Q2 Long-chain hydrocarbons are often **cracked** to produce products that are more useful.

a) What are some of the products of cracking used as?

....

b) Circle the correct word(s) in the sentence below.

Cracking is a **thermal decomposition / displacement** reaction.

Q3 Change this diagram into a **word equation**.

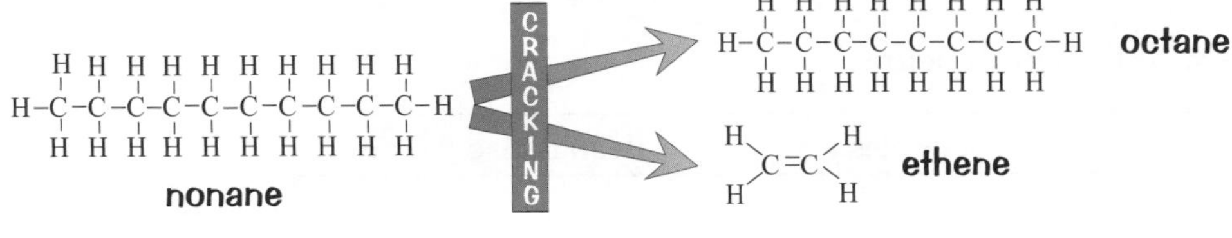

Word equation: .... → .... + ...

Q4 Put the steps of the **cracking process** in the correct order by numbering the boxes 1-4.

- [ ] The vapour is passed over a catalyst at a high temperature.
- [ ] The long-chain molecules are heated.
- [ ] The molecules are cracked on the surface of the catalyst.
- [ ] They are vaporised (turned into a gas).

Alkenes and Ethanol

Q1 Alkenes have a **general formula**. Tick the box next to the correct formula below.

☐ C_nH_{2n+2} ☐ C_nH_{2n} ☐ $C_{2n}H_{4n}$

Q2 Complete this table showing the names and formulas of some alkenes.

Name of alkene	Formula	Displayed formula
Ethene	**a)**	**b)**
c)	C_3H_6	H₂C=C(H)–C(H)(H)–H: $H_2C{=}CH{-}CH_3$

The displayed formula just shows how all the atoms are arranged.

Q3 You can test for alkenes by adding them to **bromine water**.

Fill in the gaps with the words below.

orange	colourless	decolourise

An alkene will .... the bromine water, turning it from .... to ....

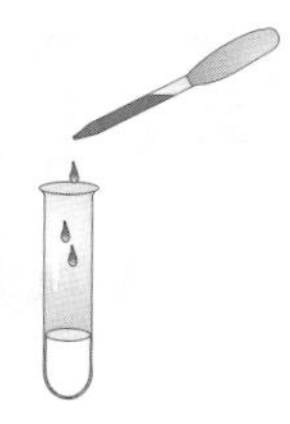

Q4 Tick the box to show which sentences are true or false.

		True	False
a)	Alkenes have double bonds between the hydrogen atoms.	☐	☐
b)	Alkenes are unsaturated.	☐	☐
c)	Ethene is useful for making ethanol.	☐	☐
d)	Ethene has three carbon atoms.	☐	☐

Alkenes and Ethanol

Q5 There are two ways of making ethanol:

Method A	Sugar → ethanol + carbon dioxide
Method B	Ethene + steam → ethanol

a) Which one of the methods describes making ethanol by **fermentation**? ....

b) Draw lines to match up the boxes.

Method A	Uses a catalyst
Method B	Uses yeast

c) Ethanol can be used as a fuel. In some countries the fermentation method is often used to produce it. Give two advantages of this method.

1. ....

2. ....

d) Give two disadvantages of the fermentation method.

1. ....

....

2. ....

....

Think about what still needs to be done to ethanol produced this way.

Q6 Ethene comes from crude oil.

Explain why making ethanol from ethene could be a problem in the future.

....

....

Top Tips: It's a cracking idea getting alkenes from crude oil because they're pretty useful for making things, like ethanol. You probably wouldn't want to drink the ethanol you get from reacting ethene with steam though. On the other hand, the ethanol you get from fermenting sugar is good for anything from your old man's pint to fuelling his car.

Burning Fuels

Q1 Answer the following questions about **burning hydrocarbons**.

a) Complete the **word equation** for the complete combustion of a hydrocarbon.

hydrocarbon + oxygen → .... + ...

b) Circle the correct words from each pair in the sentences below.

When a hydrocarbon is burnt, the carbon and hydrogen are **oxidised / reduced.**

The reaction **gives out / takes in** energy.

If there is not enough **carbon / oxygen** it is called partial combustion.

Q2 When **choosing** a fuel there are a number of things that you need to think about. Give three things that are important when choosing a fuel to be used in a car engine.

1. ....

2. ....

3. ....

Q3 **Partial combustion** can cause problems.

a) Fill in the blanks to complete the **word equation** for the partial combustion of a hydrocarbon. Use the words in the box below.

carbon monoxide	oxygen	carbon

hydrocarbon + ... →

water + carbon dioxide + ... + ...

b) Why is it dangerous if partial combustion takes place in household gas appliances?

....

....

c) Why is partial combustion messy?

....

....

Using Crude Oil as a Fuel

Q1 Use the words below to fill the gaps in the passage.

fractions	non-renewable	industry	renewable

Crude oil .... make good fuels. So extracting crude oil is a massive .... But crude oil is .... and will one day run out. Some people think we should start using .... alternatives to crude oil.

Q2 Complete the table to show some of the **environmental problems** caused by **burning** crude oil as a fuel and by **transporting** it across the sea in tankers.

Burning	Transporting crude oil across the sea in tankers

Q3 There are some **alternatives** to crude oil.

a) List three alternative ways to generate energy that **don't** rely on crude oil.

1. ....

2. ....

3. ....

b) Why do you think that crude oil is the most common source of fuel even though alternatives exist?

....

....

....

Environmental Problems

Q1 Draw lines to link the correct parts of these sentences.

In clouds sulfur dioxide reacts with water to make	acid rain.
Acid rain kills trees and	sulfuric acid.
Sulfur dioxide is produced by burning fuels which contain	makes lakes acidic
Limestone buildings and statues are affected by	sulfur dioxide.
The main cause of acid rain is	sulfur.

Q2 Give **two** ways that the amount of **acid rain** can be reduced.

Think about what can be done both before and after fuel is burnt.

1. ....

....

2. ....

....

Q3 Tick the boxes to indicate whether each statement is **true** or **false**.

		True	False
a)	When hydrocarbons are burnt, the carbon and oxygen are oxidised.	☐	☐
b)	Particles are sometimes released when fossil fuels undergo partial combustion.	☐	☐
c)	Oxides of nitrogen form if a fuel burns at low temperatures.	☐	☐
d)	Soot forms if a fuel contains sulfur.	☐	☐

Q4 Circle the correct words in the sentence below.

Global dimming is caused by **particles of soot and ash / carbon dioxide.**

Carbon Dioxide in the Atmosphere

Q1 Look at the graph and then answer the questions below.

% CO_2 in atmosphere
0.036
0.035
0.034
0.033
0.032
0.031
0.030
0.029
0.028
0.027
Year
1700 1750 1800 1850 1900 1950 2000

a) Describe the trend shown by the graph.

....

....

....

....

....

b) Give a cause of this trend.

....

c) What effect is the trend shown in the graph having on the Earth's average temperature?

....

Q2 **Carbon dioxide** and **methane** are two gases in the atmosphere which help to keep the Earth **warm**.

a) Which of A, B, C and D best explains how carbon dioxide and methane help to keep the Earth warm? Circle your answer.

A They absorb heat from the Sun.

B They stop the polar ice caps from melting.

C They stop heat escaping from the Earth.

D They cancel out acid rain.

b) Explain how you add to the amount of carbon dioxide in the atmosphere if you are driven to school in a car instead of walking.

....

Q3 Tick the boxes to show whether the following statements are **true** or **false**.

		True	False
a)	Oxygen is released when trees are burnt to clear the land.	☐	☐
b)	Living trees remove carbon dioxide from the atmosphere during photosynthesis.	☐	☐
c)	Chopping down trees helps to reduce carbon dioxide level.	☐	☐
d)	Rainfall patterns could be changed by the increasing carbon dioxide level.	☐	☐

Reducing Carbon Dioxide in the Atmosphere

Q1 Scientists are researching new ways to **remove** carbon dioxide from the atmosphere.

Use the words below to fill the gaps in the passage.

phytoplankton	poisonous	photosynthesis	seeding	ocean

Iron .... involves adding iron to the .... to make more .... grow there. These plants remove carbon dioxide from the atmosphere during .... But, there's no way of controlling which plants grow — some are ....

Q2 **Hydrogen** is often talked about as the 'fuel of the future'.

a) What is the **only product** produced when **hydrogen** is burned?

....

b) Give **one** reason why it is better for the **environment** if we burn hydrogen rather than petrol.

....

....

c) Give three problems with using hydrogen to power vehicles.

1. ....

2. ....

3. ....

Think about storage of hydrogen, where it comes from and the costs involved.

Q3 Use the words below to fill the gaps in the passage about **ethanol**.

carbon neutral	plant material	engines	water	land

Ethanol can be produced from .... and used as a fuel. It is said to be .... because the carbon dioxide produced by burning it was taken in by the plants as they grew. The only other product of burning ethanol is .... There are disadvantages of using ethanol as a fuel. For example, growing the crops to make it takes up .... needed to grow food. Also, ... need to be converted to run on ethanol.

Using Alkenes to Make Polymers

Q1 Tick the box next to the **true** statement below.

☐ The monomer of poly(ethene) is ethene.

☐ The polymer of poly(ethene) is ethane.

☐ The monomer of poly(ethene) is ethane.

We bring you gold, frankincense...
and poly-myrrh

Q2 Polymers have many uses, for example, in LYCRA® fibre for tights.

Give three other uses of polymers.

1. ....

2. ....

3. ....

Q3 Most polymers are **not** biodegradable.

Fill in the gaps with the words below.

reuse	expensive	rot	landfill	crude oil

Polymers that aren't biodegradable won't ....
This means it's difficult to get rid of them — they stay in .... sites for years and years. The best thing to do is to .... them as many times as possible and then recycle them. As .... gets used up, it will get more expensive. This means that polymers will get more ....

Top Tips: It's amazingly easy to name polymers. You just take the name of the monomer (the little molecules that are joined together) stick it in brackets, and write the word 'poly' in front of it. And Bob's your uncle (except if his name's Mike or anything else that's not Bob).

Using Alkenes to Make Polymers

Q4 Plastic bags made just from polymers don't biodegrade.

Circle the correct word(s) in the sentence below.

New biodegradable plastics are being made by adding **crude oil / cornstarch** to polymers.

Q5 Draw lines between the boxes to join the process to the correct descriptions of it.

Turns longer molecules into shorter ones.

Cracking

Turns alkenes into polymers.

Polymerisation

Turns shorter molecules into longer ones.

Splits less useful crude oil fractions into alkenes.

Q6 The equation below shows molecules of ethene joining to form **poly(ethene)**.

$$n\left(\begin{matrix} H & & H \\ | & & | \\ C & = & C \\ | & & | \\ H & & H \end{matrix}\right) \longrightarrow \left(\begin{matrix} H & & H \\ | & & | \\ -C & - & C- \\ | & & | \\ H & & H \end{matrix}\right)_n$$

many ethene molecules → **poly(ethene)**

Draw a similar equation in the box below to show propene (C_3H_6) molecules joining together to make poly(propene).

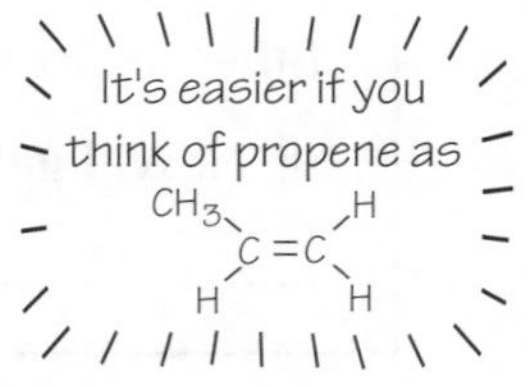

It's easier if you
think of propene as
CH_3 H
C = C
H H

Structure and Properties of Polymers

Q1 Tick the boxes to show whether the statements are **true** or **false**.

		True	False
a)	What a polymer is used for depends on its properties.	☐	☐
b)	The properties a polymer has depends only on what chemicals it's made from.	☐	☐
c)	A high density polymer has chains that are very spread out.	☐	☐
d)	You can change the properties of a polymer by changing its chain length.	☐	☐

Q2 Complete the following statements by circling the correct words.

a) Polymer chains are held **together** / **apart** by forces between the chains.

b) If these forces are weak, the chains **cannot** / **can** slide over each other easily.
This makes the polymer **rigid** / **stretchy**.

c) If these forces are strong, the chains **cannot** / **can** slide over each other easily.
This makes the polymer **rigid** / **stretchy**.

d) The stronger the forces between the polymer chains, the **more** / **less** energy is needed to break them apart, and the **lower** / **higher** the melting point.

Q3 Polymers can be **changed** to give them different properties.

Give **three** ways that a polymer can be changed to give it different properties.

1. ....

2. ....

3. ....

Q4 The diagrams on the right show the structures of two different polymers.

Polymer A

Polymer B

a) Which of the two polymers will have the **highest melting point**?

....

b) Explain your answer to part **a)**.

....

....

Plant Oils

Q1 Oil can be extracted from some **fruits**, **seeds** and **nuts**.

a) Fill in the gaps with the words below.

pressed	crushed

To extract oil from plant material it is first ....

Then the plant material is .... to squeeze the oil out.

b) Give two uses of plant oils.

1. ....

2. ....

c) After oil has been extracted from plant material, two things are often removed to leave pure oil. What are they?

1. .... 2. ....

Q2 Circle the correct words in the sentences below.

Vegetable oils provide **almost no / loads of** energy.

They provide us with **nutrients / no nutrients**.

Q3 Tick the boxes to show whether these statements are true or false.

	True	False
a) Vegetable oils have lower boiling points than water.	☐	☐
b) Vegetable oils help food cook faster.	☐	☐
c) Cooking with vegetable oils reduces the energy content of food.	☐	☐
d) Food cooked in oils has less flavour.	☐	☐

Q4 Vegetable oils can be turned into **fuels**.

a) Give the name of a fuel that can be made from vegetable oil.

....

b) Why do vegetable oils make good fuels?

....

Plant Oils

Q5 Ben and Martin both planned an experiment to identify saturated and unsaturated oils.

Ben's Method

1. Put some oil in a test tube.
2. Add some bromine water.
3. Shake vigorously.
4. Repeat for next oil.
5. When all the oils are done, write down the results.

Martin's Method

1. Put 2 ml of oil into a test tube.
2. Label the test tube with the name of the oil sample.
3. Add 5 drops of bromine water and shake.
4. Record any colour change.
5. Repeat for each oil.

a) **i)** Whose method do you think is better?

....

ii) Explain your answer.

....

....

b) Martin did the experiment using three oils — A, B and C.
He draws a table showing what happened to the bromine water.
Look at the results and use them to complete the table.

Oil	Results	Is it saturated?
A	No change	
B	Decolourised	
C	No change	

Q6 Some types of fats are considered bad for your heart.

a) Which type of fats are **less healthy**? Underline your answer.

Saturated **Unsaturated**

b) Explain why this type of fat is bad for your heart.

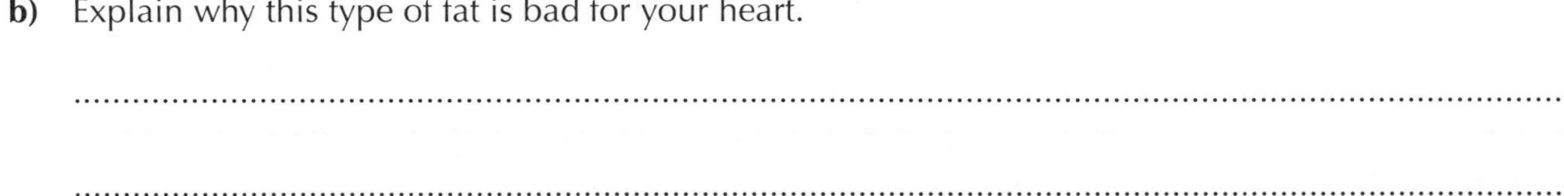

....

....

Emulsions

Q1 Circle the correct word(s) in the sentences below.

a) Oils **do / don't** dissolve in water.

b) Emulsions are **thicker / runnier** than both water and oil.

c) In an emulsion the droplets of one liquid are **suspended / dissolved** in another liquid.

d) Emulsions like salad dressing are **good / bad** at coating foods.

Q2 Emulsions are found in lots of things.

a) Give two examples of **foods** that are emulsions.

1. ....

2. ....

b) Give an example of an emulsion that **isn't a food**.

....

Q3 Adding emulsifiers to foods has **advantages** and **disadvantages**.

a) Explain why emulsifiers are added to emulsions.

....

....

b) i) Give an **advantage** of adding emulsifiers to food.

....

ii) Give a **disadvantage** of adding emulsifiers to food.

....

Top Tips: Don't get emulsions and emulsifiers muddled up. The difference is really important. So make sure you learn it. The middle of the exam isn't a good time to realise you don't know which one's which. So, you know what to do...

Mixed Questions — Section 6

Q1 **Petrol** and **diesel** are two commonly used fuels for cars.

Don't think of them as petrol and diesel — think of them as short and long-chain hydrocarbons.

a) Diesel has longer molecules than petrol. List **three** differences you would expect in the properties of petrol and diesel.

1. ....

2. ....

3. ....

b) Ethanol, hydrogen gas and biodiesel are all alternative fuels to petrol and diesel. Complete the table with the words '**yes**' or '**no**'.

Fuel	Engine needs to be converted	Burning releases carbon dioxide
Ethanol		Yes
Hydrogen gas		
Biodiesel		

Q2 Long-chain hydrocarbons can be **split up** by heating them and passing them over a catalyst.

a) What is the process of splitting up long-chain hydrocarbons called? Circle your answer.

polymerisation **electrolysis** **cracking**

b) Splitting hydrocarbons makes alkenes and alkanes. Circle the correct words in the sentence below.

Unlike alkanes, alkenes are **saturated / unsaturated** because they have **double / single** bonds.

c) Hydrocarbons can also be joined together. For example, styrene molecules can join together to form a polymer. **Name** this polymer and **draw** a diagram of part of it below.

Styrene

H H
C = C
H

Name: ....

d) Most polymers aren't biodegradable. Give one problem this causes.

....

Mixed Questions — Section 6

Q3 Tick the boxes to show whether the following statements are true or false.

		True	False
a)	Ethene can be reacted with ice to make ethanol.	☐	☐
b)	Plant sugars can be fermented to make ethanol.	☐	☐
c)	Ethanol produced by fermentation is a fairly cheap fuel.	☐	☐
d)	Using ethene to make ethanol is a renewable option.	☐	☐

Q4 The **ingredients** list from a tin of **macaroni cheese** is shown below.

> **Macaroni Cheese — Ingredients**
> Water, Durum Wheat, Cheddar Cheese, Rapeseed Oil, Salt, Sugar, Skimmed Milk Powder, Mustard, Emulsifiers, Flavour Enhancer (E621), Colour (E160)

a) Describe how rapeseed oil is extracted from rapeseed.

....

b) Rapeseed oil is an unsaturated oil. Circle the words to complete the sentence below.

Rapeseed oil **will / will not** turn bromine water from orange to colourless.

c) Cheddar cheese contains a lot of saturated fat.
Name a **health problem** that too much saturated fat can cause. ....

d) The macaroni cheese contains emulsifiers. What do emulsifiers do?

....

....

Q5 Extracting, transporting and separating crude oil is a major industry.

a) Give one problem associated with **transporting** crude oil.

....

b) Give one problem associated with **burning** crude oil.

....

Temperature and Kinetic Theory

Q1 The pictures below show particles in a **solid**, a **liquid** and a **gas**. Draw lines to match each picture and description to the correct word.

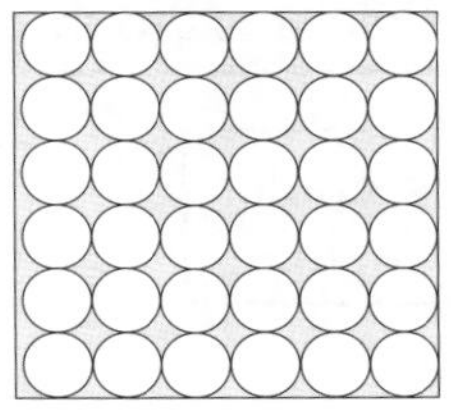

GAS

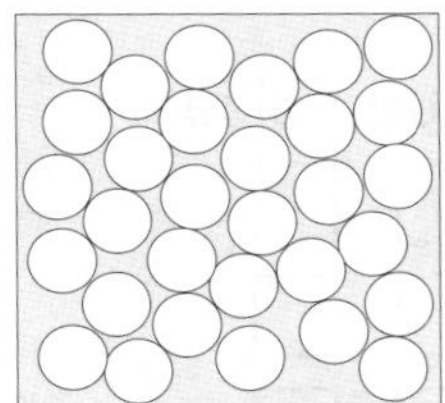

LIQUID

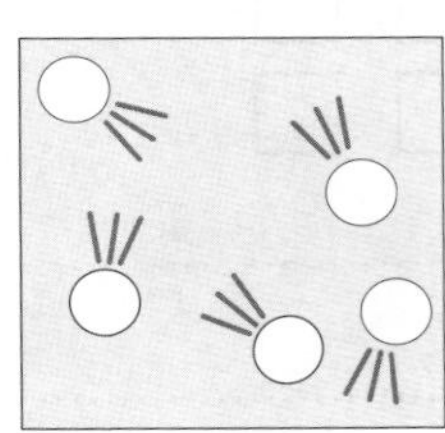

SOLID

There are weak forces of attraction between the particles.

There are almost no forces of attraction between the particles.

There are strong forces of attraction holding the particles close together.

Q2 Complete these sentences by circling the correct word from each pair.

Heat is a measure of **hotness** / **energy**.

Temperature is a measure of **hotness** / **energy**.

Heat travels from a **hot** / **cold** place to a **hot** / **cold** place.

The hotter something is, the **higher** / **lower** its temperature.

When a substance is heated its particles vibrate **more** / **less** quickly.

Temperature is measured in **°C** / **J**.

Q3 Three flasks, each containing the same amount of water at the same temperature, are left to cool in **different rooms**.

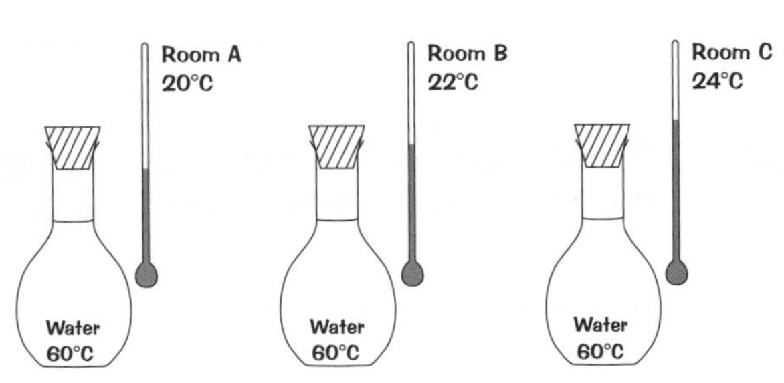

Which flask will cool **fastest**?
Give a reason for your answer.

Flask .... will cool fastest because ....

....

Conduction and Convection

Q1 Draw lines to match each type of heat transfer with the correct explanation of how it works.

Conduction

Convection

Vibrating particles pass on energy to the particles next to them.

Particles with more energy move to a cooler place, taking their heat energy with them.

Q2 Tick to show whether the sentences below are **true** or **false**.
Write a correct version of any false statements in the space below.

		True	False
a)	Conduction involves **energy** passing between **vibrating particles**.	☐	☐
b)	**Metals** are very **poor** conductors.	☐	☐
c)	**Solids** are usually better **conductors** of heat than liquids and gases.	☐	☐
d)	**Air** is a **good** insulator.	☐	☐

....

....

Q3 Jacob says, "My radiator heats the air in my room by **radiation**."

a) Why is Jacob wrong?

....

....

b) Use the words below to complete the passage.

rises	falls	spread

Radiators can .... warm air around a whole room.

When air is heated, it .... above any colder air.

The cooler air .... to take its place.

Q4 Great Aunt Marjorie knits blankets for babies. She says that a blanket **with holes** in keeps a baby **warmer** than a blanket without holes in. Why is this?

....

....

....

....

The holes contain air rather than wool. Think about why this would reduce heat flow.

Heat Radiation

Q1 Tick the correct boxes below to show whether the sentences are true or false.

		True	False
a)	The amount of heat radiation absorbed by a surface depends only on its colour.	☐	☐
b)	The hotter a surface is, the more heat it radiates.	☐	☐
c)	Good absorbers of heat are also good emitters of heat.	☐	☐
d)	Shiny surfaces like silver reflect most of the heat that falls on them.	☐	☐

Q2 Complete the following sentences by circling the correct words.

a) Dark, matt surfaces are **good** / **poor** absorbers of heat radiation.

b) The best surfaces for radiating heat are **good** / **poor** emitters.

c) The best materials for making survival blankets are **good** / **poor** emitters of heat radiation.

Q3 The **power** radiated by a system is the energy it transfers to the room per second. Draw lines to match up the boxes below.

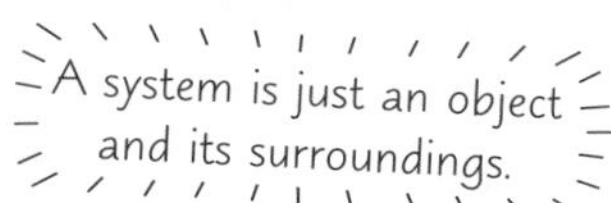

A system is just an object and its surroundings.

A system that's at a constant temperature... | ...radiates more power than it absorbs.

A system that's warming up... | ...radiates less power than it absorbs.

A system that's cooling down... | ...radiates the same average power that it absorbs.

Q4 Tim did an experiment using a **Leslie's cube** to investigate the amount of heat different surfaces radiate.

Each surface on the cube had a different colour and texture.
Tim measured the heat radiation coming from each surface. His results are shown below.

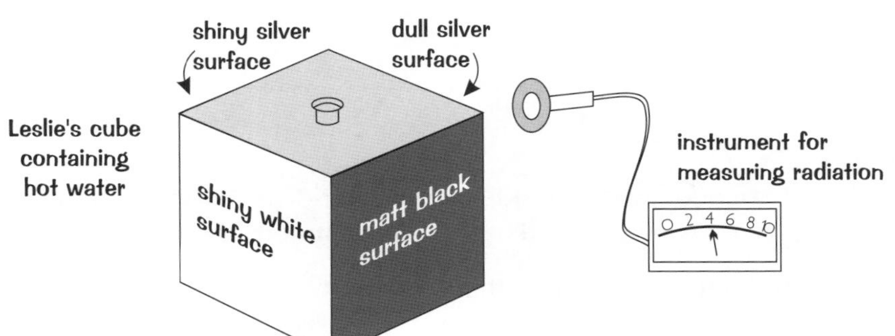

Reading	Colour and Texture
10	matt black
4	dull silver
4	shiny white
2	shiny silver

Think about which surface radiates the most heat.

Use Tim's results to write a conclusion for his experiment.

....

....

Condensation and Evaporation

Q1 Complete the passage using the words given below.

energy **liquid** **forces** **cools**

As a gas .... , the particles in the gas slow down and lose .... The particles are pulled closer together by the attractive .... between them. If the particles get close enough together, the gas will condense into a ....

Q2 Tick the boxes to show whether the sentences are **true** or **false**.

		True	False
a)	Evaporation is when particles escape from a liquid.	☐	☐
b)	The average energy of a liquid decreases when the particles with the most energy evaporate.	☐	☐
c)	The particles with the most energy are the least likely to escape from a liquid.	☐	☐

Q3 When you get hot, your skin produces **sweat**.
Sweat starts as a liquid, but leaves your skin when it becomes a gas.

a) Which of the words below describes the change from **liquid** to **gas**?
Circle the correct answer.

Condensation **Melting** **Evaporation**

b) What effect does sweat leaving your body have on your **temperature**?

....

c) Explain **in terms of particles** why sweat has the effect you described in part **b)**.

Think about the energy of the particles.

....

....

....

Q4 Steph makes a nice cup of hot tea and leaves it beside a cold window. When she comes back, she finds that some of the tea has **evaporated** and there's **condensation** on the window.

Give **one** way in which you could **decrease** the rate that:

a) the tea evaporates from the cup.

....

b) water vapour from the tea condenses on the window.

....

Rate of Heat Transfer

Q1 Engines work best if they don't get too hot. Look at the picture of the engine below. Circle the design features on the right that help the engine have a **high** rate of heat transfer.

- The engine has a small surface area.
- The engine is made from insulating materials.
- The engine is made of metal.
- Cooling fins.
- The engine has a large surface area.

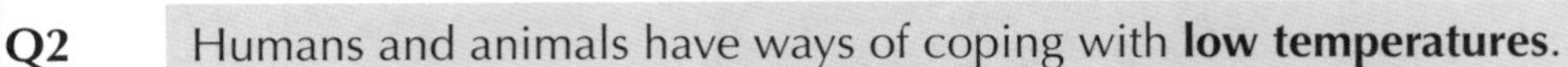

Q2 Humans and animals have ways of coping with **low temperatures**.

In the passage below, circle the correct word or phrase in each highlighted pair.

> Air is a very good **conductor / insulator** of heat energy. When you get cold, your body hairs **stand on end / lie flat** so they can trap a thicker layer of air around your body. By doing this, the amount of heat you lose to your surroundings by convection and **conduction / radiation** is reduced. Wearing a coat also helps you keep warm in this way.

Q3 Radiators are used to transfer heat to their surroundings.

a) Why do radiators have a **large** surface area?

....

b) Explain why a radiator would transfer heat quicker to a **metal spoon** in contact with it, than to the **air** surrounding it.

....

....

c) The radiators A and B have the same temperature. Which radiator will transfer heat the **fastest**? Circle the correct answer.

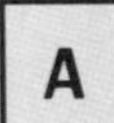

A

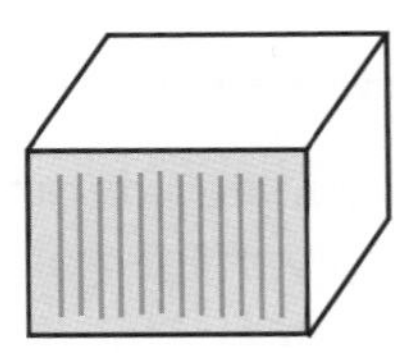

Surface area = 0.76 m^2
Volume = 0.044 m^3

B

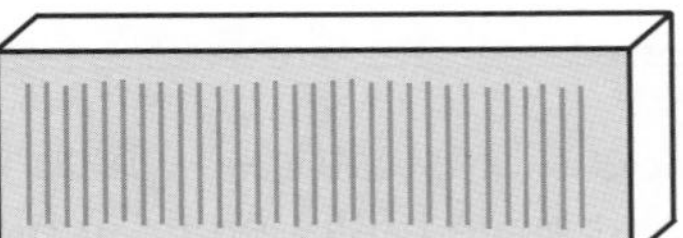

Surface area = 0.76 m^2
Volume = 0.024 m^3

Energy Efficiency in the Home

Q1 Jessy wants to reduce heat loss in her home from the **roof**, **walls** and **hot water tank**.

In the spaces on the diagram, write down **one** thing that can be fitted to reduce heat losses through each part of the house.

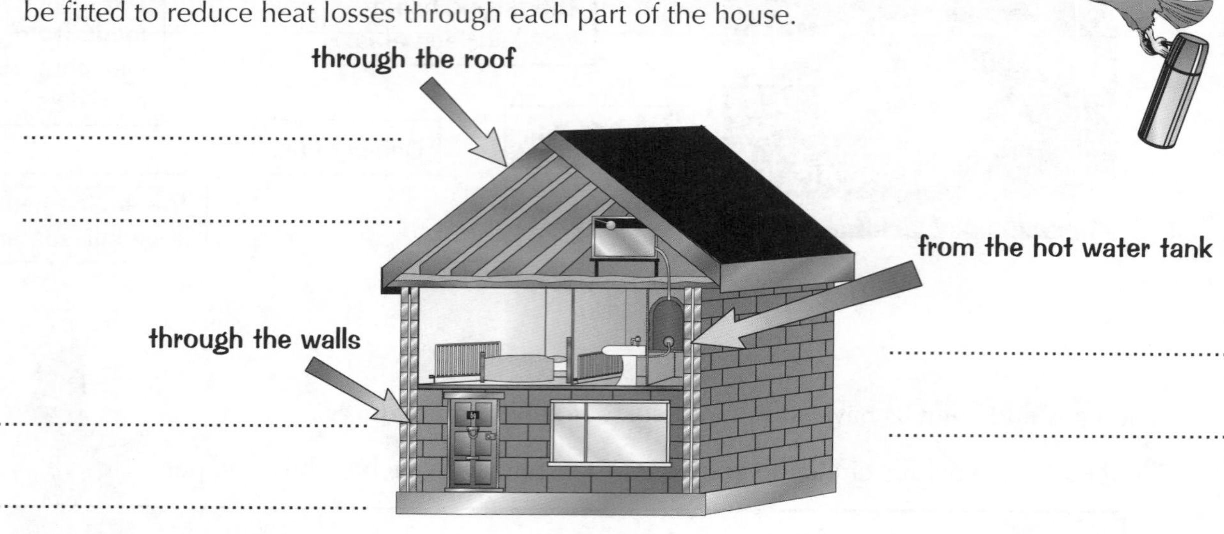

Q2 **Insulation** is used to reduce heat transfer. Use the words in the box to **fill in the gaps** in the passage below.

gap conduction wall fibreglass radiation

To insulate your loft, you can put down a thick layer of .... wool. When this is laid out across the whole loft floor it reduces heat loss by conduction and .... Cavity .... insulation can also be used to reduce heat losses in the home. Insulating foam is squirted into the .... between the bricks. This reduces heat being transferred by convection and .... across the gap.

Top Tips: Air is a great insulator — which is why many of the best insulating materials are the ones that trap air. Polar bears have hollow hairs which trap air to keep them extra toasty in the cold. With fur and air working together, you've got yourself an insulating dream team. Wowza.

Energy Efficiency in the Home

Q3 Mr Tarantino wants to buy a **hot water tank jacket** to save on his heating bills, but his friend tells him that **loft insulation** would be more **cost-effective**.

	Hot water tank jacket	Loft insulation
Initial Cost	£60	£200
Annual Saving	£15	£100
Payback time	4 years	

a) Calculate the **payback time** for loft insulation and write it in the table.

b) Is the advice correct? Give reasons for your answer.

Payback time = initial cost ÷ annual saving

....

....

....

Q4 Shona, Tim, Meena and Alison are talking about what '**cost-effectiveness**' means.

Shona: Cost-effectiveness means having a short payback time.

Alison: Cost-effectiveness means getting good value for your money.

Tim: Cost-effectiveness means getting a job done for a low price.

Meena: Cost-effectiveness just means not wasting energy.

Whose explanations do you think are right? Circle their names.

Shona Alison Tim Meena

Q5 Gary is choosing between two brands of loft insulation material. Brand A has a U-value of **0.1 W/m²K**. Brand B has a U-value of **0.2 W/m²K**.

a) What do **U-values** tell us? Tick the box next to the correct answer.

- ☐ The surface area of the material.
- ☐ The temperature of the material.
- ☐ How fast heat can transfer through the material.
- ☐ The thickness of the material.

b) If both brands are the same price, which brand should Gary buy? Explain your answer.

Gary should buy brand .... because ....

....

Specific Heat Capacity

Q1 Use the words below to complete the definition of **specific heat capacity**.

1 kg **energy** **1 °C**

Specific heat capacity is the amount of .... needed to change the temperature of .... of a substance by ....

Q2 Specific heat capacity tells you how much energy a particular material can store.

a) Which of the following is the equation for specific heat capacity? Circle the correct answer.

$$E = m \times c \times \theta$$

$$E = \frac{m \times c}{\theta}$$

E is energy transferred,
m is the mass of a material,
c is the specific heat capacity of a material,
θ is the temperature change.

b) Water has a specific heat capacity of **4200 J/kg°C**. Use the equation you circled in part **a)** to calculate how much energy is needed to heat **3 kg** of water from **10 °C** to **20 °C**.

....

....

....

Q3 To the right is a table with a list of **materials** and their **specific heat capacities**.

Material	Specific heat capacity (J/kg°C)
Concrete	880
Oil	2000
Mercury	139
Water	4200
Copper	380

Use the information in the table to help you answer the questions below.

a) Which of the materials is used in storage heaters?

....

b) Water is usually used to transfer heat around central heating systems. Give **two** reasons why this material is the best one to use.

1. ....

....

2. ....

....

Energy Transfer

Q1 Use the words below to fill in the gaps.

dissipated **transferred** **created** **Conservation**

The Principle of the .... of Energy says:

Energy can be .... usefully from one form to another, stored or

.... — but it can never be .... or destroyed.

Q2 Complete the following **energy transfer chains**. The first one has been done for you.

A solar water heating panel: light energy → heat energy

a) A gas cooker: .... → heat and light energy

b) An electric buzzer: electrical energy → ....

c) A television screen: .... → ....

Q3 For each of the electrical appliances below, draw a line to the form of **useful** energy it is designed to produce.

Electric fan	electrical energy
Iron	heat energy
Bedside table lamp	kinetic energy
	sound energy
	light energy

CGP's biggest fan

Q4 Bruce is practising weightlifting.

a) When Bruce holds the bar still, above his head, what kind of energy does the weight have?

....

b) When Bruce lets go of the weight, what happens to its energy?

....

Q5 Write down the name of an appliance which transfers:

a) electrical energy into **sound energy** ....

b) light energy into **electrical energy** ....

c) electrical energy into **heat** and **kinetic energy** ....

Efficiency of Machines

Q1 Choose from the words in the box below to complete the paragraph.

light	efficiency	wasted

A lamp transfers electrical energy into useful .... energy.
Some of the electrical energy is .... as heat energy.
The .... of the lamp is the amount of useful energy divided by the total energy supplied.

Q2 Here is an **energy flow diagram** for an electric lamp. Complete the following sentences.

a) The **total energy supplied** is .... J

b) The **energy usefully transferred** is .... J

c) The amount of energy **wasted** is ....

.... J

d) The **efficiency** of the lamp is ....

Efficiency = (Useful ÷ Total) × 100% .... %

Q3 a) Complete the **blanks** in the table below.

Appliance	Total Energy Supplied (J)	Energy Usefully Transferred (J)	Wasted Energy (J)	Efficiency (%)
A	2000	1000	1000	
B	10 000		7000	
C	4000	1000		
D	20 000	2000	18 000	

b) Circle the letter of the **most efficient** appliance in the table.

Energy Transformation Diagrams

Q1 The sketch below is an **energy transformation (Sankey) diagram** for a blender.

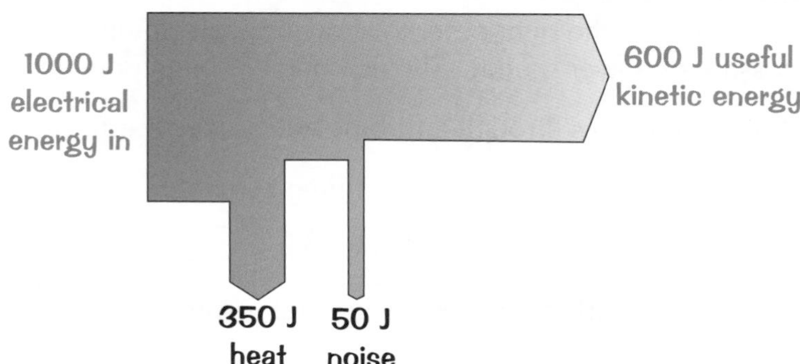

a) Circle the correct word to complete the sentence:

The thicker the arrow on a Sankey diagram, the more **energy / efficiency** is being transferred.

b) What is the **efficiency** of the blender? Give your answer as a **decimal**.

Efficiency = Useful ÷ Total

....

....

c) In what **form** is the **most** energy lost? ....

Q2 Professor Bean is testing a new car engine.
For every **100 J** of energy supplied to the engine, **50 J** are transformed into **useful kinetic energy**, **10 J** are **wasted** as **sound energy** and **the rest** is wasted as **heat energy**.

a) On the grid below, complete the **Sankey diagram** to show his results.

Use one square for every 10 J of energy.

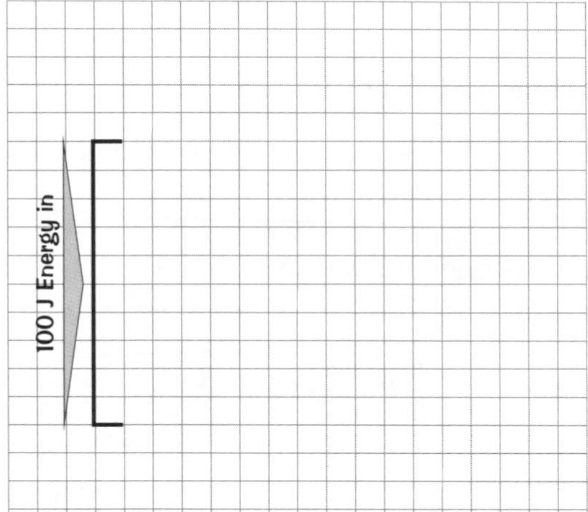

b) What is the **efficiency** of the new car engine? Give your answer as a **decimal**.

....

....

Top Tips: Energy transformation diagrams (or Sankey diagrams as they like to be known) go hand in hand with efficiency calculations. They help you to picture how energy-efficient something is. A big 'wasted energy' arrow means it's probably not very efficient, but a small one is great.

Power Stations and Nuclear Energy

Q1 **Fossil fuels** can be used to generate electricity.

a) Number these steps (1-5) in the right order to show how electricity is generated in a fossil fuel power station. The first one has been done for you.

- [ ] Hot steam rushes through a turbine and makes it spin.
- [ ] Electricity is produced by the spinning generator.
- [1] The fossil fuel is burned to release heat.
- [ ] The spinning turbine makes the generator spin too.
- [ ] Water is heated in a boiler and turned to steam.

b) Name the **three** types of fossil fuel.

1. .... 2. .... 3. ....

Q2 Choose from the words below to complete the paragraph about nuclear power.

plutonium **electricity** **steam** **burnt** **turbine** **fission**

In nuclear power stations, water is heated to produce .... This then drives a ...., which is then used to drive a generator to produce .... In a nuclear power station, no fuel is .... Instead, the heat energy used to heat the water comes from a reaction called nuclear .... The fuels used for this reaction are uranium and ....

Q3 Nuclear power has **advantages** and **disadvantages**.

a) Which of the following statements describes an **advantage** of nuclear power? Circle the **one** correct answer.

A — Nuclear fuel releases less energy than fossil fuels.

B — Nuclear power stations don't produce carbon dioxide.

C — Nuclear power stations produce radioactive waste.

b) Circle the letter of the statement below that describes a **disadvantage** of nuclear power.

A — Nuclear fuel will never run out.

B — Nuclear power stations produce radioactive waste.

C — The overall cost of nuclear power is low.

D — Nuclear power stations produce lots of carbon dioxide.

Wind and Solar Energy

Q1 People often complain about wind turbines being put up near to where they live, because wind energy has some **disadvantages**.

a) Tick the boxes to show whether the following statements are true or false.

	true	false
i) The noise from wind turbines might annoy people living near them.	☐	☐
ii) Wind turbines produce lots of carbon dioxide.	☐	☐
iii) Some people think wind turbines spoil the view of the landscape.	☐	☐
iv) Wind power has high running costs.	☐	☐

b) List **two advantages** of using wind turbines to generate electricity.

1. ....

2. ....

Q2 Geoff wanted to find out if he could get enough energy from the Sun to power a lamp with a battery. He connected a battery to a **solar cell**, then timed how **long** the lamp stayed on for using the energy stored in the battery at the end of each day. His results are shown in the table below.

Day	Mon	Tues	Wed	Thu	Fri	Sat	Sun
Time lamp stays lit (hours)	5	4	2	6	5	1	5

a) Circle the **day** in the table that you think had the **sunniest** weather.

b) Geoff did his test in **summer**.
Why might Geoff **not** be able to use the solar cell to charge the battery in **winter**?

....

....

Q3 **Solar cells** use the Sun's energy to make electricity.

a) Give **two advantages** of using solar cells.

1. ....

2. ....

b) Give **one disadvantage** of using solar cells.

....

Top Tips: Learn all the good and bad points of using wind and solar energy. Then the exam will be a breeze — like wind through a turbine. Remember — they're both renewable energy sources.

Wave and Tidal Energy

Q1 **Number** the steps below 1-4 to explain how electricity is made from wave power. The first one has been done for you.

- [ ] The air makes the turbine spin.
- [ ] The generator makes electricity.
- [1] A wave pushes air through a turbine.
- [ ] The spinning turbine drives a generator.

Q2 Tick the boxes to show whether each statement applies to **wave** power or **tidal** power or **both**.

		Wave	Tidal	Both
a)	Doesn't need steam to drive the turbine.	☐	☐	☐
b)	Suitable for use on a small scale.	☐	☐	☐
c)	Is a reliable way to make electricity.	☐	☐	☐
d)	Depends on the weather.	☐	☐	☐
e)	Is a renewable energy source.	☐	☐	☐

Q3 Which of the following statements about **tidal energy** is true? Circle the **one** correct answer.

A — Tidal barrages can affect boats and wildlife habitats.

B — Tidal energy has high running costs.

C — Tidal energy produces lots of carbon dioxide.

Q4 **Wave-powered generators** can be very useful around islands, like Britain.

a) Give **one advantage** of using wave power to make electricity.

....

b) Give **one disadvantage** of using wave power to make electricity.

....

Biofuels, Geothermal and Hydroelectricity

Q1 Complete the block diagram about **hydroelectricity** below by choosing the correct words from the list.

generator **gravity** **dam**

Water is stored in a reservoir using a	→	.... causes the water to rush through turbines.	→	A .... changes the movement of the turbine into electricity.

Q2 Number these sentences 1 to 5 to describe one possible way of generating electricity from **geothermal** energy. The first one has been done for you.

- [ ] The water is heated and turns to steam.
- [ ] Water is pumped down to the hot rocks.
- [ ] A generator driven by the turbine makes electricity.
- [1] Deep holes are drilled down into hot rocks.
- [ ] Steam comes up to the surface and powers a turbine.

Q3 **Biofuels** are made from plants and waste.

a) One of the sentences below explains why biofuels are a **renewable** source of energy. Circle the correct **one**.

A — They can be burnt in thermal power stations.

B — They will never run out as we can keep growing more.

C — They give off carbon dioxide when burnt.

b) Some advantages and disadvantages of biofuels are written below. Write each one in the **correct space** in the table.

need large areas to grow

are carbon neutral

can be made quickly

Advantages	Disadvantages

Biofuels, Geothermal and Hydroelectricity

Q4 At a public meeting, people are sharing their views about **hydroelectric power**.

We should use hydroelectric power more — it doesn't produce pollution like carbon dioxide.

Brian

And it gives us loads of free energy.

Hillary

But it makes a terrible mess of the countryside.

Sue

Say whether you agree or disagree with each person by circling the correct word.
Then explain why you agree or disagree underneath. An example has been done for you.

a) I **(agree)** / **disagree** with Brian because

hydroelectric power stations don't produce carbon dioxide when they're running.

b) I **agree** / **disagree** with Hillary because

....

....

c) I **agree** / **disagree** with Sue because

....

....

d) Give **two advantages** of hydroelectric power that were **not** mentioned at the meeting.

1. ....

2. ....

e) Give **two disadvantages** of hydroelectric power **not** mentioned at the meeting.

1. ....

2. ....

Top Tips: Biofuels, geothermal energy and hydroelectricity are all renewable energy sources. One uses steam coming from hot rocks underground, one uses rainwater trapped behind a dam, and the other is burning stuff like wood and cow muck. How lovely.

Energy Sources and the Environment

Q1 Draw lines to match up each environmental problem below with something that causes it.

Acid rain	Releasing carbon dioxide by burning fossil fuels
Climate change	Coal mining
Dangerous radioactive waste	Sulfur dioxide formed by burning oil and coal
Spoiling of natural landscapes	Using nuclear power

Q2 '**Carbon capture**' helps reduce the damage done by burning fossil fuels on the environment.

a) Complete the paragraph below by circling the correct word from each pair.

> Carbon capture and storage (CCS) is used to **reduce / increase** the amount of carbon dioxide (CO_2) released into the atmosphere. This helps **reduce / increase** the strength of the greenhouse effect. CCS works by collecting the CO_2 from power stations **before / after** it is released into the atmosphere.

b) Give **one** example of where captured carbon dioxide can be stored.

....

Q3 Lisa says: "Using nuclear power to make electricity is too dangerous."
Ben says: "Using fossil fuels is even more dangerous in the long run."

a) Who do you think is right? ....

b) Explain why you think the person you chose in part **a)** is right.

....

....

Q4 Biofuels are **burnt** to produce steam that drives turbines and generates electricity.
Biofuels are often made from plants that take in CO_2 from the atmosphere as they grow.

Burning biofuels releases CO_2 into the atmosphere.
Explain why using biofuels **doesn't increase** the overall amount of CO_2 in the atmosphere.

....

....

....

Comparison of Energy Resources

Q1 Which of the following fossil fuel power stations has the **shortest start-up time**? Circle the correct answer.

Coal **Oil** **Gas**

Q2 Use the words in the box to complete the passage on energy resources.

safe | run out | non-renewable | unreliable | pollution | renewable | expensive

.... resources need bigger power stations than .... resources for the same energy output. Renewable energy resources are generally .... as they often depend on the weather. However, non-renewable energy resources release harmful .... into the atmosphere and will .... one day. Nuclear and hydroelectric power stations both need a lot of work to make them .... This makes them .... to build.

Q3 Different types of power station have different **running costs**.

a) Tick the box to show which type of energy resource usually has the **higher running costs** when used to generate electricity.

☐ **Renewable** ☐ **Non-renewable**

b) Explain your answer.

....

....

Q4 Tidal power, geothermal power and biofuels are all renewable energy resources. Suggest **one** reason why they're generally **more reliable** than **other** renewable energy resources.

....

....

Top Tips: Phew, there's a lot to think about when deciding what energy source to use. You've got to think about the running costs, how reliable it is and whether it harms the environment. I know how much you enjoy comparing energy resources. That's why there is plenty more of it coming up on the next page. There's no need to thank me...

Comparison of Energy Resources

Q5 The city of Fakeville decides to replace its old coal-fired power station. They have to choose between using gas, nuclear, wind or geothermal.

Fill in the table below to give one **disadvantage** of each choice:

	Energy resource	Disadvantage
a)	Gas	
b)	Nuclear	
c)	Wind	
d)	Geothermal	

Q6 It can cost a lot of money to **decommission** a power station.

a) What is meant by the term **decommission**?

....

....

b) Tick the box below to show which of the following power stations **costs the most** to decommission.

☐ Coal-fired power stations ☐ Nuclear power stations ☐ Hydroelectric power stations

Q7 Read the **statement** below and then answer the **question** that follows.

I think tidal power is a **reliable** source of energy.

Do you agree with the statement above? Explain your answer.

I **agree** / **disagree** because ....

....

....

....

Mixed Questions — Section 7

Q1 Paul wants to buy some new windows. He reads that **double glazed** windows **reduce** heat loss by trapping a **thin layer of air** in between two sheets of glass.

a) Name the type of **heat transfer** that double glazed windows help to **reduce**.

....

b) Paul compares some different brands of double glazed windows.
Brand A windows have a U value of **0.5 W/m²K**. Brand B windows have a U value of **0.3 W/m²K**.
Which brand of windows is the better insulator? Circle the correct answer.

A B

c) Paul notices condensation on the inside of his single glazed windows.
Use the words in the box to fill in the gaps in the passage describing how condensation happens.

liquid	energy	cools	attraction

Water vapour in the air .... as it comes into contact with the cold surface of the windows. The particles of water vapour slow down as they lose .... Eventually, the particles don't have enough energy to escape the forces of .... between them, and the vapour condenses into a ....

Q2 In Bogville coal-fired power station, for every **1000 J** of energy input to the power station, **650 J** are wasted.

a) What **type** of energy is contained in the **coal**? ....

b) Calculate the **efficiency** of the power station.

Efficiency = Useful ÷ Total.

....

....

c) Bogville is thinking of building a **nuclear power station** to replace the coal one.
Tick the box next to the **one** statement that describes an **advantage** of nuclear power.

- [ ] Nuclear fuel releases much more energy than the same amount of fossil fuels.
- [ ] Nuclear power is a renewable energy source.
- [ ] Nuclear power does not produce any waste.

d) Why is radioactive waste from nuclear power stations **dangerous**?

....

....

Mixed Questions — Section 7

Q3 A group of farmers live on an island, growing potatoes and farming llamas. They decide to put **solar cells** on the roofs of their houses and **wind turbines** in their fields.

a) Why do you think the farmers have chosen to use:

i) solar power ....

....

....

ii) wind power ....

....

....

b) Name **one** other **renewable source** of energy the farmers could use.

....

c) Why couldn't most people in the UK **just** use solar and wind power to power their homes?

....

....

Q4 Ben sets up an experiment to investigate **heat radiation** using a Bunsen burner, thermometers and coated metal plates as shown. After waiting for 5 minutes, he takes readings from the **two thermometers**, A and B.

a) Complete Ben's conclusion to his experiment by choosing the correct word in each highlighted pair.

matt black surface
shiny silver surface
A
B
coated metal plates
Bunsen burner

Heat radiation from the Bunsen burner is transferred to the thermometers by being **absorbed / reflected** and then **emitted / refracted** by the metal plates. Thermometer **A / B** is heated to a higher temperature. This is because the metal plate in front of it is coated with a **matt black / shiny silver** surface which is a good **reflector / absorber** and emitter of heat radiation.

b) Complete the energy transfer chain below for the Bunsen burner used in Ben's experiment.

Chemical energy → .... + ... + ...

c) Explain why metals are good conductors of heat.

....

....

Mixed Questions — Section 7

Q5 Steve has bought a new fridge. It has a thermometer inside, level with the top shelf.

a) Steve puts a hot pie on the **bottom shelf** of the fridge and the temperature on the **top shelf** rises. What is the **name** of this type of heat flow?

....

b) Most fridges have a light which comes on when the door is opened. The light in Steve's new fridge wastes 68 J of energy for every 100 J of useful output energy. Calculate the light's efficiency.

....

.... %

Q6 Jonny investigates ways of saving energy in his grandma's house. He calculates the annual savings that could be made on his grandma's fuel bills, and the cost of doing the work.

Work needed	Annual Saving (£)	Cost of work (£)	Payback time (years)
Hot water tank jacket	15	15	
Draught-proofing	80	100	
Cavity wall insulation	70	560	
Thermostatic controls	30	120	

a) Use the equation for **payback time** to complete the table.

Payback time = initial cost ÷ annual saving.

b) Which of these energy-saving measures has the shortest **payback time**?

....

c) Jonny's grandma decides to buy some draught-proofing for her house. How much money will she save **over 5 years**? Show your working.

Don't forget that she had to pay for the draught-proofing.

....

....

....

d) Jonny's grandma likes to have a hot bath in the evenings. How much energy is needed to heat **100 kg** of water from **20 °C** to **40 °C** ? (The specific heat capacity of water is **4200 J/kg°C**.)

Energy transferred = mass × specific heat capacity × temperature change

....

....

....

Generating Electricity

Q1 Adrian is using the equipment in the diagram below to show **electromagnetic induction**.

Choose from the following words to complete the passage below.

An ammeter measures the amount of electric current.

current	field	wire	alternating

As Adrian moves the .... near the magnet,

it passes through a magnetic ....

This produces a .... in the wire.

By moving the wire in and out of the magnetic field Adrian produces an .... current in the wire.

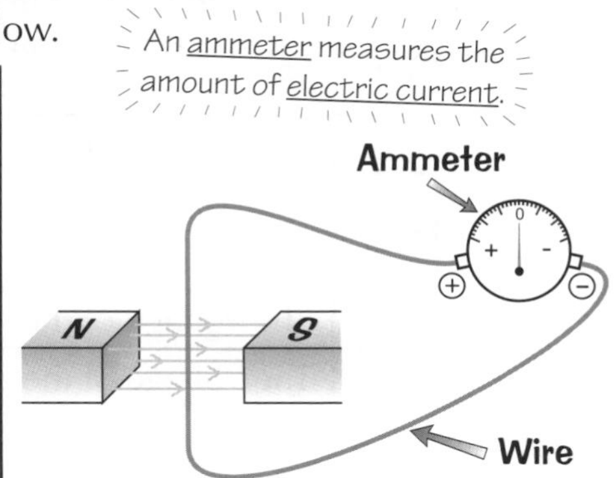

Q2 Look at the simple **generators** sketched below.

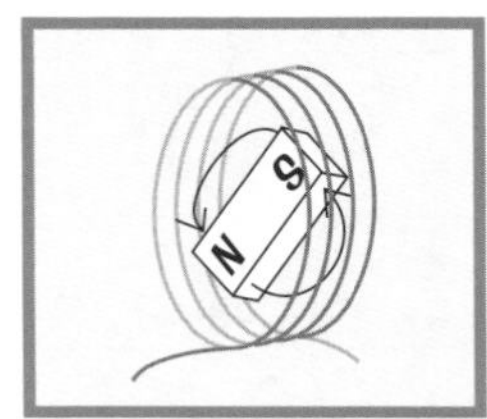

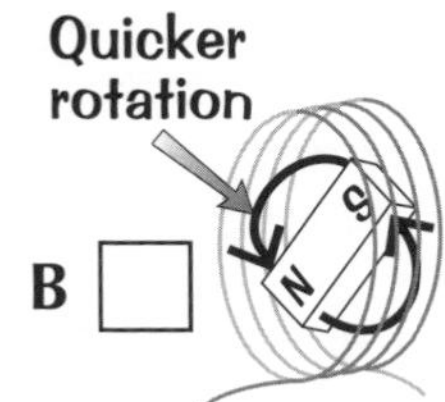

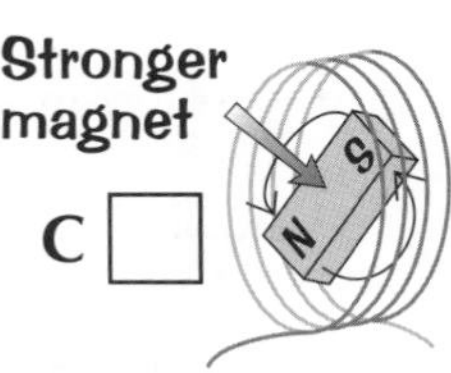

One of the generators labelled A - C will **not** produce a higher current than the generator in the box on the left. Tick the box next to that generator.

Q3 Moving a **magnet** inside a **coil** of **wire** can produce an image on a **display**.

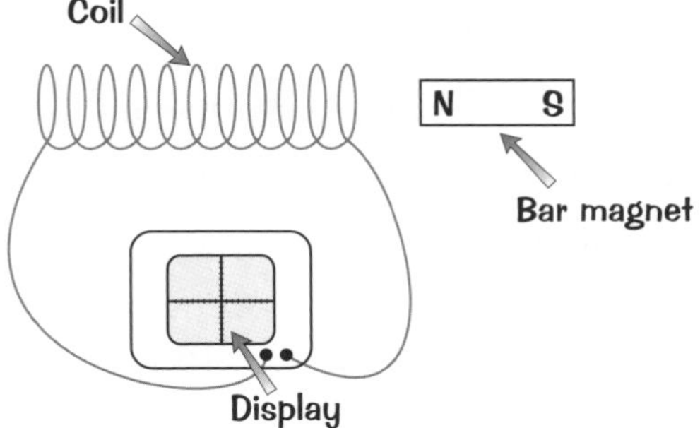

Images on display screen

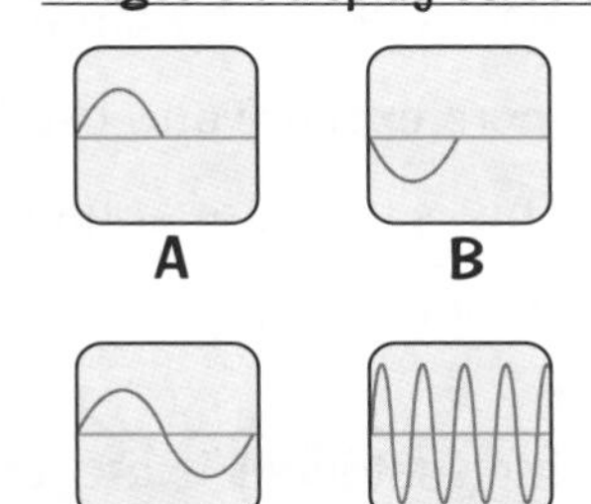

When the magnet was **pushed inside** the coil, image **A** was produced on the display.

Draw lines to match the images to how they could have been produced:

Image B	Pushing the magnet in and pulling it out again straight away.
Image C	Quickly moving the magnet in and out of the coil a few times.
Image D	By pulling the magnet out of the coil.

Electricity and the National Grid

Q1 Number these statements 1 to 5 to show the order of the steps that are needed to deliver energy to Mrs Miggins' house so that she can boil the kettle. The first one has been done for you.

	An electrical current flows through power cables across the country.
	Mrs Miggins boils the kettle for tea.
1	Electrical energy is generated in power stations.
	The voltage of the supply is raised.
	The voltage of the supply is reduced.

Q2 Using **high voltages** in power cables means you need some **expensive** equipment.

a) Add labels to complete the diagram below showing the equipment used for **high-voltage transmission**, by choosing the correct words from the box.

pylons	step-up transformer	power station	step-down transformer

i) ....

....

iii) ....

ii) ....

iv) ....

b) Complete the sentences below by circling the correct word from each pair.

It is **cheaper / more expensive** to use high voltages for transmission, even though the equipment is expensive. This is because at higher voltages **less / more** energy is wasted as heat. This saves **less / more** money than the cost of the equipment.

Q3 Each of the following sentences is **incorrect**. Write a correct version of each.

a) The National Grid transmits energy at **high voltage** and **high current**.

....

b) A step-up transformer is used to **reduce the voltage** of the supply before electricity is transmitted.

....

c) Using a **high current** makes sure there is not much energy **wasted**.

....

Power and the Cost of Electricity

Q1 Tick to show whether the following statements are **true** or **false**.

		True	False
a)	Power is measured in watts.	☐	☐
b)	Voltage is measured in watts.	☐	☐
c)	The cost of using an electric kettle depends only on its power rating.	☐	☐

Q2 The **current** an appliance uses depends on its **power** rating. Complete the table below to show the power rating of various appliances at mains voltage — **230 V**.

Appliance	Current (A)	Power (W)
Kettle	10	2300
Radio	0.1	
Laptop computer	0.35	
Lamp	0.17	

Power = voltage × current

Q3 Luigi cooks a pizza for his tea. It takes him **half an hour** to cook his pizza in a **2.3 kW** oven.

a) How much **energy** is used to cook the pizza? Circle the correct answer.

Energy = power × time

1.5 kWh **2.3 kWh** **1.15 kWh**

b) Luigi has to pay 12p per kWh. How much does it **cost** him to cook his pizza?

....

Cost = number of kWh × price per kWh

Q4 A tumble drier operating on a **230 V** household supply uses a current of **8 A**.

1 kW = 1000 W

a) Calculate the **power rating** of the tumble drier in kW.

....

.... kW

b) How much **energy** does the tumble drier use in 2 hours? Give your answer in kWh.

.... kWh

c) Electricity costs 11.5p per kWh. How much does it **cost** to use the tumble drier for 2 hours?

.... p

Power and the Cost of Electricity

Q5 Mr Havel recently received his **electricity bill**. Unfortunately, he tore off the bottom part.

Customer : Mr. V. Havel

Date	**Meter Reading**
June 11th	34259
September 10th	34783

Total Cost @ 9.7p per kWh

a) The bill uses units of **kilowatt-hours** (kWh). What is a kilowatt-hour?

....

....

b) How many **kWh** of energy did Mr Havel use in the three months from June to September?

Work out the difference between the meter readings.

.... kWh

c) Calculate the **total cost** of Mr. Havel's electricity bill.

.... p

Q6 Boris puts his **2 kW** electric heater on for 3 hours.

a) Calculate how many **kilowatt-hours** of electrical energy the heater uses.

.... kWh.

b) Boris's electricity costs 7p per kilowatt-hour. Work out the **cost** of the energy calculated in part **a)**.

.... p

c) Boris leaves a 60 W lamp on for 9 hours every day. Boris's wife uses an 8 kW shower for 15 mins every day.

Who uses the **most energy** per day? Calculate how much energy each person uses and compare your results.

Make sure the units are right before you do any calculations.

i) Boris uses:

....

.... kWh

ii) Boris's wife uses:

....

.... kWh

iii) Circle the name of the person who uses the most energy: **Boris / Boris's wife.**

Top Tips: Lots of maths on these pages, but practice makes perfect. One day you'll have your own electricity bills to sort out and then you'll be glad you learnt all this (and it could be on the exam).

Choosing Electrical Appliances

Q1 Cheryl wants to buy a new hair dryer to take on **holiday** with her. The two hair dryers she is choosing between are shown below.

Hair dryer A:
Cost: £25.00
Power: 2.2 kW
Weight: 130 g
Special features: 5 speeds and temperature control

Hair dryer B:
Cost: £12.99
Power: 1.2 kW
Weight: 95 g
Special features: Handle folds away

Use the information given above to answer the following questions.

a) Suggest **one** reason why Cheryl might choose to buy hair dryer B, rather than hair dryer A.

....

b) Suggest **one** reason why Cheryl might choose hair dryer A.

....

Q2 Tick the correct box(es) below to show why somebody going on a camping trip might take a **wind-up radio** instead of a **mains powered radio**.

There might not be an electricity supply where they are camping. ☐

A wind-up radio will need winding up regularly, to keep working. ☐

Wind-up radios don't have power cords that might get in the way. ☐

Q3 June wants to buy a new tumble dryer. In an average week, **dryer A** would use **17 kWh** of energy and **dryer B** would use **16 kWh**.

June's electricity supplier charges **12p** per kWh.
How much money would June save each week if she bought dryer B, rather than dryer A?

....

....

....

Find the difference between the energy used by dryers A and B, then times this by the cost per kWh.

Q4 Some people living in the world's **poorest countries** don't have **access to electricity**. This can have a big **effect** on their **health**.

Give **two** examples of how electricity is used in hospitals.

1. ....

2. ....

Wave Basics

Q1 Complete the sentences below by circling the correct word in each pair.

a) Waves transfer **energy** / **matter** without transferring any **energy** / **matter**.

b) Wavelength is the distance from crest to **crest** / **trough**.

c) Amplitude is the distance from the **trough** / **rest position** to the crest.

d) Frequency is the number of waves produced by a source every **second** / **minute**.

Q2 Diagrams A, B and C represent **electromagnetic waves**.

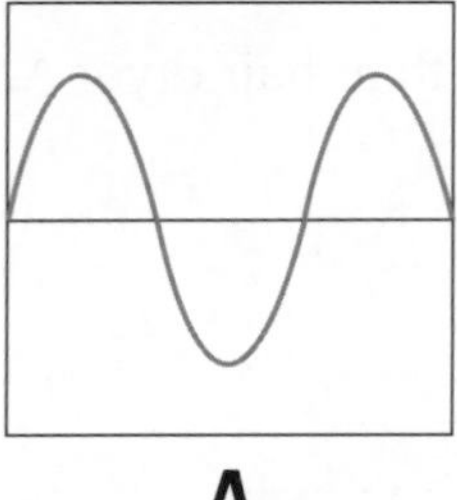

A

B

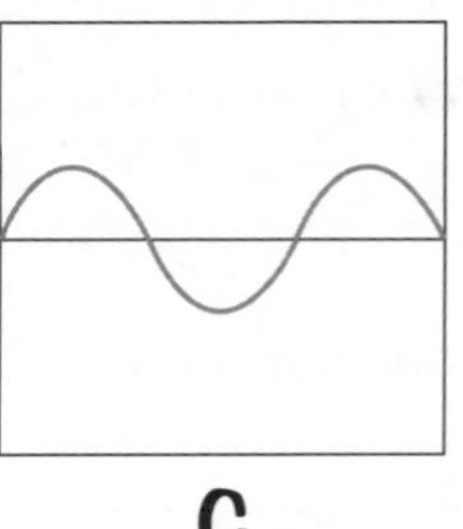

C

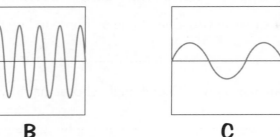

a) Which two diagrams show waves with the same **frequency**? ...... and ......

b) Which two diagrams show waves with the same **amplitude**? ...... and ......

c) Which two diagrams show waves with the same **wavelength**? ...... and ......

Q3 Astronauts on the Moon hear a message from Earth **1.3 seconds** after it was sent. The message was sent using EM radiation.

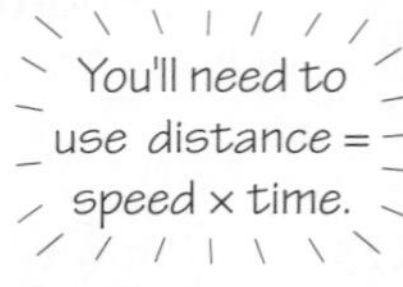

You'll need to use distance = speed × time.

EM radiation travels at **300 000 km/s**.
How **far away** is the Moon from the Earth?

....

....

Q4 There are **two ways** in which you can make waves on a **slinky** spring.

a) Which diagram shows a **transverse** wave, and which one shows a **longitudinal** wave?

Transverse: ....

Longitudinal: ....

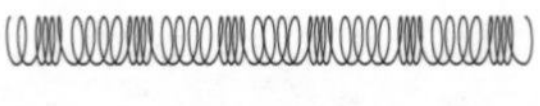

1

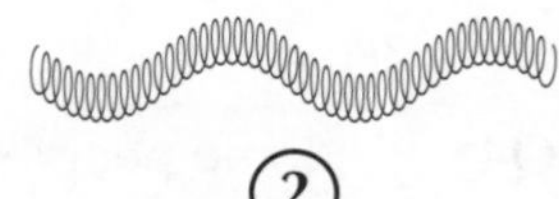

2

b) Write down **one** difference between these two types of wave.

....

....

Wave Basics

Q5 A **P-wave** has a wavelength of about 250 m and a frequency of 20 Hz.

Calculate the **speed** of this P-wave. Give the correct unit in your answer.

....

....

....

You'll need to use speed = frequency × wavelength

Q6 A ripple in a pond makes a duck bob up and down **twice every second**.

a) What is the **frequency** of the duck's bobbing?

....

b) The distance between the crests of one ripple and the next is 0.5 m.
What is the speed of the ripples?

....

....

Think about what the distance from crest to crest is a measure of.

Q7 Jason draws the graph below to show a wave with an **amplitude** of **4 m** and a **wavelength** of **2 m**.

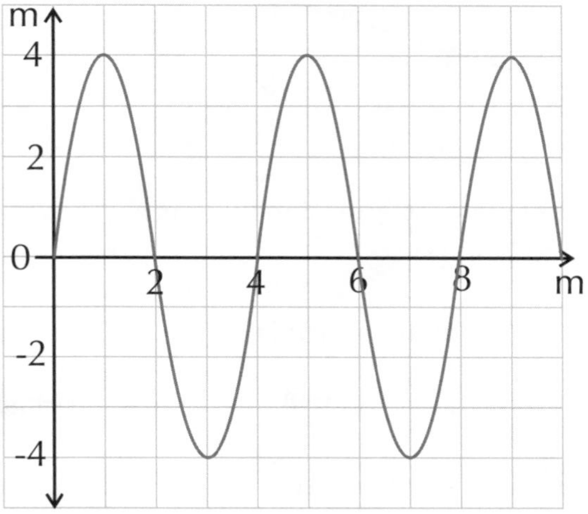

m
4
2
0
-2
-4
2 4 6 8 m

a) What has Jason done wrong?

....

....

b) Draw a wave with a **wavelength** of **5 m** and an **amplitude** of **3 m** on the **same graph** above.

Reflection

Q1 Harriet spends at least an hour looking at herself in a **mirror** every day. The image she sees is formed from light **reflected** by the mirror.

a) Tick the box which correctly describes what is meant by a **normal**.

- [ ] It is a line drawn **at right angles** to the mirror where the incident ray hits.
- [ ] It is a line drawn **parallel** to the mirror where the incident ray hits.

b) Complete the diagram to show an incident ray of light being reflected by the mirror. Label the **angle of incidence**, **i**, the **normal**, and the **angle of reflection**, **r**.

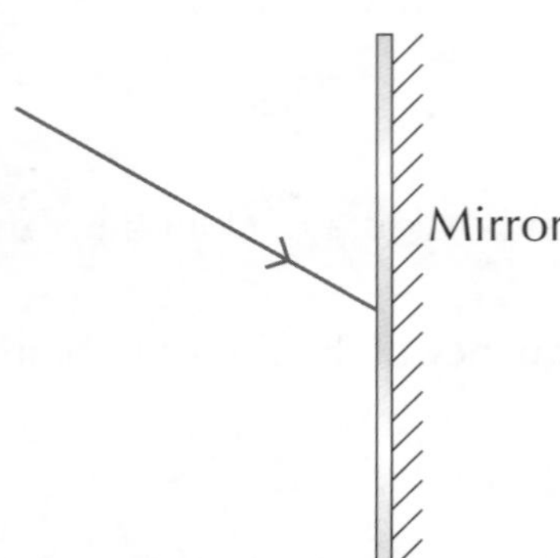

Q2 The diagram below shows a pencil being reflected in a **plane mirror**.

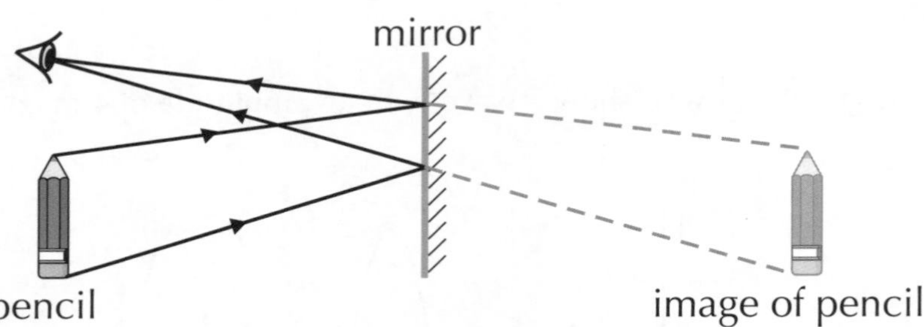

Complete each of the sentences by choosing the correct word from the words listed below them. Use the diagram above to help you.

a) The image of the pencil in the plane mirror is a .... image.

real   normal   virtual

b) The image of the pencil is laterally inverted and ....

upright   upside down   at 90° to the pencil

Top Tips: If you get asked a question about constructing ray diagrams, remember the important rule for drawing reflections in a plane mirror: angle of incidence = angle of reflection. Always use a ruler to draw your ray diagrams too — examiners love a line drawn with a ruler.

Diffraction and Refraction

Q1 An important property of waves is **diffraction**.

a) Circle the correct word from each pair below to explain what **diffraction** means.

Diffraction is where a wave **slows down** / **spreads out** as it passes through a **gap** / **different substance** or when it meets an obstacle in its path.

b) A ripple tank is used to study diffraction of waves through gaps.

In ① there's a small gap that would cause **lots** of diffraction.

In ② there's a larger gap that would cause much **less** diffraction.

Complete both diagrams to show what happens to the waves after they pass through the gap.

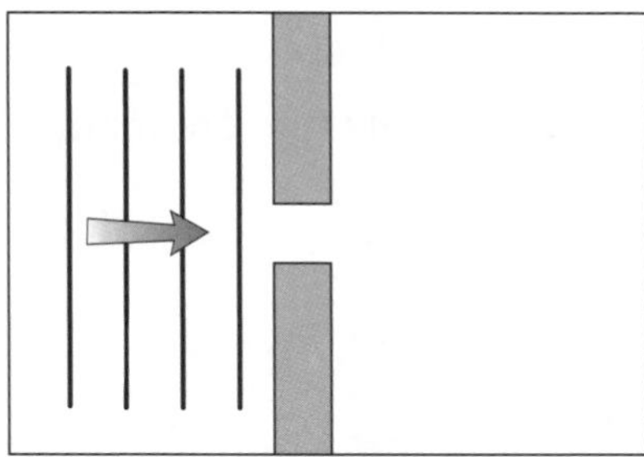

Lots of diffraction

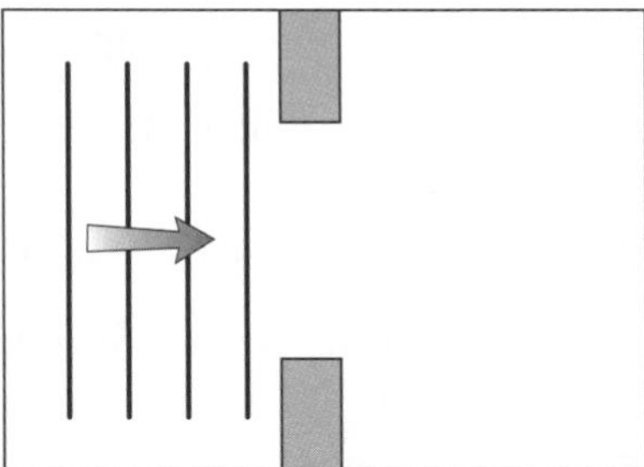

Little diffraction

Q2 Diagrams A and B show waves travelling from one substance to another.

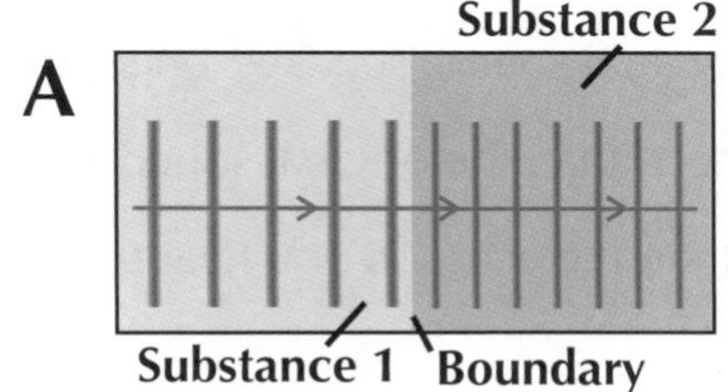

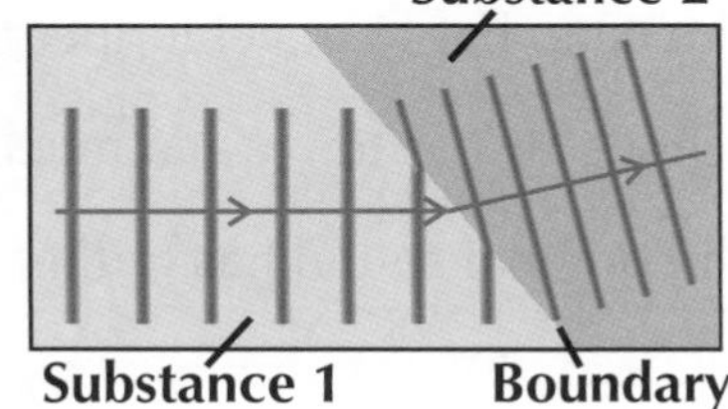

a) Which diagram shows the waves being **refracted**? ....

b) Why does refraction **not happen** in the other diagram?

....

c) Tick **one** box that explains why waves refract at boundaries.

☐ Because the waves change colour.

☐ Because the waves change speed.

☐ Because the waves change temperature.

FACT: Chameleons change colour to stay on-trend in the fashion world. This season they are mostly wearing grey.

Sound Waves

Q1 Number these processes 1 to 4 in the correct order to explain how the sound of a drumbeat is made and reaches our ears. The first one has been done for you.

- [ ] The vibration of the drum sets the air molecules next to it vibrating too.
- [ ] We hear the sound when the vibrations in the air reach our ears.
- [1] When someone beats a drum, the skin on top of the drum vibrates.
- [ ] A series of compressions and rarefactions travel outwards through the air as a longitudinal wave.

Q2 Choose from the words below to fill in the spaces in the passage.

high **low** **vibrate**

A sound wave makes air molecules .... If there are many vibrations per second the frequency or pitch of the sound is .... If there are only a few vibrations per second the pitch of the sound is ....

Q3 Mina sings in her school choir. When practising in a large, empty practice room at school, Mina hears an **echo** of her voice.

a) What is an echo?

....

b) Tick the correct box to describe why there is a delay before you hear an echo.

- [ ] The echo has to travel further than the original sound, so takes longer to reach your ears.
- [ ] Echoes always travel at a much lower speed than the original sound.
- [ ] The original sound has further to travel than the echo, so you hear that first.

Q4 In an experiment, a ringing alarm clock is placed in a glass bell jar. Air is sucked out of the jar by a vacuum pump.

Ringing bell
Glass bell jar
Foam
air
To vacuum pump

Hint: the vacuum pump is sucking all the air out, so there are fewer and fewer particles in the jar.

a) What happens to the sound you can hear?

....

....

b) Explain the reason behind your answer to part **a)**.

....

....

....

Analogue and Digital Signals

Q1 Data can be sent either as an **analogue** signal or a **digital** one.

a) Analogue signals **vary continuously**. What does this mean?

....

b) How are digital signals **different** to analogue signals?

....

c) The diagrams below show a 'clean' digital signal and a 'clean' analogue signal. Below each diagram, sketch how the signal might look with 'noise' added to it.

Clean digital signal

Clean analogue signal

The same signal with noise

The same signal with noise

Q2 Using **digital** signals instead of analogue signals for communications has **advantages**. Choose the correct word to fill in the blanks below.

1. Digital signals are affected less by .... than analogue signals.

signal pulses noise

2. Digital signals are better when using computers because they're .... devices.

analogue digital noisy

Q3 Fill in the blanks, choosing from the words below.

noise	analogue	original	bytes

All signals pick up .... as they travel. Digital signals are higher quality than .... signals because the information is the same as the .... The amount of information stored in a digital signal is measured in ....

EM Waves and Communication

Q1 The table below shows the different possible wavelengths of **electromagnetic radiation**.

a) Use the words in the box to complete the table showing the seven types of electromagnetic waves:

ultraviolet infrared microwaves
X-rays gamma rays radio waves

			VISIBLE LIGHT			
Wavelength → $1\text{m}-10^{4}\text{m}$	10^{-2}m (1 cm)	10^{-5}m (0.01 mm)	10^{-7}m	10^{-8}m	10^{-10}m	$10^{-12}\text{m} - 10^{-15}\text{m}$

b) In which direction does the **energy** of the electromagnetic radiation **increase** across the table? Tick the box next to the correct answer.

☐ The energy of the waves **increases** from **left to right** across the table.

☐ The energy of the waves **increases** from **right to left** across the table.

Q2 Tick the correct boxes to show whether each of the following statements is true or false.

		True	False
a)	Visible light travels faster in a vacuum than both X-rays and radio waves.	☐	☐
b)	Microwaves have a higher frequency than X-rays.	☐	☐
c)	Radio waves have the shortest wavelength of all electromagnetic waves.	☐	☐
d)	All electromagnetic waves can travel through space.	☐	☐
e)	Infrared waves have a higher energy than ultraviolet waves.	☐	☐
f)	Gamma rays have a shorter wavelength than X-rays.	☐	☐

Q3 Red and violet are at opposite ends of the spectrum of **visible** light. Tick the boxes to show the things that red and violet light waves have **in common**.

☐ frequency ☐ they are both transverse waves

☐ speed in a vacuum ☐ wavelength

Mr. Red

Ms. Violet

EM Waves and Communication

Q4 The house shown below receives radio signals from a nearby transmitter, even though there is a mountain between the house and the transmitter.

radio transmitter

Use the words below to fill in the blanks in the passage.

atmosphere **short-wave** **long-wave** **FM**

The house can receive .... signals because they can bend around the mountain. It also receives .... signals because they are reflected by the .... However, the mountain blocks .... signals and stops them reaching the house.

Q5 Circle the letter next to the statements below that are **true**.

A Long waves such as radio waves are good for transmitting information over long distances.

B Some wavelengths of radio wave are reflected by the atmosphere and come back to Earth.

C Short wavelength EM waves can travel large distances because they diffract around the curved surface of the Earth.

Top Tips: You may have realised by now that radio waves are really important for communication. I don't want to panic you, but you're more than likely being hit by loads of radio waves right now, there's pretty much nowhere to hide. Luckily, radio waves are harmless, and they'll only affect you if you don't know all about them for your exams. So get learning.

Microwaves

Q1 Complete the sentences below by circling the correct word from each pair.

a) Satellite TV uses **infrared / microwaves** to send signals. The signals from a transmitter are sent into space where they're picked up by the satellite's receiver **transmitter / dish**.

b) The satellite transmits the signal back to **space / Earth** in a different direction, where it is received by a satellite dish on the ground.

Q2 Mr Schwarzenegger and Mr Stallone are arguing about a **mobile phone mast** being put up near their homes.

a) Mr Stallone wants the mast to be put up.
Give **one advantage** to having the mast put up.

....

b) Mr Schwarzenegger says, 'A mobile mast near our homes would **definitely** damage our health.'

i) Is he right? **yes** **no**

ii) Explain your answer.

....

Q3 Sharon is heating up some ready-made curry in her **microwave** oven.

a) Briefly describe how microwaves heat up the curry.

....

....

....

b) The curry comes in a **plastic** container.
Explain why Sharon can leave the curry in its container and her curry will still cook.

....

....

c) Microwave ovens have a **metal lining** to stop microwaves getting out.
What effect does this have on the microwaves? Circle the correct answer below.

A They're **absorbed** by the metal lining

B They're **reflected** by the metal lining

C They're **transmitted** by the metal lining

Infrared and Visible Light

Q1 EM radiation is used in **photography**.
Choose from the words below to complete the sentences below.

more Cameras visible

a) .... use a lens to focus .... light onto a light-sensitive film or electronic sensor.

b) The longer the film or sensor is open to the light, the .... light there will be in the photograph.

Q2 Television **remote controls** use EM waves to send signals to a TV.

Tick the correct box to show what type of radiation is used in wireless remote controls.

Gamma rays	☐	Infrared radiation	☐
Ultraviolet radiation	☐	Visible light	☐

Q3 Infrared sensors can be used in **security systems**.

Circle the **one** correct statement below that explains why infrared can be used.

A — Intruders would give off infrared radiation that can be picked up by sensors which detect body heat, even if the person can't be seen.

B — Light waves reflect off people and on to the infrared sensor, allowing them to be seen on the security system.

C — Infrared sensors emit heat radiation to make it too hot for someone to break in to a building.

Q4 Tick the boxes to show whether these statements are **true** or **false**.

		True	False
a)	Infrared radiation can be used to send information between phones.	☐	☐
b)	Infrared is too dangerous to be used in the home.	☐	☐
c)	Infrared radiation is also known as heat radiation.	☐	☐
d)	Automatic doors use infrared radiation.	☐	☐
e)	Infrared radiation can't be used in optical fibres.	☐	☐

X-rays and Gamma Rays

Q1 Some types of electromagnetic radiation can be dangerous because they are **ionising**.

a) Circle the **three** types of **ionising** electromagnetic radiation.

ultraviolet | visible light | gamma rays | microwaves | X-rays | radio waves | infrared

b) Why do **only** these types of EM radiation cause ionisation?

....

Q2 **X-rays** are one type of ionising radiation used in hospitals.

a) Complete the paragraph below, choosing from the words in the box.

bones	dense	flesh	pictures

Hospitals use X-rays to produce .... to see if a patient has any broken bones. X-rays cannot pass easily through .... and metal because they are absorbed by them. X-rays pass through .... more easily because it's less ....

b) Write down **one** other use of X-rays.

....

Certificate of Birth
Ray

Q3 Tick the boxes to show whether the sentences below are true or false.

	True	False
a) Your cells can be damaged by ionising radiation.	☐	☐
b) The longer you're exposed to ionising radiation the less damage it causes.	☐	☐
c) High doses of ionising radiation can cause cancer.	☐	☐

Top Tips: All EM radiation is the same sort of thing, but it's the ionising types that do serious damage. Learn what ionisation does to molecules and the effects on the body's cells.

X-rays and Gamma Rays

Q4 Use the words below to complete the paragraph.

carefully	kill	cells	cancer	normal

High doses of gamma radiation will .... living ....

Because of this, gamma radiation is used to treat ....

The gamma rays have to be .... directed so that they don't kill too many .... cells.

Q5 Number these processes 1-3 in the correct order to explain how **gamma rays** can be used to **detect** cancer.

- ☐ The camera creates an image which can be used to detect where there might be cancer.
- ☐ A radioactive isotope is injected into the patient.
- ☐ A camera is used to 'see' where the radioactive isotope has travelled to in the body.

Q6 Doctors sometimes use **X-rays** to help them diagnose a patient's injury or illness.

Taking X-rays involves risks for both patients and hospital staff.

a) Explain why the hospital staff taking an X-ray wear **lead aprons** and stand behind **concrete**.

....

....

....

....

b) What can be done to reduce the risk **to the patient**?

....

....

....

UV Radiation and Ozone

Q1 Spending too much time in the **Sun** gives us a higher risk of **skin cancer**.

a) Which part of the radiation from the Sun causes the damage?
Circle the correct answer.

Ultraviolet **Visible light** **Infrared**

b) Give **two other** health problems this radiation can cause.

1. ....

2. ....

Q2 Marie has **darker skin** than her friend, so she has slightly more protection from harmful radiation.

a) **How** does darker skin give this protection?

Think about how much radiation is absorbed.

....

....

b) **i)** Marie uses a sun cream with '**SPF 25**' on the label. What does 'SPF 25' mean?

....

....

ii) If Marie normally burns after **30 minutes** in the sun, how many **minutes** will she be able to stay in the sun for after applying the sun cream?

....

....

Q3 Scientists discovered a '**hole**' in the **ozone layer** over **Antarctica**.

a) How does the ozone layer help protect life on Earth?

....

....

b) How did the scientists make sure their findings were **accurate**?
Tick the boxes next to the **two** correct answers below.

- [ ] They carried out just one study.
- [ ] They used lots of different equipment.
- [ ] They carried out many different studies.
- [ ] They didn't tell anyone about their results.

The Greenhouse Effect

Q1 The diagram below shows how the **greenhouse effect** keeps the Earth warm. Use the descriptions **A** to **C** to label the diagram with the correct letters.

A
The Earth gives off some of the heat radiation.

B
Greenhouse gases absorb radiation from Earth, stopping it radiating back into space.

C
The Earth absorbs radiation from the Sun.

Q2 Tick the boxes next to the **three** greenhouse gases below.

nitrogen ☐ water vapour ☐ carbon dioxide ☐

oxygen ☐ methane ☐ helium ☐

Q3 Which of the statements below best describes the **greenhouse effect**? Circle the **one** correct statement.

A Global warming is caused by humans releasing more greenhouse gases.

B A process which keeps the Earth warm.

C A chemical reaction in the atmosphere which releases heat.

D The natural heating effect of the Sun.

Q4 Greenhouse gases can come from **natural** and **man-made** sources.

a) **i)** Give **one natural source** of carbon dioxide in the atmosphere.

....

ii) Give **two man-made sources** of carbon dioxide.

1. ....

2. ....

b) List **one natural** and **one man-made** source of the greenhouse gas methane.

Natural: ....

Man-made: ....

Global Warming and Climate Change

Q1 Complete the passage by choosing from the words below.

carbon	greenhouse	temperatures

Global .... have risen in recent years.

This is due to an increased .... effect caused

by too much .... dioxide in the atmosphere.

Q2 Below are five statements about climate change.
Tick the boxes to show whether each statement is true or false.

		True	False
a)	Global temperatures are decreasing.	☐	☐
b)	The amount of carbon dioxide in the atmosphere has been increasing.	☐	☐
c)	Global warming is caused by climate change.	☐	☐
d)	Humans are definitely not to blame for global warming.	☐	☐
e)	Global warming can affect the weather.	☐	☐

Q3 Map A shows the coastline of Great Britain **now**. Map B shows how it might look in a **thousand years' time** because of **global warming**.

Map A

Map B

a) Describe the **differences** between Map A and Map B.

....

....

....

b) Explain why the coastline might change because of global warming.

....

....

c) Give **two** other possible effects of global warming.

1. ....

2. ....

Top Tips: You need to know how global warming and climate change affect the Earth. It's not just so you can pass exams — serious changes could happen in your lifetime.

Seismic Waves

Q1 **Underline** the correct words from each pair to complete the following sentences.

Earthquakes / **Mountains** produce shock waves.

These **EM** / **seismic** waves can travel inside and on the surface of the Earth.

Q2 Earthquakes can produce both **S-waves** and **P-waves**.

a) Which of these types of wave travels **faster**?

....

b) Which type of wave **cannot** travel through the **liquid outer core** of the Earth?

....

Q3 Circle the letter next to the **one** statement below which is **true**.

A Both P and S waves can travel from the North Pole to the South Pole.

B P-waves cannot be detected by instruments on the Earth's surface.

C S-waves can only travel through solids.

D P-waves are transverse waves.

Q4 P-waves can quickly **change direction** as they travel through the Earth.

a) Why does this happen?

....

....

b) **i)** Which type of wave doesn't reach the opposite point of the Earth to the site of an earthquake?

....

ii) What does this tell scientists about the structure of the Earth's core?

....

Top Tips: The Mexican Wave has been known to trigger earthquakes at large sports stadiums all over the world. Scientists say that the long-term effects of the Mexican Wave are unknown.

Mixed Questions — Section 8

Q1 The waves A, B and C represent **infrared**, **visible light** and **ultraviolet** radiation (not in that order).

Tick the box next to any of the following statements which are **true**.

- ☐ B represents ultraviolet radiation.
- ☐ A represents infrared radiation.
- ☐ C has the highest frequency.
- ☐ C has the shortest wavelength.
- ☐ A has the largest amplitude.

A

B

C

Q2 Infrared radiation is used by TV **remote controls**. Jake can change the TV channel by pointing the remote control at a mirror on the opposite wall.

a) What property of EM rays does this show? Circle the correct answer.

reflection **refraction** **diffraction**

b) Draw a ray diagram below to show the path of the radiation emitted from the remote control to the TV.

TV remote sensor

mirror

TV remote

Q3 Carbon dioxide is a **greenhouse gas**. Over the last 200 years the amount of carbon dioxide in the atmosphere has **increased**.

a) Circle **two** processes that **release** carbon dioxide into the atmosphere.

respiration **eating vegetables** **photosynthesis** **burning trees** **painting trees**

b) Having more carbon dioxide in the atmosphere is **increasing** global temperatures. The rising temperature could cause changes in the **climate** in some places.

How might climate change affect food production?

....

....

....

Mixed Questions — Section 8

Q4 Jemima wants to sand some floorboards. She can hire **sander A**, which has a power rating of **0.36 kW** and will do the job in **45 minutes**. Or she can hire **sander B**, which has a power rating of **0.4 kW** and will do the job in **30 minutes**.

a) Jemima wants to hire the sander that will use the **least** amount of electrical energy.

i) Calculate how much energy **sander A** would use to do the job.

....

....

Don't forget to convert from minutes to hours — energy use is measured in kilowatt-hours.

ii) Calculate how much energy **sander B** would use to do the job.

....

....

b) Jemima's electricity supplier charges **15p per kWh**. Tick the correct box to show how much it would cost if she used **sander A** for the job (to the nearest penny).

☐ 3p ☐ 1p ☐ 4p ☐ 56p

Q5 EM radiation can be very **useful** but also **dangerous**.

a) Using the boxes below, **number** the following types of EM radiation 1-3 in order of **decreasing** frequency (1 = highest frequency).

☐ Microwaves

☐ X-rays

☐ Infrared

b) A pie is being heated up in a microwave. What happens to **microwaves** when they hit each of these things? Draw a line to match each word to the correct explanation below.

Metal case	reflects microwaves
Food	transmits microwaves
Plastic container	absorbs microwaves

c) The sentences below each contain **one mistake**. Write a correct version of each sentence.

i) Ionising radiation isn't dangerous.

....

ii) Radioactive materials give out non-ionising radiation all the time.

....

Galileo and Copernicus

Q1 Circle the correct word in the following sentences.

a) The planets all orbit the Earth in the **Ptolemaic / Copernican** model.

b) **Ptolemy / Copernicus** said the Sun was at the centre of the Universe.

c) The Copernican model says that the planets all orbit the **Sun / Moon**.

d) The orbits of the planets in the Copernican model are all perfect **circles / ellipses**.

e) Evidence for the Copernican model was found by **Ptolemy / Galileo**.

f) The Ptolemaic model is also a **heliocentric / geocentric** model.

An egocentric model.

Q2 Galileo made some observations of **Jupiter** and **Venus** that helped to provide evidence for the **Copernican** model of the Solar System.

a) What technological advance helped Galileo? Circle the correct answer.

Unmanned probes **Telescopes** **Telephones**

b) Choose the **two** correct statements below to describe what Galileo saw when looking at Jupiter and Venus.

- ☐ The moons of Jupiter
- ☐ The moons of Venus
- ☐ The phases of Jupiter
- ☐ The phases of Venus

c) Complete the passage below using words from the list.

Ptolemaic	Earth	Jupiter	Venus	small	big

Galileo saw moons orbiting .... This showed not everything was in orbit around the .... — so the .... model was wrong. Galileo also noticed that .... has phases (like the Moon). If the Ptolemaic model was right then the changes would be .... But if a Copernican model was right, the changes would be .... — this is what Galileo saw.

Top Tips: New technology changed our idea of how the Solar System worked. Make sure that you know what Copernicus' great idea was, and what Galileo saw that showed it might be right.

The Solar System

Q1 This diagram shows the most important objects in the **Solar System**. It isn't to scale.

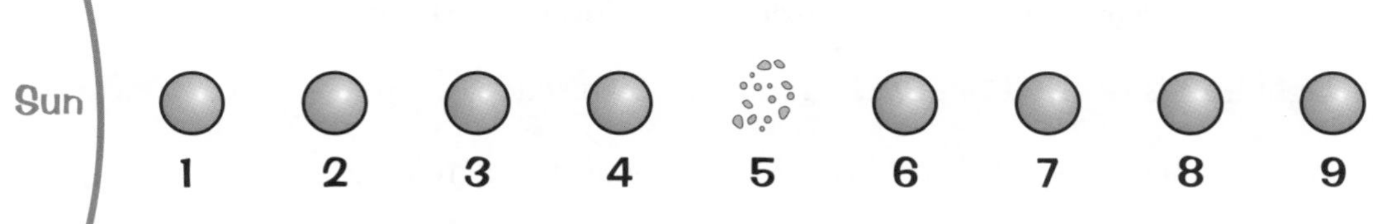

In the table below, write the correct number under each name to show its position in the Solar System. One has been done for you.

Body	Mars	Jupiter	Asteroids	Venus	Saturn	Neptune	Earth	Mercury	Uranus
Number						9			

Q2 As well as planets, there are **asteroids** and **comets** in the Solar System.

a) What are asteroids made of?

....

b) Circle the correct word in each pair.

Comets are made of ice and **black holes** / **dust**.

The tail of a comet is a trail of **asteroids** / **debris**.

c) Where do comets come from?

Q3 The diagram shows the orbit of a **comet** around the Sun.

a) What is the name of the **shape** of the comet's orbit?

....

b) Write down the **letter** that shows at what point (**A** to **D**) the comet is travelling fastest and slowest.

i) The comet is travelling fastest at point: ....

ii) The comet is travelling slowest at point: ....

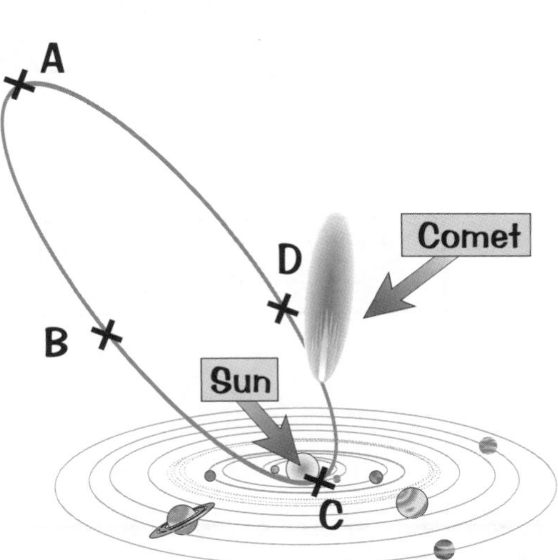

Beyond the Solar System

Q1 Fill in the **blanks** in the sentences below using some of the words from the list.

light years quickly slowly metres

a) Light travels really .... in space.

b) The distances in space are so big that we measure them in ....

Q2 What is a **light year**?

....

....

HINT: just say what you see — with light years it's all in the name.

Q3 The sentences below are **wrong**. Write out correct versions below them.

a) Our Sun is one of thousands of millions of stars in the Solar System.

....

b) The Milky Way is a collection of galaxies.

....

c) There are only a hundred galaxies in the Universe.

....

Q4 Circle the **two** correct statements below about measuring the **distances** to stars.

A — You can measure the distance to a star using parallax.

B — You can measure the distance to a star using fusion.

C — You can measure the distance to a star by counting how many moons it has.

D — You can measure the distance to a star by looking at its brightness.

Top Tips: Wow. The Universe is really old and really, really big. Trying to imagine how big and old it is makes me go mad. Keep yourself safe and just learn that it's really big instead.

Looking into Space

Q1 Some stars look **brighter** than others in the night sky.

a) Circle the correct word in the statements below.

i) We can tell a lot about stars by studying the **radiation** / **convection** coming from them.

ii) When we see things in space we are looking **forwards** / **backwards** in time.

b) When looking at stars, astronomers often complain about light pollution.

i) What is light pollution?

....

ii) Why is light pollution a problem?

....

c) Why does the Earth's atmosphere make it harder to see things in space?

....

Q2 Choose from the words below to complete the paragraphs.

structure   visible   X-ray   all   microwaves

a) Modern telescopes can detect .... parts of the electromagnetic spectrum.

So we can now 'see' things in the Universe that we couldn't see just using .... light.

b) This means we can learn more about the Universe, e.g. its ....

c) .... telescopes are a good way to 'see' violent, high-temperature events in space, e.g. exploding stars.

d) It wasn't until we could detect .... from space that we discovered cosmic microwave background radiation (CMBR).

Q3 When we look into space, we see things as they were in the **past**.

Explain why we see things as they were in the past.

....

....

The Life Cycle of Stars

Q1 Complete each of the sentences about how stars are formed by choosing the correct word from the words listed below them.

a) At first, stars form from clouds of dust and gas called ....

red giants fusion nebulas

b) The force of .... makes the gas and dust spiral in together, which causes the temperature to rise.

pressure gravity mass

c) When the temperature is high enough, ... nuclei fuse (join) together to make .... nuclei.

hydrogen oxygen helium

d) When they fuse, they give out huge amounts of .... and a star is born.

gravity energy steam

Q2 Choose from the words below to complete the paragraph.

white	hydrogen	red giant	fades	unstable	nebula

A star in its stable phase will eventually run out of .... It then swells into a .... The star will then become .... and will eject gas and dust as a planetary ...., leaving a hot, dense core called a .... dwarf. This cools down and eventually ....

Due to printing restrictions, red giants are unavailable.

Q3 A star in its **stable** phase **doesn't change size**, even though there are forces pushing it outwards and forces pulling everything inwards.

a) What causes the **outward** pressure on the star?

....

b) What is the force pulling the star **inwards**? ....

c) Why doesn't the star change size?

....

d) What is another name for a star in its stable phase? ....

Top Tips: The life cycle of a star is by far the saddest thing I've heard all week. If you've got no idea what I'm talking about, then you probably haven't answered question two. Off you pop.

The Life of the Universe

Q1 Complete the sentence below by circling the correct word in each pair.

The Universe is getting **bigger / smaller**.

Almost all its galaxies seem to be moving **away from / towards** each other.

Q2 Francesca is standing by a busy street when an ambulance rushes past, with its sirens on.

a) Tick the box(es) to say what will happen to the sound reaching Francesca as the ambulance **moves away**.

- ☐ The **frequency** of sound **becomes higher** as the ambulance passes Francesca.
- ☐ The **wavelength** of the sound **seems longer** to Francesca as the ambulance moves away.
- ☐ As the ambulance moves away, the **frequency** of sound **seems lower** to Francesca.
- ☐ The **wavelength** of the ambulance's siren **becomes shorter** as it moves past Francesca.

b) The ambulance turns around and heads back up the road towards Francesca. Complete the sentences below by circling the correct word from each pair.

> As the ambulance moves towards Francesca, the frequency of the sound will seem **higher / lower** to her and the wavelength of the sound will **increase / decrease**.

c) What is the name of the **effect** described in parts **a)** and **b)**?

....

d) Tick the boxes to show whether each statement about the effect given in part **c)** is **true** or **false**.

	True	False
The effect only happens to longitudinal waves.	☐	☐
The effect can happen to light waves and microwaves.	☐	☐

Q3 **Red-shift** provides evidence that the Universe is **expanding**.

a) Light from distant galaxies is red-shifted. What has happened to the wavelength of the light from these galaxies?

....

....

b) Explain how red-shift shows the Universe is expanding.

....

....

....

The Life of the Universe

Q4 Complete this passage using the words supplied below.

matter	Red-shift	energy	expand	explosion

Many scientists believe that the Universe started with all the .... and .... in one small space. There was a huge ...., and space and the material in it started to .... This is the Big Bang theory. .... measurements provide evidence for the Big Bang theory, as it supports the idea that the Universe is expanding.

Q5 Tick the correct box to say whether each of the following statements are true or false.

		True	False
a)	CMBR is mostly made up of radio waves.	☐	☐
b)	The Big Bang theory is the only theory that can explain CMBR.	☐	☐
c)	The CMBR comes from radiation that was around shortly after the beginning of the Universe.	☐	☐

Q6 Describe **one** thing the Big Bang theory can't be used to explain about the start of the Universe.

....

....

Q7 It is difficult to work out **how** and **when** the Universe will end.
This is because it's **hard** to work out how fast the Universe is expanding.

a) Circle the **two** things below we need to measure and observe to work out how fast it's expanding.

Friction in the Universe

The distances between objects

How objects in the Universe move

Temperature of the Universe

b) Explain why it's difficult to measure these things.

....

....

....

Mixed Questions — Section 9

Q1 The **Sun** is at the centre of our Solar System.

a) Circle the **one** correct statement below.

A — The Moon orbits comets.

C — The Milky Way orbits the Sun.

B — There are eight planets that orbit the Sun.

b) Which galaxy is the Sun in?

....

Q2 Tick the boxes to show which of these statements are **true** and which are **false**.

		True	False
a)	The Ptolemaic model has the Sun at the centre of the Solar System.	☐	☐
b)	There are eight planets that orbit the Earth.	☐	☐
c)	The asteroid belt in our Solar System is between Jupiter and Saturn.	☐	☐
d)	Comets have small, circular orbits around the Sun.	☐	☐

Q3 **Astronomers** watch the night sky to find out about **stars** and **galaxies**.

a) Choose from the words below to complete the paragraph.

absorbs **radiation** **pollution**

Scientists use .... coming from space to learn more about stars. The Earth's atmosphere .... some light before it can reach us on Earth. Light .... makes it hard to see dim objects.

b) About how many stars are there in the Milky Way galaxy?

....

Don't panic. Just give a really rough estimate.

c) CMBR is detected coming from all parts of the Universe.
It is mainly in the **microwave** part of the EM spectrum.

Complete each of the sentences by choosing the correct word from the words listed below.

expanding **CMBR** **red-shift**

The Big Bang theory is the only theory that can explain the existence of the .... The .... of light from distant galaxies also supports the Big Bang theory, as it is evidence that the Universe is ....

Answers

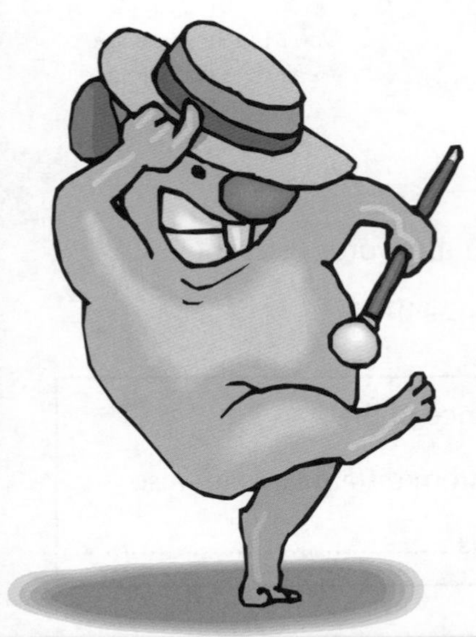

Section 1 — Nerves and Hormones

Section 1 — Nerves and Hormones

Pages 1-2 — The Nervous System

Q1 E.g. so they can react/respond to the changes in their surroundings.
Q2 Light receptor cells contain a nucleus, cytoplasm and a cell membrane.
Q3 hearing
Q4 a) five
b) receptors
c) balance, body position
d) skin, temperature
e) electrical
f) eye, light
g) CNS
Q5 a) central nervous system
b) brain and spinal cord
Q6 a) muscle
b) hormones
Q7 receptor, sensory neurone, CNS, motor neurone, effector
Q8 a) Chemical receptor. **Tongue** underlined.
b) Chemical receptor. **Nose** underlined.
c) Sound receptor. **Ears** underlined.
d) Pain receptor. **Skin** underlined.

Page 3 — Synapses and Reflexes

Q1 a) quickly
b) protect
c) without
d) neurones
e) chemicals
Q2 a) V = sensory neurone, W = synapse, X = relay neurone, Y = synapse, Z = motor neurone
b) electrically
c) i) effector
ii) contracting
Q3 The nerve signal is taken across the gap by chemicals. These chemicals set off a new electrical signal in the next neurone.

Page 4 — Hormones

Q1 chemical, glands, blood, target
Q2 a) e.g. FSH / LH
b) e.g. oestrogen
Q3 a) slower
b) longer
c) in a general way
d) on a precise area
Q4 a) blood
b) oestrogen
c) FSH
d) glands
e) LH

Page 5 — The Menstrual Cycle

Q1 FSH — pituitary gland
oestrogen — ovaries
Q2 a) FSH — causes an egg to mature in one of the ovaries
LH — causes the release of an egg from the ovaries
Oestrogen — inhibits FSH
b) FSH
Q3 a) & b)

Stage 1 | Stage 2 | Stage 3 | Stage 4 | Next cycle
D | A | C | B
Day 1 | Day 4 | Day 14 | Day 28

Pages 6-7 — Controlling Fertility

Q1 a) too low
b) stimulate
c) to get pregnant
Q2 contraceptive, high, progesterone, side effects, blood clots, lower, side effects
Q3 a) E.g. it's very effective at preventing pregnancy.
It reduces the risk of getting some types of cancer.
b) Because it has fewer side effects.
Q4 The contraceptive pill — any two from e.g.: there's still a very slight chance of getting pregnant. / Causes side effects like headaches. / Doesn't protect against STDs.
FSH / LH — e.g. it doesn't always work / it can cause multiple pregnancies.
Q5 a) 2. The woman's eggs are collected from her ovaries and fertilised in a lab using a man's sperm.
3. The fertilised eggs are grown into embryos.
4. Once the embryos are tiny balls of cells, one or two of them are transferred to the woman's womb.
b) **Advantages** — It allows infertile couples to have children.
Disadvantages — There can be reactions to the hormones, e.g. vomiting. It may result in multiple births, which can be risky.

Page 8 — Plant Hormones

Q1 a) False
b) True
c) False
d) True
e) True
f) False
Q2 a) E.g. the growth of shoots / the growth of roots / flowering
b) i) auxins
ii) in solution
Q3 a)

b) The plant shoots will grow towards the light.

Page 9 — Commercial Use of Plant Hormones

Q1 E.g. as selective weedkillers / growing cuttings with rooting powder / controlling the ripening of fruit / controlling dormancy.
Q2 a)

Concentration of growth hormone (parts per million)	0	0.001	0.01	0.1	1
Length of root at start of investigation (mm)	20	20	20	20	20
Length of root 1 week after investigation started (mm)	26	32	28	23	21
Increase of root length (mm)	6	12	8	3	1

Section 2 — Diet and Health

b)

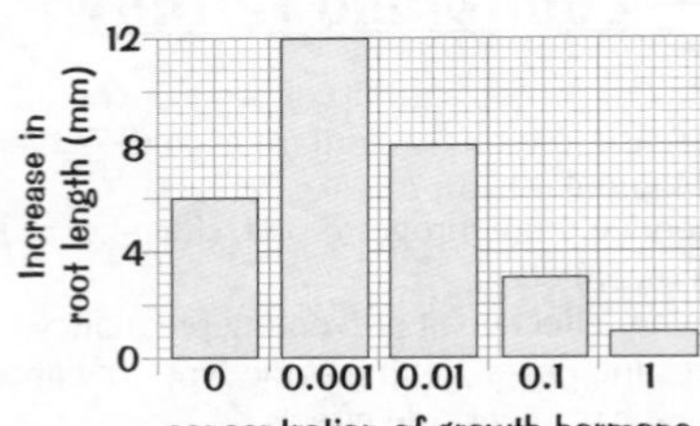

c) 0.001 parts per million

Q3 a) It increased crop yield.

b) The weedkillers change the weeds' normal growth patterns, which soon kills them. Grass and crops aren't affected by these weedkillers.

Page 10 — Homeostasis and Body Temperature

Q1 a) warm up

b) cool down

c) warm up

d) warm up

Q2 a) The maintenance of a constant internal environment in the body.

b) They need steady conditions in order to function properly.

c) The nervous communication system

d) Receptors — detect a change in the internal environment.
Processing centres — receive information on the change in the internal environment and organise the response.
Effectors — produce the response to the change.

Q3 a) 37 °C

b) i) E.g. heat stroke / dehydration

ii) E.g. hypothermia

c) When sweat evaporates it uses heat from the skin. This transfers heat to the environment, cooling you down.

Page 11 — Controlling Ion Levels and Water Content

Q1 The following should be ticked:
Ronald loses salt in his sweat.
Ronald's kidneys remove salt from his blood.
Ronald gets rid of salt in his urine.

Q2 a) To keep the water level in the cells just right for them to work properly.

b) In food / in drinks / from respiration

Q3 a) E.g. exercise / external temperature / intake of fluids/salts

b) i) concentrated

ii) more concentrated

iii) large

c) When you exercise you get hot and sweat more. Water is lost in the sweat, so the kidneys reabsorb more water into the blood and produce concentrated urine.

Page 12 — Controlling Blood Sugar

Q1 a) insulin

b) i) pancreas

ii)

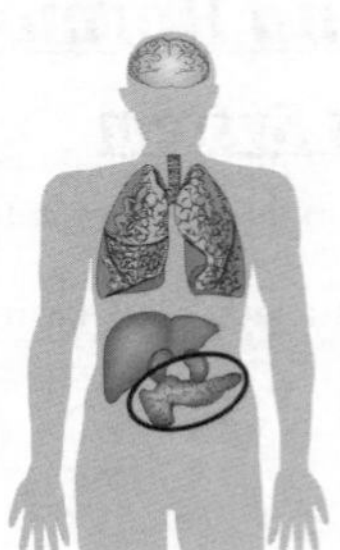

Q2 two, pancreas, rise, diet, sugary foods, insulin

Q3 a) Eating foods containing carbohydrates.

b) To provide the body's cells with a constant supply of energy.

Pages 13-14 — Mixed Questions — Section 1

Q1 a) In the blood.

b) slow response, response lasts for a long time

c) i) auxins

ii) Negative phototropism is when— plant roots grow away from light.
Positive geotropism is when — roots grow in the direction of gravity.
Negative geotropism is when — plant shoots grow away from gravity.

Q2 a) 28 days

b) An egg is released / ovulation.

c) FSH / LH.

d) It inhibits FSH, so no eggs mature.

Q3 a) The sense organs are the ears, and they contain sound and balance receptors.

b) i) Sensory neurones carry impulses from receptors to the CNS. Motor neurones carry impulses from the CNS to the effectors (muscles and glands).

ii) synapse

Q4 a) i) Skin — water is lost when we sweat.

ii) Lungs — water is lost as we breathe.

iii) Kidneys — water is lost as urine.

b) i) More water. The exercise will increase his temperature, so he will have to sweat more to cool down.

ii) More water. The exercise will make him breathe harder, so more water will be lost via the lungs.

iii) Less water. More will be lost as sweat and in the breath, so to balance this the kidneys will give out less water in the urine.

Section 2 — Diet and Health

Page 15 — Diet and Metabolic Rate

Q1 a) teenagers

b) They're still growing.

Q2 a) build, repair (in either order)

b) energy

c) warm, energy

d) minerals, tiny

Q3 a) speed, reactions

b) proportion of muscle to fat in the body, inherited factors, amount of exercise

Q4 a) Alice — she has a more active job, so needs more energy, so will have a higher metabolic rate.

b) David — he has more muscle than fat, so needs more energy, so will have a higher metabolic rate.

Section 2 — Diet and Health

Page 16 — Factors Affecting Health

Q1 Eating too much fat or carbohydrate can cause obesity. Not eating enough vitamins or minerals can cause deficiency diseases.
Obesity can cause type 2 diabetes.
Q2 a) i) energy
ii) obesity
b) i) inherited
ii) heart disease
Q3 healthier, energy, fat, muscle, metabolic, less, obesity

Page 17 — Evaluating Food, Lifestyle and Diet

Q1 less, use, less, increases
Q2 a) Burger B
b) It contains more fat (including saturated fat) and carbohydrate than Burger A, and has a higher energy content.
Q3 a) Report B
b) It was published in a science journal. It used a large sample size.

Page 18 — The Circulatory System

Q1 a) i) right
ii) left
b) i) muscle cells
ii) They need a supply of nutrients and oxygen to keep the heart beating continually.
Q2 a) A = Artery, B = Vein, C = Capillary
b) i) Arteries carry blood away from the heart at high pressure so they need to be strong and elastic to withstand this pressure.
ii) Capillaries supply cells with substances. Walls that are one cell thick allow substances to move in and out quickly and easily.
iii) Veins carry blood back to the heart. Valves prevent the blood flowing back in the wrong direction.

Page 19 — Heart Rate and Blood Pressure

Q1 artery, two, higher, relaxes
Q2 a) The number of times your heart beats in one minute.
b) Arteries pulse when blood is pumped through them by a heart beat, so you can measure your pulse rate to work out your heart rate.
Q3 a) three
b) Because individuals vary.
c) Nigel
d) Damage caused by fatty deposits could cause the artery to become blocked. If the artery is supplying the heart then an area of heart muscle will be totally cut off from its blood supply. This causes a heart attack.

Page 20 — Factors Affecting Heart Disease

Q1 a) Lifestyle
b) Lifestyle
c) Non-lifestyle
d) Lifestyle
e) Lifestyle
Q2 Regular
Q3 People in poorer countries eat less junk food and so have a lower fat diet.
Poorer people in poorer countries will have to walk more because they cannot afford cars and so they get more exercise.
Q4 a) Studies that look at the patterns of disease and the factors that affect them.
b) E.g. You could study a group of people who all died from heart disease to look for similarities in their lifestyle that may be linked to heart disease.

Page 21 — Drugs

Q1 a) A chemical that alters the reactions in your body.
b) i) You want a drug really badly. You can get withdrawal symptoms if the drug is not taken.
ii) E.g. heroin
c) To lower the risk of heart and circulatory disease.
Q2 a) E.g. steroids, stimulants
b) They may not know all the health risks.
It makes sporting competitions unfair.
Q3 a) In the group that were given statins.
b) Statins combined with lifestyle changes helps to reduce cholesterol levels more than just lifestyle changes alone.
c) The group that wasn't given statins act as the control.

Page 22 — Testing Medicinal Drugs

Q1 1. Drug is tested on human cells and tissues
2. Drug is tested on live animals
3. Human volunteers are used to test the drug
Q2 sleeping pill, morning sickness, tested, unborn, arm, leg, banned, leprosy
Q3 a) E.g. to find the optimum dose / to test how well the drug works.
b) A placebo is a substance that's like a drug being tested but contains no drug.
c) A double blind trial is one where neither the scientist doing the test nor the patient knows whether they are getting a drug or a placebo.

Page 23 — Recreational Drugs

Q1 a) Liver disease, unconsciousness and addiction should be underlined.
b) Cancer, addiction, lung disease should be underlined.
Q2 a) Any two from: e.g. for enjoyment / relaxation / stress relief.
b) E.g. they can cause problems with the heart / circulatory system.
Q3 People are more likely to use cannabis than hard drugs.
Q4 a) Because so many more people take them.
b) E.g. the NHS spends large amounts each year on treating patients with drinking-related problems.

Page 24 — Fighting Disease

Q1 microorganism, infectious
Q2 small, damaging, toxins, cells, copies, bursts, damage
Q3 a) They engulf and digest pathogens. They produce antitoxins.
b) white, antigen, antibodies, antigen, antibodies
Q4 Tiny bits of cells help the blood clot quickly to stop anything else getting in.

Page 25 — Fighting Disease — Vaccination

Q1 a) false
b) true
c) false
d) true
Q2 a) measles, mumps and rubella

Section 3 — Genetics, Evolution and the Environment

b) 2. The inactive MMR pathogens had antigens on their surface.
3. John's white blood cells learnt to make the antibodies specific to these antigens.
4. If he is later infected with any of the MMR pathogens, John's memory cells will quickly make antibodies specific to the antigens on that pathogen.
5. The antibodies will kill the pathogen so John won't get ill.

Q3 a) E.g. they've helped to control lots of infectious diseases that used to be common in the UK. / Epidemics can be prevented if lots of people are vaccinated.
b) E.g. Some people do not become immune after vaccination. You can sometimes have a bad reaction, e.g. swelling at the injection site.

Pages 26-27 — Fighting Disease — Drugs

Q1 A drug that kills bacteria.
Q2 reproduce, drugs, killing, mutations, resistant, antibiotic-resistant, natural selection
Q3 E.g. MRSA
Q4 A lid should be taped on the Petri dish to stop any microorganisms in the air getting in.
The Petri dish and culture medium should be sterilised to kill any unwanted microorganisms.
The inoculating loop should be sterilised by passing it through a flame.
Q5 a) The medicine doesn't kill the virus causing the cold — it just relieves the symptoms.
b) Colds are caused by a virus and antibiotics only kill bacteria.
c) Different antibiotics kill different types of bacteria, so a patient needs to be treated with the right antibiotic for it to have an effect.
Q6 a) It started to decrease in number.
b) i) 37 °C
ii) 25 °C, because harmful pathogens won't grow.
iii) 37 °C, so that microorganisms can grow a lot faster.

Page 28 — Fighting Disease — Past and Future

Q1 a) 12%
b) i) He asked all the doctors to wash their hands using antiseptic solution before seeing patients.
ii) The antiseptic solution killed bacteria on the doctors' hands.
Q2 a) Mutations
b) won't
c) immune
d) an epidemic
e) antigens
f) a pandemic
Q3 a) It's fallen dramatically.
b) i) E.g. by not overusing antibiotics.
ii) E.g. they're trying to develop new antibiotics that will kill resistant strains of bacteria.

Pages 29-30 — Mixed Questions — Section 2

Q1 a) Vitamins
b) Overeating
c) more
d) energy
Q2 true, false, false, true, false
Q3 a) i) E.g. to increase muscle size
ii) E.g. high blood pressure
b) Ecstasy can increase your heart rate and blood pressure which increases the risk of heart disease.

Q4 Any three from, e.g: Whether it is published in a well-known science journal. / Whether it was written by a qualified person. / How large a sample was used. / Whether there have been other studies that have found similar results.
Q5 valves in veins — keep blood flowing in the right direction
thin walls of capillaries — allow the blood to exchange substances with cells
thick, elastic walls of arteries — cope with the high pressure of blood leaving the heart
Q6 a) kwashiorkor
b) Any three from: carbohydrates / fats / vitamins / minerals / water / fibre
Q7 a) The bacteria have been killed by the antibiotic.
b) i) Antibiotic 3.
ii) Flu and colds are caused by viruses but antibiotics don't kill viruses.

Section 3 — Genetics, Evolution and the Environment

Page 31 — Genes, Chromosomes and DNA

Q1 nucleus, chromosomes, genes
Q2 gene, chromosome, nucleus, cell
Q3 a) 'Alleles' are different forms of the same gene.
b) Alleles give different versions of a characteristic.
Q4 There are two chromosome 7s in a human nucleus, one from each parent.

Pages 32-33 — Genetic Diagrams

Q1 a) B — white
C — yellow
D — white
b) 50%
Q2 a) True
b) False
c) True
d) False
Q3 recessive, are two copies, rr
Q4 two, one, dominant, recessive, two
Q5 a)

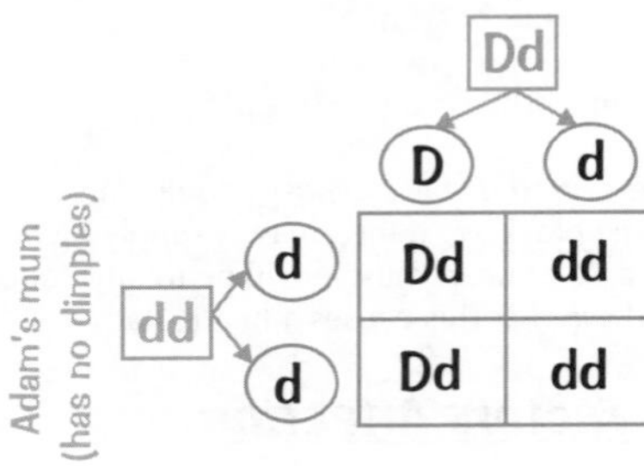

b) i) 50%
ii) 100%

Page 34 — Genetic Disorders and Sex Chromosomes

Q1 sex, X, Y, males
Q2 a) Susan is a carrier of cystic fibrosis so she only has one recessive allele. She would need two recessive alleles to be a sufferer.
b) i) No
ii) Yes

Section 3 — Genetics, Evolution and the Environment

Page 35 — Reproduction

Q1 a) two
b) gametes
c) identical
d) Sexual
e) asexual

Q2 a) clones
b) sperm
c) fuse together

Q3 a) Sexual reproduction

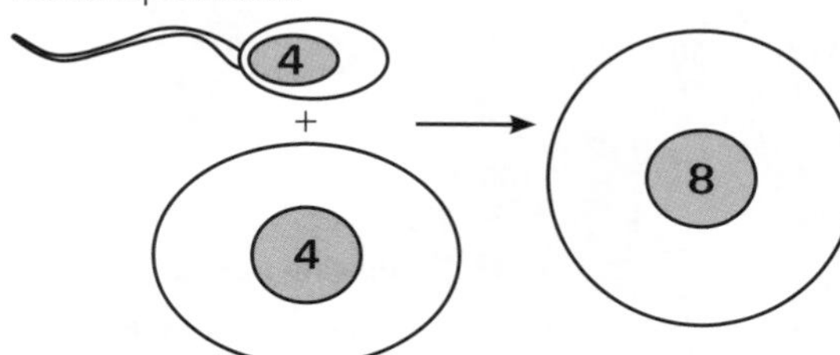

b) Asexual reproduction

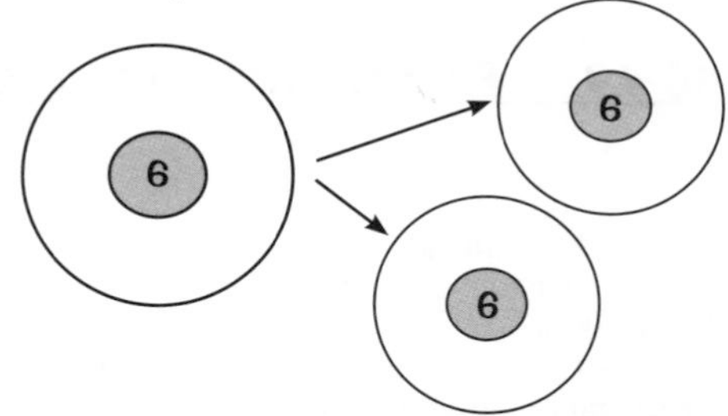

Q4 Asexual reproduction produces cells with identical genes to the parent cells.

Page 36 — Cloning

Q1 Prize bull and cow are mated. → An embryo develops. → The embryo is then split many times, before any cells become specialised. → The embryos are put into the wombs of (implanted into) lots of other cows. → The embryos are clones, so all the baby calves will have the same genes.

Q2 a) You take a few plant cells and grow them into new plants — clones of the parent plant.
b) E.g. it's quick / it's cheap

Q3 implantation in an adult female = **D**
useful nucleus removed = **B**
putting the useful nucleus into an empty egg cell = **C**

Page 37 — Genetic Engineering

Q1 A gene in human DNA → Enzymes cut the gene out of human DNA → Enzymes cut the DNA of bacteria → Then enzymes insert the useful gene into the DNA of bacteria

Q2 very early, develop, genetically modified, changed

Q3 viruses, insects, herbicides

Q4 Pro: GM crops can increase — the yield of a crop.
Con: GM crops might decrease — the number of flowers that live by the crops.
Pro: GM crops can include extra nutrients to — prevent deficiency diseases.
Con: some people worry GM crops aren't — safe to eat.

Page 38 — Classification

Q1 a) class, order, family, genus
b) A supporting rod up the back of their body.

Q2 a) Plants — Contain chlorophyll
Fungi — Are saprophytes
Protoctists — Are unicellular and have a nucleus
Prokaryotes — Are unicellular but don't have a nucleus
b) Animals
c) Because they're non-living.

Q3 a) i) breed together
ii) breed
iii) can
b) Not all organisms interbreed — some reproduce asexually. Some hybrids are fertile.

Pages 39-40 — Adaptations

Q1 a) hot
b) cold
c) dry
d) salty

Q2 extremophiles, pressure, temperature

Q3 a) In the desert.
b) i) E.g. the cactus has spines instead of leaves, because the small surface area reduces water loss.
ii) E.g. the cactus has a thick stem where it can store water.
iii) E.g. the cactus roots spread out over a large area to absorb water quickly.

Q4 a) i) white fur
ii) It provides camouflage (white colour makes it hard to spot against a snowy background).
b) It is a warning colour to scare off predators.
c) E.g. poison in their stings.

Q5 a) The kangaroo rat.
b) The polar bear.
c) Less heat.
d) It would be bigger than the polar bear's because the desert is very hot, so the kangaroo rat needs to lose more heat than the polar bear, which lives in a cold climate.

Page 41 — Variation

Q1 have differences, genes, gametes, hair style, environment, a mixture of genetic and environmental factors, variation

Q2 a) True
b) False
c) True

Q3 a) Yes. Features like blood group are controlled by genes, so I would expect the girls to have the same blood group.
b) I don't think that birthmarks are caused by genes. Identical twins have exactly the same genes, so if Stephanie had a birthmark then Helen should too if it was genetic.
c) No. Intelligence is determined by both genes and environment.

Page 42 — Evolution

Q1 A mutation is a change in an organism's DNA.
Useful characteristics may give an organism a better chance of surviving and reproducing.
A helpful mutation is more likely to be passed on to future generations by natural selection.

Q2 a) Rays and Sharks
b) They could be in competition.

Section 3 — Genetics, Evolution and the Environment

Q3 2. Short-sighted birds in poor light didn't spot the stick-like moths.
3. So the stick-like moths were more likely to survive and reproduce.
4. Genes that made the moths look like sticks were more likely to be passed on to the next generation.

Page 43 — More About Evolution

Q1 A, D, E
Q2 Lamarck, more developed, longer, the next generation
Q3 a) True
b) False
c) True
d) True
Q4 Any two from, e.g. because they have different beliefs / because they have been influenced by different people / because they think differently.

Pages 44-45 — Competition and Environmental Change

Q1 a) Light — Plants
Minerals from the soil — Plants
Space — Plants and Animals
Water — Plants and Animals
Food — Animals
Mates — Animals
b) The two species would have to compete for it.
c) E.g. as a source of food.
Q2 a) April
b) Boxes ticked: Water temperature, Lower number of predator fish
Q3 a)

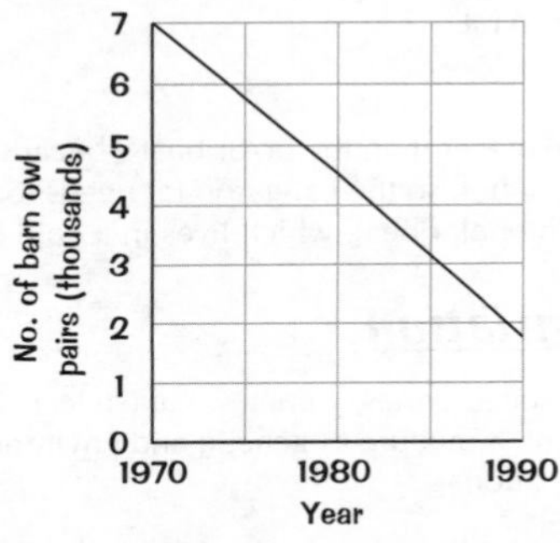

b) The number of barn owls decreased between 1970 and 1990.
c) E.g. fewer prey / more diseases / increase in competitors.
Q4 a) It means a change in where the organism lives.
b) The maximum height up the mountain where the snail was found has increased over the last 100 years.
c) E.g. average rainfall

Page 46 — Measuring Environmental Change

Q1 a) True
b) True
c) False
Q2 a) Indicator species.
b) Collect the samples in the same way
c) Mayfly larvae prefer clean water.
d) It leads to less oxygen in the water.
Q3 a) 1970.
b) About 1 million tonnes.
c) lichen

Page 47 — Pyramids of Biomass and Energy Transfer

Q1 a) crab
b) algae
c) it decreases
Q2 a) true
b) true
c) false
d) false
e) false
Q3 a) 50 g
b) i) C
ii)

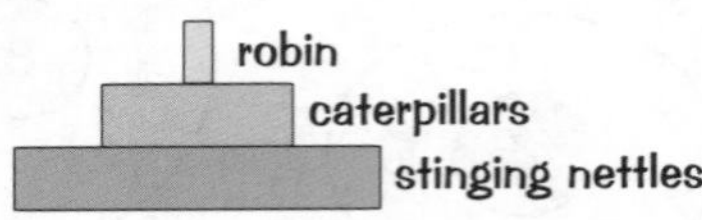

c) The total mass of the organisms decreases at each step as shown by this pyramid.
d) 500 ÷ 25 = **20 g**

Pages 48-49 — Energy Efficiency and Decay

Q1 a) i) 50 000 – 8000 = **42 000 kJ**
ii) 8000 – 500 = **7500 kJ**
b) i) (8000 ÷ 50 000) × 100 = **16%**
ii) (500 ÷ 8000) × 100 = **6.25%**
Q2 take, waste products, dead organisms, decay, microorganisms, soil, plants
Q3 Any two from:
Shredded waste — Shredding the waste gives more surface area for the microorganisms to work on.
Mesh sides — These allow contact with the air, so plenty of oxygen is available to help the microorganisms work faster.
Open top — This allows contact with the air, so plenty of oxygen is available to help the microorganisms work faster.
Q4 (2070 ÷ 103 500) × 100 = **2%**
Q5 a) not stable
b) stable
c) not stable
d) stable

Page 50 — The Carbon Cycle

Q1 carbon dioxide, photosynthesis, respire, microorganisms, eating, carbohydrates, waste, detritus
Q2 Plants use — carbon dioxide to build complex molecules.
Microorganisms release carbon dioxide by — respiration whilst decaying waste and dead tissue.
Animals and plants release — carbon dioxide through respiration.
Animals take in — carbon through feeding.
Plants take in carbon by — photosynthesis.
Q3 a) fossil fuel (accept coal or oil)
b) combustion / burning

Page 51 — The Nitrogen Cycle

Q1 Plants — By absorbing nitrates from the soil
Animals — By eating other organisms
Q2 a) eating
b) proteins
c) i) decomposition
ii) decomposers / bacteria and fungi

Section 4 — Atoms, Elements and Compounds

Pages 52-53 — Mixed Questions — Section 3

Q1 a) i) It increased.
ii) It stayed constant.
b) The goat.
c) natural selection
Q2 a) i) DNA
ii) cut
iii) enzymes
b) asexual
Q3 a) Egg A.
b) The parents of egg A provided the genetic material that was inserted into egg B, so the toad inherited its features from these parents.
c) E.g. space and food
d) Species that are very sensitive to changes in their environment e.g. they can't live in some conditions.
Q4 Any three from e.g.: cloning quickly gets you lots of ideal offspring. / Studying clones could help us understand some diseases. / Cloned organisms all have the same genes, so if a disease appears they could all be wiped out. / It's possible that cloned animals might not be as healthy as normal ones.

Section 4 — Atoms, Elements and Compounds

Page 54 — Atoms and Elements

Q1 a) zero
b) element
c) protons, electrons (in either order)
d) protons
Q2

Particle	Charge
Proton	+1
Neutron	0
Electron	-1

Q3 a) nucleus
b) electron
c) proton
d) neutron
e) proton
Q4

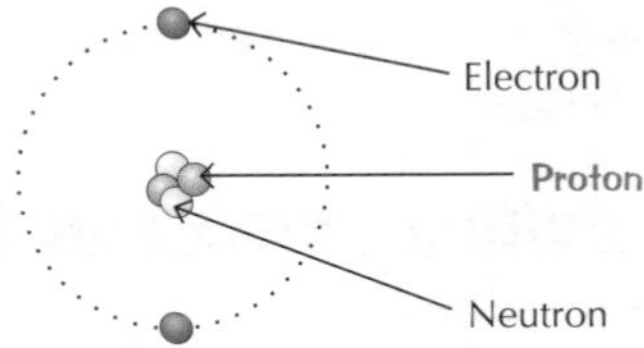

Q5 copper and oxygen should be circled

Page 55 — The Periodic Table

Q1 a) A group in the periodic table is a **vertical** column of elements.
b) Metals are on the **left** side of the periodic table.
c) There are about 100 different **elements** in the periodic table.
d) Each element has a different **symbol**.
e) Elements in the same group have **similar** properties.
f) The symbol for copper is **Cu** and the symbol for calcium is **Ca**.

Q2 a)

b) 11
c) 11
d) 23 – 11 = 12
Q3 a) The following should be ticked: **A** and **D**
b) Group I, outer electrons, properties
Q4 a) false
b) true
c) true
d) true

Pages 56-57 — Electron Shells

Q1 a) true
b) false
c) false
d) false
Q2 E.g. The inner most electron shell should be filled first / there should be two electrons in the inner shell.
The outer shell contains too many electrons, it only holds a maximum of 8 electrons.
Q3 a) 2,2
b) 2,6
c) 2,8,4
Q4 Missing words are: outer shell, unreactive, reactive, unreactive, reactive.
Q5 a) 2,8,7
b)

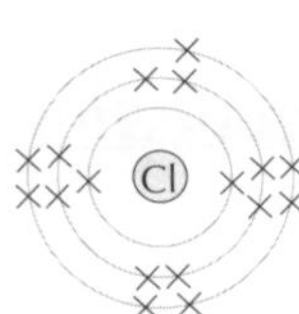

c) Its outer shell isn't full (it's keen to get an extra electron).
Q6

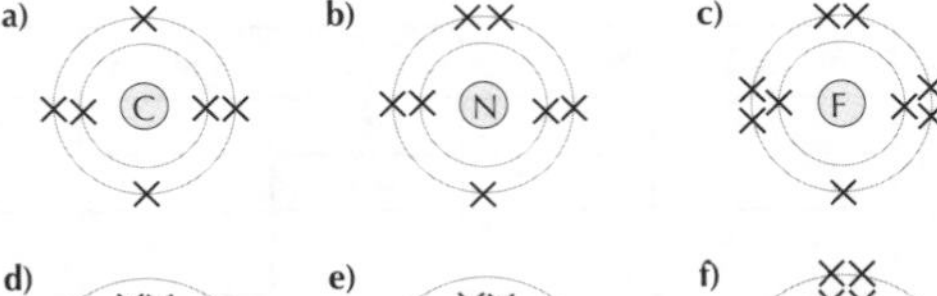

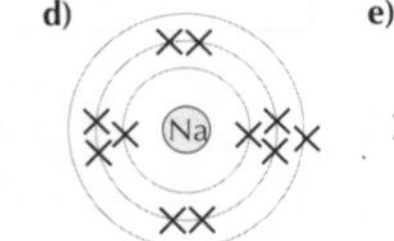

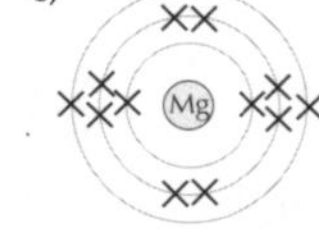

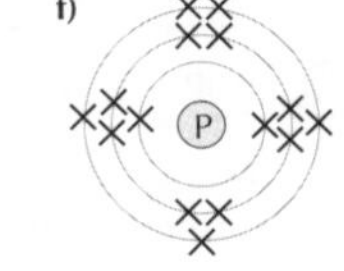

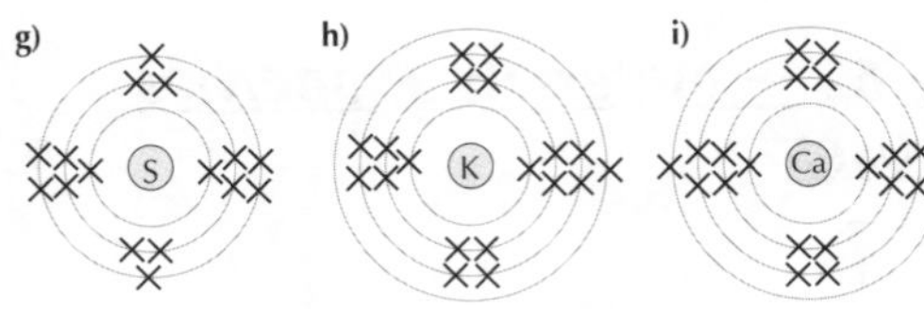

Page 58 — Compounds and Formulas

Q1 Missing words are: electrons, molecules, covalent.
Q2 a) True
b) False
c) True
Q3 a) C_2H_5OH (accept C_2H_6O)
b) 2
c) 9
Q4 a) CH_4
b) C_2H_6
c) C_3H_8

Section 4 — Atoms, Elements and Compounds

Pages 59-60 — Chemical Reactions

Q1

Equation	Reactants	Products
$C + O_2 \rightarrow CO_2$	C and O_2	CO_2
nitrogen + hydrogen → ammonia	nitrogen and hydrogen	ammonia
$2Na + Cl_2 \rightarrow 2NaCl$	(2)Na and Cl_2	(2)NaCl

Q2 a) four H atoms and two O atoms
b) four H atoms and two O atoms
c) Yes, because there are the same number of each type of atom on each side.
Q3 a) Correctly balanced
b) Incorrectly balanced
c) Incorrectly balanced
d) Correctly balanced
e) Correctly balanced
Q4 $2C + O_2 \rightarrow 2CO$
Q5 a) Reactants: magnesium and oxygen
Products: magnesium oxide
b) magnesium + oxygen → magnesium oxide
c) $2Mg + O_2 \rightarrow 2MgO$
Q6 a) calcium oxide + water → calcium hydroxide
b) Atoms aren't made or lost during a reaction. So, the mass of the reactants is the same as the mass of the products.
c) 11 g (29 – 18 = 11).
Q7 a) $CO_2 + \mathbf{4}H_2 \rightarrow CH_4 + \mathbf{2}H_2O$
b) $K_2O + H_2O \rightarrow \mathbf{2}KOH$
c) $MgCO_3 + \mathbf{2}HCl \rightarrow MgCl_2 + H_2O + CO_2$
d) $\mathbf{2}Li + \mathbf{2}H_2O \rightarrow \mathbf{2}LiOH + H_2$

Page 61 — Materials and Properties

Q1 a) strong
b) break
c) pulling
d) pushing
e) high
Q2

Substance	Water	Sulfur	Propanone	Sodium chloride
Melting point (°C)	0	115	-95	801
Boiling point (°C)	100	444	56	1465
State at room temperature	**liquid**	**solid**	**liquid**	**solid**

Q3 a) True
b) False
c) True
Q4 a) Compressive strength.
b) B — Diamond is very hard.

Page 62 — Materials, Properties and Uses

Q1 a) B
b) D
c) A
d) C
Q2 Slate is used for making roof tiles because — it lasts a long time.
Stainless steel is used for making knives and forks because — it is non-toxic.
Rubber is used for making car tyres because — it is strong but flexible.
Q3 a) E.g. the saucepan needs to be strong. / The saucepan needs to be stiff. / Metal conducts heat well, so food in the pan will heat up quickly.
b) E.g. a wooden handle will be strong. / A wooden handle will be stiff. / Wood does not conduct heat, so the handle will stay cool.
Q4 a) pyjamas
b) E.g. soft / long lasting / low density / non-toxic / flame resistant.
c) E.g. tents are used outside, so the material they're made from must be waterproof.

Page 63 — Properties of Metals

Q1 a) Metal 3 (because it has the best heat conduction, and is strong and resistant to corrosion).
b) Metal 2 (because it is the strongest, isn't too expensive and won't corrode too much). (Accept metal 3.)
c) Metal 1 (because it is most resistant to corrosion so it will last a long time).
Q2 a) It can be bent to make pipes and tanks. It doesn't react with water.
b) It is a good conductor of electricity.
Q3 a)

Property	Aluminium	Titanium
Density	**low**	**low**
Strength	low	high
Corrosion resistance	**high**	**high**

b) transition metals

Page 64 — Alloys

Q1 Missing words are: pure, properties, alloys.
Q2 a) True
b) False
c) True
d) False
e) True
Q3

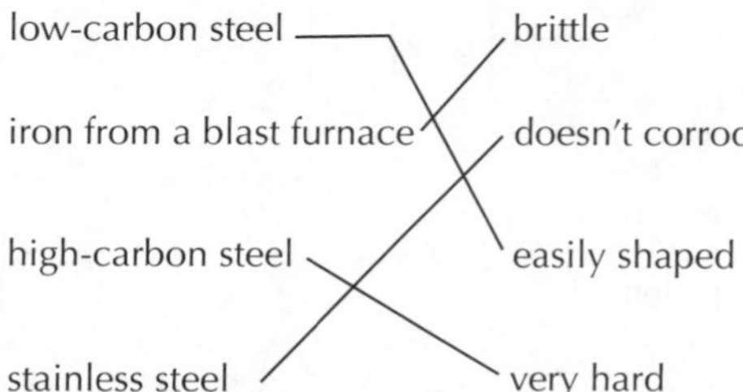

Q4 It makes the gold harder.

Pages 65-67 — Getting Metals from Rocks

Q1 unreactive, compounds, ores.
Q2 a) reduction
b) iron oxide + **carbon** → **iron** + carbon dioxide
c) electrolysis
Q3 **bodium**, carbon, **candium**, **antium**
Q4 Missing words are: electricity, liquid, negative.
Q5 A high temperature is needed to melt aluminium oxide. This uses a lot of energy which is expensive.
Q6 a) Year 1
b) cost of extraction = 75/100 x £2.00 = £1.50, so **year 6**
Q7 a) Because iron is more reactive than copper.
b) Because iron is less reactive than aluminium so it wouldn't be able to push the aluminium out.
Q8 copper, leaves, ash

Section 5 — Chemicals and Rocks

Q9 a) Bioleaching uses bacteria to separate copper from copper sulfide. The leachate (the solution produced by the process) contains copper. The copper can be extracted from the leachate, e.g. by filtering.

b) E.g. the supply of copper-rich ores is limited and the demand for copper is growing. / These alternative methods can extract copper from low-grade ores.

Page 68 — Impacts of Extracting Metals

Q1 Any three from: e.g. new jobs available for locals, improved local services, more money in local area, more goods made from the extracted metal are available, pollution such as dust and noise, habitat destruction, damage to the landscape.

Q2 E.g. there's only a fixed amount of metal in the Earth, which could one day run out if we don't recycle. If metal isn't recycled, it ends up in landfill sites, which take up space and pollute the surroundings. Mining and extracting new metals uses lots of energy / involves burning fossil fuels. Burning fossil fuels causes global warming, global dimming and acid rain.

Page 69 — Nanotechnology

Q1 a) 1-100 nanometres
b) E.g. seaspray
c) E.g. they make the plastic stronger and they make the plastic last longer.

Q2 We don't know what long-term effects nanoparticles might have on human health.

Q3 B and C are true.

Q4 a) molecules
b) soot
c) can, can't
d) bandages

Pages 70-71 — Mixed Questions — Section 4

Q1 a) **A** should be ticked.
b) The following should be ticked:
Metals are generally strong but also malleable.
Metals conduct electricity well.
Properties of a metal can be altered by mixing it with another metal to form an alloy.
c) i) R.
ii) The material needs to be as light and as strong as possible with a high melting point and a reasonable price.

Q2 a) 20
b)

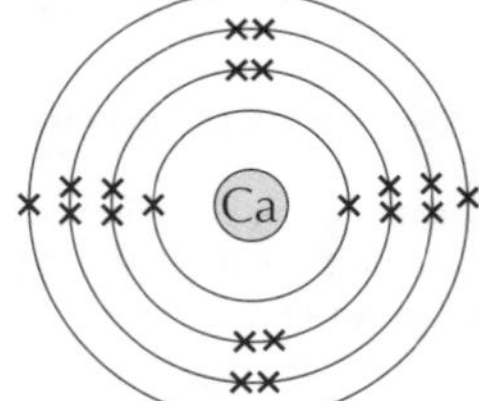

Q3 a) There is a limited amount of metals in the Earth.
b) i) It is purified by electrolysis.
ii) Any one from: e.g. zinc / iron / tin.
c) i) Aluminium is more reactive than carbon, and so cannot be extracted by reduction with carbon.
ii) Any one from: e.g. magnesium / calcium / sodium / potassium.

Q4 a)

Product	Material	Property
Frying pan	Stainless steel	E.g. rigid / high melting point / conducts heat well
Window	Glass	E.g. transparent / stiff / waterproof
Surgical masks	Silver nanoparticles	antibacterial properties
Cushion cover	Cotton	E.g. soft / flexible / light
Bookcase	Oak	E.g. strong / stiff / attractive appearance

b) i) false
ii) true
iii) false

Section 5 — Chemicals and Rocks

Pages 72-73 — The Earth's Structure

Q1 1. crust
2. mantle
3. core

Q2 The main earthquake zones are along the plate boundaries.

Q3 1.6 × 10 000 = 16 000 cm = 0.16 km

Q4 Crust — Thinnest of the Earth's layers
Mantle — Slowly flowing, mostly solid layer that plates float on
Convection current — Caused by heat from radioactive decay in the mantle
Tectonic plates — Large pieces of crust and upper mantle
Earthquakes — Caused by sudden movements of plates

Q5 E.g. tectonic plates stay still for a long time and then suddenly lurch forwards. It's impossible to know exactly when they'll move.

Page 74 — Plate Tectonics

Q1 continental drift, fossils, land bridges, Pangaea, spinning.

Q2 True, True, False, True

Page 75 — The Three Different Types of Rock

Q1 igneous rocks — formed when magma cools — granite
metamorphic rocks — formed under intense heat and pressure — marble
sedimentary rocks — formed from layers of sediment — limestone

Q2 crust, cools, size, cooled

Q3 a) Limestone
b) Limestone is the only one of the three rocks listed that can contain fossils because it is the only sedimentary rock.

Q4 a) False
b) False
c) True
d) False
e) True

Pages 76-77 — Using Limestone

Q1 calcium carbonate

Q2 a) i) calcium oxide, carbon dioxide
ii) thermal decomposition
b) i) False
ii) True

Q3 a) calcium carbonate → calcium oxide + carbon dioxide
b) To neutralise soils that are acidic.

Section 5 — Chemicals and Rocks

c) i) carbon dioxide
ii) The limewater goes cloudy.
Q4 The missing words are: limestone, mortar, concrete.
Q5 a) carbon dioxide, water
b) magnesium carbonate + sulfuric acid → magnesium sulfate + carbon dioxide + water
c) Any two from: e.g. copper/zinc/calcium/sodium
d) Limestone is made of calcium carbonate. The calcium carbonate reacts with the acid in acid rain which erodes/damages the building.
Q6 a) Any three from: e.g. increased traffic, spoiling the look of the landscape, putting off tourists, noise
b) E.g. they provide jobs / bring money into the area.

Page 78 — Salt

Q1 a) False
b) False
c) True
d) True
e) True
Q2 Chlorine and sodium hydroxide.
Q3 a) i) negative
ii) positive
b) So they don't react with anything.
c) A — brine
B — Cl_2
C — H_2
Q4 Chlorine — plastics such as PVC, solvents, used to sterilise water
Sodium hydroxide — soap
Hydrogen — margarine

Page 79 — Salt in the Food Industry

Q1 It's used as a preservative.
It's used to improve the flavour.
Q2 a) E.g. there's lots of salt in many processed foods, like breakfast cereals, sauces, soups, crisps, etc.
b) 1.2 + 4.4 = 5.6
6 – 5.6 = 0.4
She could eat 0.4 grams of salt without going over the recommended limit.
Q3 a) high blood pressure, strokes, osteoporosis
b) E.g. because it may cost a lot to change the recipe / the products might not taste as good or last as long.
Q4 1. They look at the health risk of chemicals in food to make sure they're safe.
2. They tell the public about how food affects their health.

Page 80 — Chlorination

Q1 chlorine, drinking water, chlorination, kills, microorganisms, algae, smells
Q2 a) It can be made from the reaction between hydrogen chloride and oxygen.
b) The properties of compounds are different from the properties of elements from which they're made.
So although chlorine will kill microorganisms, compounds that contain chlorine, such as sodium chloride, may not.
Q3 a) E.g. When chlorination was introduced the number of cases of typhoid decreased rapidly.
b) This is because chlorination is a water treatment that kills disease-causing microorganisms.
c) E.g. chlorine can react with organic compounds in the water to make chemicals that can cause cancer.

Page 81 — Impacts of Chemical Production

Q1 a) carbon, hydrogen, chlorine
b) Any one from: e.g. the plasticisers may leach out of the PVC into the environment, where they may have harmful effects. / Plasticisers are toxic, and can build up in animals like fish and end up being eaten by humans.
Q2 a) The amount of chemical in each animal increases as you go along the food chain.
b) All of them.
Q3 No. E.g. some of the chemicals used to make the monitors may not have been tested thoroughly to see if they cause any long term problems to the environment or human health. As there are so many chemicals, they can't all be tested as much as we'd like. This means there's not enough data to tell if some chemicals are a risk to the environment or public health.

Page 82 — Hazard Symbols, Acids and Alkalis

Q1 a) — corrosive — damages living tissue, like eyes and skin.
b) — irritant — causes reddening or blistering of the skin.
c) — toxic — can cause death if swallowed, breathed in, or if it seeps through the skin.
d) — oxidising — provides oxygen which allows other materials to burn more strongly.
e) — harmful — like toxic but not quite as dangerous.
Q2 a) acidic
b) acid
c) base
d) water
e) 7
Q3 5/6 — weak acid
8/9 — weak alkali
14 — strong alkali
7 — neutral
1 — strong acid

Pages 83-84 — Reactions of Acids

Q1 a) hydrochloric acid + lead oxide → **lead** chloride + water
b) hydrochloric acid + **nickel** oxide → nickel **chloride** + water
Q2 a) **ii)** and **iv)** should be ticked.
b) i) hydrochloric acid + sodium hydroxide → sodium chloride + water
ii) sulfuric acid + copper oxide → copper sulfate + water
Q3 a) Baking soda/soap powder.
b) Baking soda/soap powder is a weak base and so would neutralise the acid but wouldn't irritate or harm the skin.
Q4 a) acid + metal oxide → **salt** + **water**
b) Copper oxide and hydrochloric acid.
Q5 The following should be circled:
copper oxide, lead hydroxide, potassium hydroxide, tin oxide
Q6 a) i) sulfuric acid + **copper** carbonate → copper **sulfate** + water + **carbon dioxide**
ii) **hydrochloric** acid + potassium **carbonate** → **potassium** chloride + **water** + carbon dioxide
b) sulfuric acid + lithium carbonate → **lithium sulfate** + **water** + **carbon dioxide**

Section 6 — Chemicals from Oil

Pages 85-86 — The Evolution of the Atmosphere

Q1 a) True
b) False
c) True
d) True

Q2 The statements should be in this order (from the top of the timeline):
1. The atmosphere is about 80% nitrogen and 20% oxygen.
2. Green plants and algae evolve over the Earth. The green plants and algae absorb some of the carbon dioxide and produce oxygen by photosynthesis. A lot of the carbon dioxide also dissolves into the oceans.
3. Water vapour condenses to form oceans.
4. The Earth cools down slightly. A thin crust forms. There are lots of volcanoes erupting.
5. The Earth's surface is molten — it's so hot that any atmosphere just 'boils away' into space.

Q3 Largest sector is Nitrogen, second largest is Oxygen, smallest is Carbon dioxide and other gases.

Q4 a) Burning fossil fuels
b) i) Generally increased (although it has gone up and down).
ii) Global warming

Q5 acidic, coral, carbon dioxide

Pages 87-88 — Mixed Questions — Section 5

Q1 a) i)

calcium carbonate —(+ HEAT)→ **calcium oxide** —(+ WATER)→ calcium hydroxide

ii) E.g. neutralising acidic soil in fields / acidity in lakes.

b)

Limestone —(heat with clay)→ **cement** —(add sand and aggregate)→ **concrete**

c) sand and water

Q2 a) surface, evidence, tectonic plates, tidal forces, convection currents
b) Earthquakes and volcanic eruptions

Q3 a) There was no oxygen.
b) i) Green plants and algae.
ii) The oceans absorbed CO_2.

Q4 a) Chlorine: PVC, disinfecting water, bleach, solvents
Hydrogen: margarine
Sodium hydroxide: soap, bleach
b) i) chlorine
ii) hydrogen

Section 6 — Chemicals from Oil

Page 89 — Fractional Distillation of Crude Oil

Q1 a) Crude oil is a **mixture** of different molecules.
b) Most of the compounds in crude oil are **hydrocarbon** molecules.
c) The molecules in crude oil **aren't** chemically bonded to each other.
d) Physical methods **can** be used to separate out the molecules in crude oil.

Q2

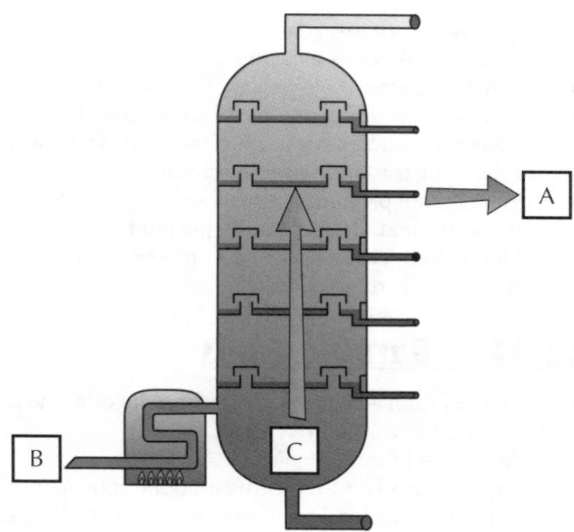

Q3 Each fraction contains molecules of a similar size / with a similar number of carbon atoms.

Page 90 — Properties and Uses of Crude Oil

Q1 a) C_nH_{2n+2} should be ticked.
b)

```
1.          2.            3.
  H           H H           H H H
  |           | |           | | |
H-C-H       H-C-C-H       H-C-C-C-H
  |           | |           | | |
  H           H H           H H H
methane      ethane        propane
```

c) Alkanes are saturated hydrocarbons.

Q2 a) The longer the alkane molecule the **more** viscous (gloopy) it is
b) The shorter the alkane molecule the **lower** its boiling point.
c) The shorter the alkane molecule the **more** flammable it is.

Q3 They would boil when the engine got hot / could catch fire easily.

Page 91 — Cracking Crude Oil

Q1 shorter, petrol, diesel, long, high, catalyst, molecules, cracking

Q2 a) E.g. fuels
b) Cracking is a thermal decomposition reaction.

Q3 nonane → octane + ethene

Q4
1. The long-chain molecules are heated.
2. They are vaporised (turned into a gas).
3. The vapour is passed over a catalyst at a high temperature.
4. The molecules are cracked on the surface of the catalyst.

Pages 92-93 — Alkenes and Ethanol

Q1 C_nH_{2n}

Q2 a) C_2H_4
b)

```
H       H
 \     /
  C = C
 /     \
H       H
```

c) Propene

Q3 Missing words are: decolourise, orange, colourless.

Q4 a) False
b) True
c) True
d) False

Section 6 — Chemicals from Oil

Q5 a) A
b) Method A — Uses yeast.
Method B — Uses a catalyst.
c) Any two from:
Needs lower temperatures so is cheaper. Can use simpler equipment. Uses sugar which is often grown as a major crop. Sugar is a renewable resource.
d) The ethanol produced is not very concentrated so it needs to be distilled. It needs to be purified.
Q6 Ethene from crude oil is a non-renewable resource and will one day run out.

Page 94 — Burning Fuels

Q1 a) hydrocarbon + oxygen → **carbon dioxide** + **water**
b) oxidised, gives out, oxygen
Q2 Any three from:
E.g. how easily it burns / the amount of heat energy it gives out / how much ash or smoke it produces / how easy it is to store or transport.
Q3 a) hydrocarbon + **oxygen** → water + carbon dioxide + **carbon** + **carbon monoxide**
b) Carbon monoxide is produced which is a very toxic (poisonous) gas.
c) Soot (carbon) is a black powder which will leave black marks.

Page 95 — Using Crude Oil as a Fuel

Q1 Missing words are: fractions, industry, non-renewable, renewable.
Q2 Burning: e.g. burning crude oil is thought to cause global warming, global dimming and acid rain.
Transporting crude oil across the sea in tankers: e.g. when oil is transported by ship there is the possibility of spills into the sea. Crude oil is poisonous to birds and sea creatures.
Q3 a) E.g. wind power, solar power, tidal power
b) E.g. most technology around today is set up to use crude oil fractions as fuel so they're often the cheapest and easiest things to use. / We need more energy than can currently be created using alternatives alone. / Crude oil fractions are often more reliable than some alternatives, e.g. solar and wind power won't work without the right weather conditions.

Page 96 — Environmental Problems

Q1 In clouds sulfur dioxide reacts with water to make... sulfuric acid.
Acid rain kills trees and... makes lakes acidic.
Sulfur dioxide is produced by burning fuels which contain... sulfur.
Limestone buildings and statues are affected by... acid rain.
The main cause of acid rain is... sulfur dioxide.
Q2 Any two from:
Removing the sulfur from the fuel before it is burnt. / Using less fossil fuels. / Removing sulfur dioxide from the waste gases after fuels are burnt, e.g. in power station chimneys.
Q3 a) false
b) true
c) false
d) false
Q4 Global dimming is caused by particles of soot and ash.

Page 97 — Carbon Dioxide in the Atmosphere

Q1 a) The percentage of carbon dioxide in the atmosphere is increasing at an increasing rate.
b) E.g. the burning of fossil fuels / deforestation.
c) It's causing the average temperature to increase.
Q2 a) C
b) Cars burn fossil fuels and give out carbon dioxide in their exhaust gases.
Q3 a) False
b) True
c) False
d) True

Page 98 — Reducing Carbon Dioxide in the Atmosphere

Q1 Missing words are: seeding, ocean, phytoplankton, photosynthesis, poisonous.
Q2 a) water
b) Any one from: e.g. when hydrogen is used as a fuel no carbon dioxide is produced so it doesn't contribute to global warming. / It doesn't produce particles so it doesn't cause global dimming. / It doesn't produce sulfur dioxide so it doesn't cause acid rain.
c) Any three from: e.g. you need a special, expensive engine. / Hydrogen isn't widely available. / You still need to use energy from another source to make hydrogen (e.g. from fossil fuels). / Hydrogen is hard to store.
Q3 plant material, carbon neutral, water, land, engines

Pages 99-100 — Using Alkenes to Make Polymers

Q1 The monomer of poly(ethene) is ethene.
Q2 Any three from:
e.g. plastic bags, waterproof coatings for fabrics, tooth fillings, hydrogel wound dressings, memory foam, packaging materials
Q3 Missing words are: rot, landfill, reuse, crude oil, expensive.
Q4 New biodegradable plastics are being made by adding cornstarch to polymers.
Q5 Cracking: Splits less useful crude oil fractions into alkenes. Turns longer molecules into shorter ones.
Polymerisation: Turns alkenes into polymers. Turns shorter molecules into longer ones.
Q6

$$n\begin{pmatrix} CH_3 & H \\ | & | \\ C & = & C \\ | & | \\ H & H \end{pmatrix} \longrightarrow \begin{pmatrix} CH_3 & H \\ | & | \\ -C & - & C- \\ | & | \\ H & H \end{pmatrix}_n$$

many propene molecules → poly(propene)

Page 101 — Structure and Properties of Polymers

Q1 a) true
b) false
c) false
d) true
Q2 a) together
b) can, stretchy
c) cannot, rigid
d) more, higher
Q3 E.g. increasing the length of the polymer chain, adding cross-linking agents, adding plasticisers

Section 7 — Heat and Energy

Q4 a) Polymer A
b) Polymer A has stronger forces / cross-linking agents holding the polymer chains together. So it will have a higher melting point.

Pages 102-103 — Plant Oils

Q1 a) Missing words are: crushed, pressed
b) Any two from: e.g. in food / in cooking / as a fuel
c) water and impurities
Q2 Vegetable oils provide loads of energy.
They provide us with nutrients.
Q3 a) False
b) True
c) False
d) False
Q4 a) biodiesel
b) They contain lots of energy.
Q5 a) i) Martin's.
ii) E.g. His method is more detailed. He gives accurate quantities of oil and bromine water. He labels his equipment so there is less opportunity for mistakes. He writes down the results after each individual experiment.
b) A: yes
B: no
C: yes
Q6 a) saturated
b) They increase the amount of cholesterol in the blood. Cholesterol can block arteries and lead to heart disease.

Page 104 — Emulsions

Q1 a) Oils don't dissolve in water.
b) Emulsions are thicker than both water and oil.
c) In an emulsion the droplets of one liquid are suspended in another liquid.
d) Emulsions like salad dressing are good at coating foods.
Q2 a) Any two from: e.g. salad dressing / whipped cream / ice cream.
b) Any one from: e.g. paint / moisturiser.
Q3 a) Emulsifiers make emulsions more stable and stop them from separating out.
b) i) Any one from: e.g. they give food a better texture, they give emulsions a longer shelf life.
ii) Some people are allergic to certain emulsifiers.

Pages 105-106 — Mixed Questions — Section 6

Q1 a) The following can be in any order:
Petrol has a lower boiling point than diesel. Petrol is more flammable (ignites more easily) than diesel. Petrol is less viscous (is runnier) than diesel.
b)

Fuel	Engine needs to be converted	Burning releases carbon dioxide
Ethanol	Yes	Yes
Hydrogen gas	Yes	No
Biodiesel	No	Yes

Q2 a) cracking
b) Unlike alkanes, alkenes are **unsaturated** because they have **double** bonds.
c) Name: poly(styrene)

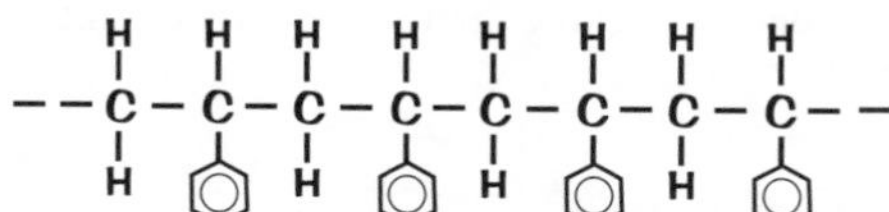

d) E.g. it's difficult to get rid of them / they fill up landfill sites.
Q3 a) False
b) True
c) True
d) False
Q4 a) Rapeseed is crushed and then pressed between metal plates to squeeze the oil out.
b) Rapeseed oil will turn bromine water from orange to colourless.
c) E.g. heart disease.
d) An emulsifier stops the oil and water in an emulsion from separating out / makes an emulsion more stable.
Q5 a) You could get oil spills, which damage the environment.
b) Any one from: e.g. global dimming / global warming / acid rain

Section 7 — Heat and Energy

Page 107 — Temperature and Kinetic Theory

Q1

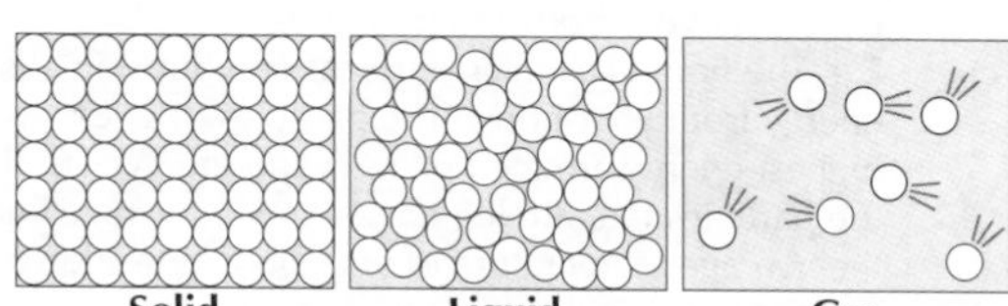

Gas — There are almost no forces of attraction between the particles.
Liquid — There are weak forces of attraction between the particles.
Solid — There are strong forces of attraction holding the particles close together.
Q2 Heat is a measure of **energy**.
Temperature is a measure of **hotness**.
Heat travels from a **hot** place to a **cold** place.
The hotter something is, the **higher** its temperature.
When a substance is heated its particles vibrate **more** quickly.
Temperature is measured in **°C**.
Q3 A — there is the largest temperature difference between it and the room.

Page 108 — Conduction and Convection

Q1 Conduction — Vibrating particles pass on energy to the particles next to them.
Convection — Particles with more energy move to a cooler place, taking their heat energy with them.
Q2 a) True
b) False — e.g. metals are very **good** conductors.
c) True
d) True
Q3 a) Jacob is wrong because the radiator will transfer most of its heat through convection.
b) spread, rises, falls
Q4 E.g. air is a gas so it's a very good insulator. This means it doesn't conduct heat as well as the wool would so there'll be less conduction of heat away from the baby.

Page 109 — Heat Radiation

Q1 a) False
b) True
c) True
d) True
Q2 a) Dark, matt surfaces are **good** absorbers of heat radiation.
b) The best surfaces for radiating heat are **good** emitters.
c) The best materials for making survival blankets are **poor** emitters of heat radiation.

Section 7 — Heat and Energy

Q3 A system that's at a constant temperature — radiates the same average power that it absorbs.
A system that's warming up — radiates less power than it absorbs.
A system that's cooling down — radiates more power than it absorbs.

Q4 E.g. Tim's experiment showed that of the four surfaces, the matt black surface was the best emitter of heat radiation. The shiny silver surface was the poorest emitter of heat radiation.

Page 110 — Condensation and Evaporation

Q1 cools, energy, forces, liquid

Q2 a) True
b) True
c) False

Q3 a) evaporation
b) When sweat evaporates, it has a cooling effect — it decreases your body temperature.
c) E.g. The liquid particles of sweat on your skin absorb heat energy from your body. The particles of sweat with the highest energy are the first to evaporate. When they do, the particles that are left have a lower average energy and the average temperature of your body goes down.

Q4 a) E.g. Put tea in a slimmer cup so that the surface area of the tea is reduced. / Have colder tea. / Reduce the airflow over the tea.
b) E.g. Increase the temperature of the window space. / Decrease the surface area of the window exposed (e.g. by drawing the curtains).

Page 111 — Rate of Heat Transfer

Q1 Cooling fins.
The engine is made of metal.
The engine has a large surface area.

Q2 Air is a very good **insulator** of heat energy. When you get cold, your body hairs **stand on end** so they can trap a thicker layer of air around your body. By doing this, the amount of heat you lose to your surroundings by convection and **conduction** is reduced. Wearing a coat also helps you keep warm in this way.

Q3 a) To maximise the amount of heat transfer.
b) Metal is a good conductor so it will conduct heat away from the radiator much faster than air, as air is an insulator.
c) B (because although it has the same surface area, it has a smaller volume.)

Pages 112-113 — Energy Efficiency in the Home

Q1 Through the roof — e.g. loft insulation.
Through the walls — e.g. cavity wall insulation.
From the hot water tank — e.g insulating hot water tank jacket.

Q2 fibreglass, radiation, wall, gap, conduction

Q3 a) Payback time = 200 ÷ 100 = 2 years.
b) Yes, loft insulation is more cost-effective because it has a shorter payback time.

Q4 Shona and Alison are right.
(Shona is right — a method that pays for itself faster will start saving you money sooner.
Alison is right — good value means getting a good effect from the money spent.
Tim is wrong — cheap or badly installed insulation might not work very well.
Meena is wrong — cost-effectiveness means getting a good energy saving per pound spent.)

Q5 a) How fast heat can transfer through the material.
b) Gary should buy brand **A** because it has a lower U-value — the lower the U-value, the better the material is as an insulator, so heat transfer will be less.

Page 114 — Specific Heat Capacity

Q1 energy, 1 kg, 1 °C

Q2 a) $E = m \times c \times \theta$
b) m = 3 kg
c = 4200 J/kg°C
θ = 20 °C – 10 °C = 10 °C
E = 3 × 4200 × 10 = **126 000 J** (= 126 kJ)

Q3 a) Concrete
b) E.g.
1. It has a really high specific heat capacity so it can store large amounts of heat.
2. It can be easily pumped around pipes because it is a liquid.

Page 115 — Energy Transfer

Q1 Conservation, transferred, dissipated, created

Q2 a) **chemical energy** → heat and light energy.
b) electrical energy → **sound and heat energy**.
c) **electrical energy** → **light and heat energy**.

Q3 Electric fan — kinetic energy
Iron — heat energy
Bedside table lamp — light energy

Q4 a) Gravitational potential energy.
b) The gravitational potential energy is transferred into kinetic energy as it falls downwards.

Q5 a) E.g. loudspeaker or buzzer/bell
b) E.g. solar cell or photocell
c) E.g. hairdryer or electric fan heater

Page 116 — Efficiency of Machines

Q1 light, wasted, efficiency

Q2 a) 100 J
b) 5 J
c) 100 – 5 = **95 J**
d) Efficiency = (useful ÷ total) × 100%
= (5 ÷ 100) × 100% = **5%**

Q3 a)

	Total Energy Supplied (J)	Energy Usefully Transferred (J)	Wasted Energy (J)	Efficiency (%)
A	2000	1000	1000	**50**
B	10 000	**3000**	7000	**30**
C	4000	1000	**3000**	**25**
D	20 000	2000	18 000	**10**

b) A

Page 117 — Energy Transformation Diagrams

Q1 a) energy
b) Efficiency = Useful ÷ Total = 600 ÷ 1000 = **0.6**.
c) heat

Section 7 — Heat and Energy

Q2 a) See diagram below.

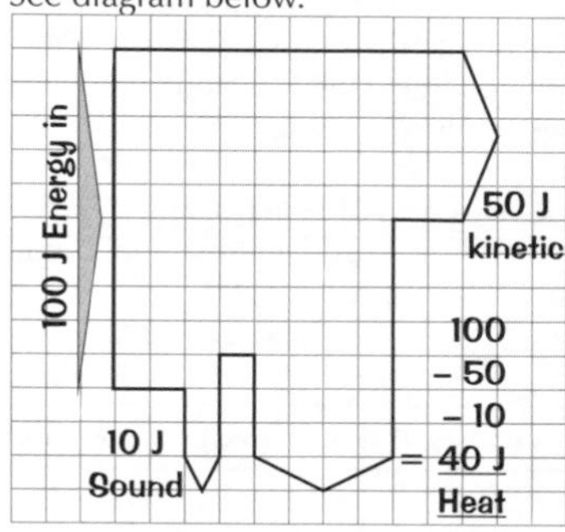

b) Efficiency = Useful ÷ Total = 50 J ÷ 100 J = **0.5**

Page 118 — Power Stations and Nuclear Energy

Q1 a) 1. The fossil fuel is burned to release heat.
2. Water is heated in a boiler and turned to steam.
3. Hot steam rushes through a turbine and makes it spin.
4. The spinning turbine makes the generator spin too.
5. Electricity is produced by the spinning generator.

b) Coal, oil and natural gas.

Q2 steam, turbine, electricity, burnt, fission, plutonium

Q3 a) B

b) B

Page 119 — Wind and Solar Energy

Q1 a) i) true

ii) false

iii) true

iv) false

b) Any two from: e.g. there's no pollution/carbon dioxide produced. / There's no permanent damage to the landscape. / It's a renewable source of energy. / There are no fuel/running costs.

Q2 a) Thursday

b) E.g. there isn't as much sun in winter so there won't be enough solar energy to charge the battery.

Q3 a) Any two from: e.g. they use a renewable source of energy. / There are no fuel/running costs. / They work well in sunny places in the daytime. / There is no pollution/carbon dioxide when they are in use.

b) E.g. the initial costs are high. / They depend on the weather. / They need a lot of energy to make. / They produce pollution when they're made. / It's not always easy to connect them to the National Grid.

Page 120 — Wave and Tidal Energy

Q1 1. A wave pushes air through a turbine.
2. The air makes the turbine spin.
3. The spinning turbine drives a generator.
4. The generator makes electricity.

Q2 a) both

b) wave

c) tidal

d) wave

e) both

Q3 A

Q4 a) E.g. there's no pollution/carbon dioxide produced. / There are no fuel/running costs. / It's good for small-scale use. / It's renewable.

b) E.g. it has high initial costs. / Wave generators can spoil the view. / Wave power can be unreliable because waves depend on winds. / Wave generators can be a danger to boats.

Pages 121-122 — Biofuels, Geothermal and Hydroelectricity

Q1 dam, gravity, generator

Q2 1. Deep holes are drilled down into hot rocks.
2. Water is pumped down to the hot rocks.
3. The water is heated and turns to steam.
4. Steam comes up to the surface and powers a turbine.
5. A generator driven by the turbine makes electricity.

Q3 a) B

b)

Advantages	Disadvantages
are carbon neutral can be made quickly	need large areas to grow

Q4 b) Either:
Agree — e.g. fuel and running costs for hydroelectric power are low.
OR:
Disagree — e.g. initial costs for hydroelectric power are high.

c) Agree — e.g. the dams are ugly. / The dams destroy wildlife habitats.

d) Any two from: e.g. it is a renewable source of energy. / Electricity can be made whenever it's needed. / It's fairly reliable.

e) Any two from: e.g. rotting vegetation releases carbon dioxide when the valley is flooded. / Reservoirs look ugly when they dry up. / Initial costs are high. / Wildlife can lose their habitat. / People may be required to move from their homes in a flooded valley.

Page 123 — Energy Sources and the Environment

Q1 Acid rain — sulfur dioxide formed by burning oil and coal.
Climate change — releasing carbon dioxide by burning fossil fuels.
Dangerous radioactive waste — using nuclear power.
Spoiling of natural landscapes — coal mining OR sulfur dioxide formed by burning oil and coal.

Q2 a) Carbon capture and storage (CCS) is used to **reduce** the amount of carbon dioxide (CO_2) released into the atmosphere. This helps **reduce** the strength of the greenhouse effect. CCS works by collecting the CO_2 from power stations **before** it is released into the atmosphere.

b) E.g. in empty gas fields/oil fields, like those under the North Sea.

Q3 Answer will depend on student's opinion but should include an explanation of their reasoning, e.g.
Lisa because nuclear power produces long-lasting, dangerous, radioactive waste.
Or Ben because nuclear power doesn't produce any carbon dioxide, whereas using fossil fuels adds to the carbon dioxide in the atmosphere, leading to climate change / an increased greenhouse effect / global warming.

Q4 Plants that are used to produce biofuels (or to feed animals that produce biofuels) take in CO_2 from the atmosphere as they grow. Burning the biofuel puts the carbon back into the atmosphere as carbon dioxide, so overall there is no change to the amount of CO_2 in the atmosphere.

Section 8 — Electricity and Waves

Pages 124-125 — Comparison of Energy Resources

Q1 gas
Q2 renewable, non-renewable, unreliable, pollution, run out, safe, expensive
Q3 a) Non-renewable
b) Non-renewable energy resources have higher costs as they require a fuel that has to be mined and transported. Renewable energy resources don't usually use a fuel.
Q4 E.g. They're more reliable as they don't depend on the weather like other renewable energy resources do.
Q5 a) E.g. Gas will run out eventually. / Burning gas causes atmospheric pollution and contributes to global warming.
b) E.g. High set-up costs. / High maintenance and/or decommissioning costs. / Long set-up times. / Dangerous radioactive waste. / Risk of accidents.
c) E.g. It's dependent on the weather. / Only works when the wind is blowing. / Unreliable. / Visual pollution. / Spoils the view. / Noise pollution.
d) E.g. It costs a lot to drill down to the rocks. / High set-up costs.
Q6 a) Shutting down the power station so that it is no longer used to generate electricity.
b) Nuclear power stations
Q7 Answer will depend on student's opinion. 'I agree' could be backed up by saying that sea levels change in a predictable and reliable way, twice every day. 'I disagree' could be backed up by saying that there are only a few suitable estuaries, or that the height of the tides isn't always the same, so at low tides there is not as much energy available as when there are high tides.

Pages 126-128 — Mixed Questions — Section 7

Q1 a) conduction
b) Brand B
c) cools, energy, attraction, liquid
Q2 a) chemical energy
b) Useful energy out = 1000 J – 650 J = 350 J.
So efficiency = 350 ÷ 1000 = **0.35** (or 35%).
c) Nuclear fuel releases much more energy than the same amount of fossil fuels.
d) Radioactive waste is dangerous because it gives out ionising radiation which can damage cells in the body.
Q3 a) i) E.g. solar cells don't need any fuel which might be difficult and expensive to get hold of on a remote island. / Solar power is a renewable source of energy so it won't run out. / Solar power won't produce pollution or damage the island in any way. / Solar cells work well in sunny places and the island might be really sunny.
ii) E.g. wind power doesn't need any fuel which might be difficult and expensive to get hold of on a remote island. / Wind power is a renewable source of energy so it won't run out. / Wind power won't produce pollution or damage the island in any way. / The island is likely to be windy.
b) Wave power / biofuels / hydroelectric power / tidal power / geothermal energy.
c) E.g. Both solar and wind power are unreliable/dependent on the weather. / On days which weren't sunny or windy, there would be little or no electricity.
Q4 a) Heat radiation from the Bunsen burner is transferred to the thermometers by being **absorbed** and then **emitted** by the metal plates. Thermometer **A** is heated to a higher temperature. This is because the metal plate in front of it is coated with a **matt black** surface which is a good **absorber** and emitter of heat radiation.
b) chemical energy → **heat energy** + **light energy** + **sound energy**
c) E.g. Metals have free electrons which can carry heat energy quickly due to their movement and collisions. Also, there are no large gaps between particles in a solid metal, making conduction easier.
Q5 a) convection
b) Efficiency = (Useful ÷ Total) × 100%.
The total input energy must equal the total output energy = 100 J useful + 68 J wasted = 168 J.
So efficiency = 100 ÷ 168 × 100% = **60%**.
Q6 a)

Work needed	Annual Saving (£)	Cost of work (£)	Payback time (years)
Hot water tank jacket	15	15	**1**
Draught-proofing	80	100	**1.25**
Cavity wall insulation	70	560	**8**
Thermostatic controls	30	120	**4**

b) Hot water tank jacket
c) Draught proofing saves £80 per year.
Over 5 years that is a saving of 5 × £80 = £400
But there is an initial cost of £100
So total saving over 5 years = £400 – £100 = **£300**
d) Energy = mass × specific heat capacity × temperature change
E = 100 × 4200 × 20 = **8 400 000 J** (= 8400 kJ)

Section 8 — Electricity and Waves

Page 129 — Generating Electricity

Q1 wire, field, current, alternating
Q2 A
Q3 Image **B** — By pulling the magnet out of the coil.
Image **C** — Pushing the magnet in and pulling it out again straight away.
Image **D** — Quickly moving the magnet in and out of the coil a few times.

Page 130 — Electricity and the National Grid

Q1
1. Electrical energy is generated in power stations.
2. The voltage of the supply is raised.
3. An electrical current flows through power cables across the country.
4. The voltage of the supply is reduced.
5. Mrs Miggins boils the kettle for tea.

Q2 a) i) power station
ii) step-up transformer
iii) pylons
iv) step-down transformer
b) It is **cheaper** to use high voltages for transmission, even though the equipment is expensive. This is because at higher voltages **less** energy is wasted as heat. This saves **more** money than the cost of the equipment.
Q3 a) The National Grid transmits energy at high voltage and **low current**.
b) A step-up transformer is used to **increase** the voltage of the supply (OR reduce the **current**) before electricity is transmitted.
c) Using a **low current** (OR high **voltage**) makes sure there is not much energy wasted.

Section 8 — Electricity and Waves

Pages 131-132 — Power and the Cost of Electricity

Q1 a) True
b) False
c) False

Q2

Appliance	Current (A)	Power (W)
Kettle	10	2300
Radio	0.1	**23**
Laptop computer	0.35	**80.5**
Lamp	0.17	**39.1**

Q3 a) Energy = power × time:
Half an hour = 0.5 h
Energy = 2.3 kW × 0.5 h = **1.15 kWh**
b) Cost = number of kWh × price per kWh:
1.15 × 12p = **13.8p**

Q4 a) Power = voltage × current:
Power = 230 V × 8 A = 1840 W
Convert W to kW = answer ÷ 1000
= 1840 ÷ 1000 = **1.84 kW**
b) Energy = power × time:
Energy = 1.84 kW × 2 h = **3.68 kWh**
c) Cost = number of kWh × price per kWh:
Cost = 3.68 kWh × 11.5p = **42.32p**

Q5 a) The amount of electrical energy used by a 1 kW appliance left on for 1 hour.
b) Meter reading from September – meter reading from June = electricity used between June and September:
= 34783 – 34259 = 524 kWh
c) Cost = number of kWh × price per kWh:
Cost = 524 kWh × 9.7p = **5082.8p** (or £50.83)

Q6 a) Energy = power × time:
Energy = 2 kW × 3 h = **6 kWh**
b) Cost = number of kWh × price per kWh:
Cost = 6 kWh × 7p = **42p**
c) i) Power in kW = power in W ÷ 1000:
Power in kW = 60 W ÷ 1000 = 0.06 kW
Energy = power × time:
Energy = 0.06 kW × 9 h = **0.54 kWh**
ii) Time in hours = time in minutes ÷ 60:
Time in hours = 15 ÷ 60 = 0.25 h
Energy = power × time:
Energy = 8 kW × 0.25 h = **2 kWh**
iii) Boris's wife

Page 133 — Choosing Electrical Appliances

Q1 a) E.g. It's cheaper to buy. / It weighs less. / It has a foldable handle so it won't take up much room in a suitcase.
b) E.g. It's more powerful. / You can change the speed and temperature settings.

Q2 The following two sentences should be ticked:
There might not be an electricity supply where they are camping.
Wind-up radios don't have power cords that might get in the way.

Q3 Difference in energy used = 17 – 16 = 1 kWh.
So June would save = 1 × 12 = **12p**.

Q4 Any two from: e.g. can be used to power X-ray machines / refrigeration of medicines/vaccines / can power lighting/ equipment for operations.

Pages 134-135 — Wave Basics

Q1 a) energy, matter
b) crest
c) rest position
d) second

Q2 a) A and C
b) A and B
c) A and C

Q3 Distance = speed × time, so,
distance = 300 000 × 1.3 = **390 000 km**.

Q4 a) Transverse — 2, Longitudinal — 1.
b) E.g. Transverse waves vibrate at 90° to the direction the wave is travelling in. Longitudinal waves vibrate in the same direction as the wave is travelling in.

Q5 speed = frequency × wavelength
speed = 20 × 250 = **5000 m/s**

Q6 a) 2 Hz, because the duck bobs up and down (moves through a complete wave) twice every second.

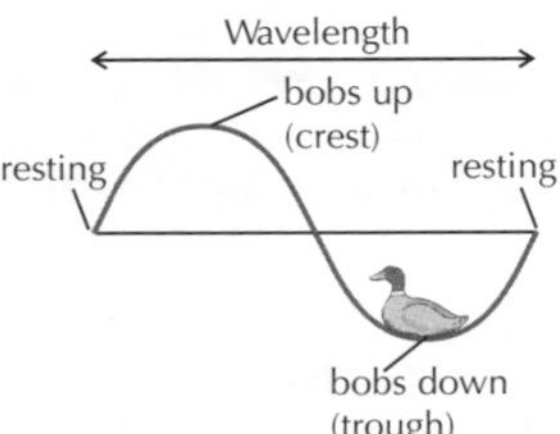

b) Crest to crest is one wavelength.
So use speed = frequency × wavelength
speed = 2 × 0.5 = **1 m/s**

Q7 a) He has drawn a wave with a wavelength of 4 m rather than 2 m.
b) E.g.

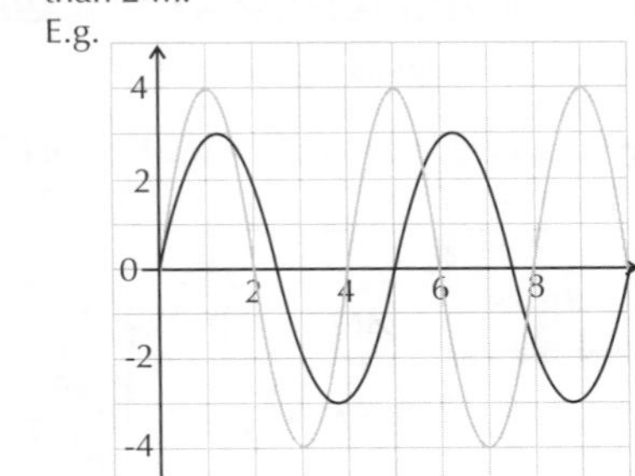

Page 136 — Reflection

Q1 a) It is a line drawn **at right angles** to the mirror where the incident ray hits.
b)

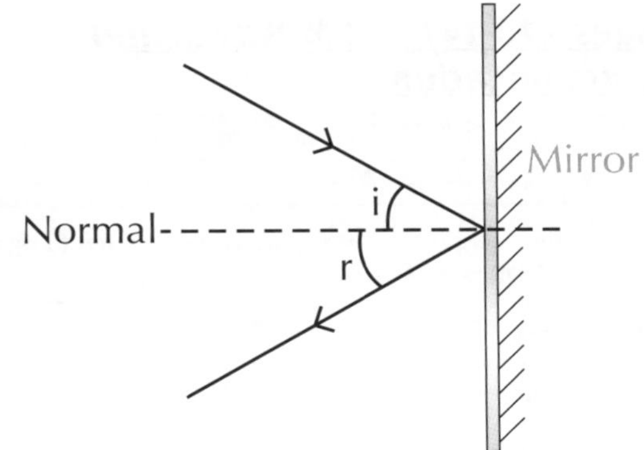

Q2 a) virtual
b) upright

Section 8 — Electricity and Waves

Page 137 — Diffraction and Refraction

Q1 a) Diffraction is where a wave **spreads out** as it passes through a **gap** or when it meets an obstacle in its path.

b)

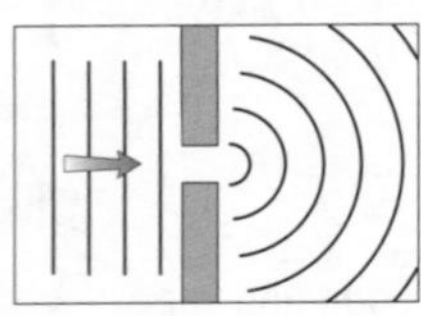

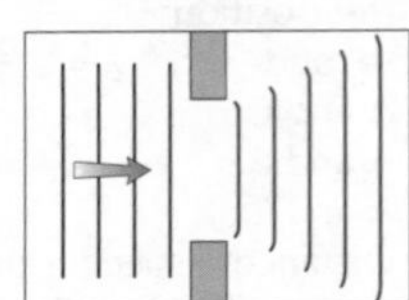

Q2 a) B

b) Because the wave met the boundary at a right angle.

c) Because the waves change speed.

Page 138 — Sound Waves

Q1 1 — When someone beats a drum, the skin on top of the drum vibrates.
2 — The vibration of the drum sets the air molecules next to it vibrating too.
3 — A series of compressions and rarefactions travel outwards through the air as a longitudinal wave.
4 — We hear the sound when the vibrations in the air reach our ears.

Q2 vibrate, high, low

Q3 a) A reflected sound wave.

b) The echo has to travel further than the original sound, so takes longer to reach your ears.

Q4 a) It gets quieter and eventually stops.

b) Sound can't travel in a vacuum because there are no particles to pass on the vibrations.

Page 139 — Analogue and Digital Signals

Q1 a) That analogue signals can have any value in a particular range.

b) Digital signals can only take one of a small number of value (usually two).

c) E.g.

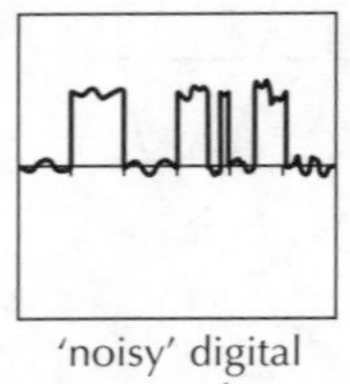

'noisy' digital signal

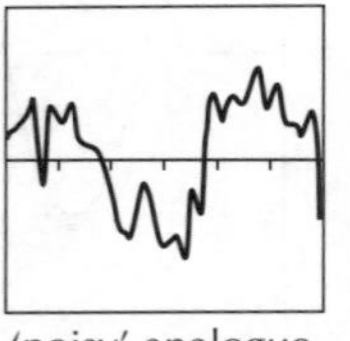

'noisy' analogue signal

Q2 1. noise
2. digital

Q3 noise, analogue, original, bytes

Pages 140-141 — EM Waves and Communication

Q1 a)

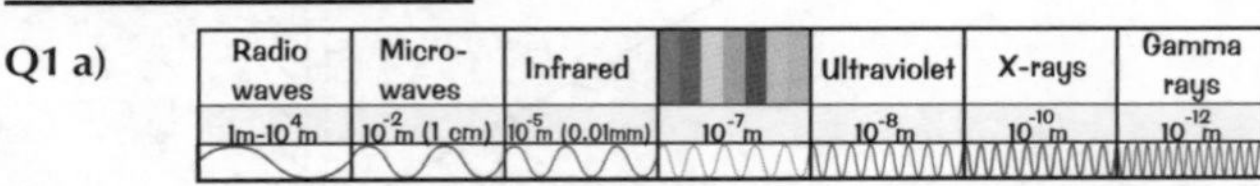

Radio waves	Micro-waves	Infrared		Ultraviolet	X-rays	Gamma rays
$1m-10^4 m$	$10^{-2} m$ (1 cm)	$10^{-5} m$ (0.01mm)	$10^{-7} m$	$10^{-8} m$	$10^{-10} m$	$10^{-12} m$

b) The energy of the waves **increases** from **left to right** across the table.

Q2 a) False

b) False

c) False

d) True

e) False

f) True

Q3 speed in a vacuum, they are both transverse waves

Q4 long-wave, short-wave, atmosphere, FM

Q5 A and B

Page 142 — Microwaves

Q1 a) Satellite TV uses **microwaves** to send signals. The signals from a transmitter are sent into space, where they're picked up by the satellite's receiver **dish**.

b) The satellite transmits the signal back to **Earth** in a different direction, where it is received by a satellite dish on the ground.

Q2 a) E.g. there would be a strong mobile phone signal in the surrounding area.

b) i) no

ii) He is wrong to say 'definitely' as there is no definite proof.

Q3 a) Microwaves are absorbed by water (or fat) molecules in the curry, which heats the water. The heat is conducted or convected throughout the curry.

b) Microwaves can pass through plastic, so the microwaves can still get through to the food.

c) B

Page 143 — Infrared and Visible Light

Q1 a) Cameras, visible

b) more

Q2 Infrared radiation

Q3 A

Q4 a) True

b) False

c) True

d) True

e) False

Pages 144-145 — X-rays and Gamma Rays

Q1 a) ultraviolet, X-rays, gamma rays

b) They're the only ones with enough energy to cause ionisation.

Q2 a) pictures, bones, flesh, dense

b) E.g. scanning luggage in airports.

Q3 a) True

b) False

c) True

Q4 kill, cells, cancer, carefully, normal

Q5 1 — A radioactive isotope is injected into the patient.
2 — A camera is used to 'see' where the radioactive isotope has travelled to in the body.
3 — The camera creates an image which can be used to detect where there might be cancer.

Q6 a) Lead and concrete absorb X-rays so hospital staff use them to protect themselves.

b) E.g. Lead shielding can be placed over the parts of the patient's body that aren't injured.

Page 146 — UV Radiation and Ozone

Q1 a) Ultraviolet

b) Any two from: e.g. sunburn / cataracts / premature skin aging.

Q2 a) Darker skin absorbs more UV radiation than pale skin, so less reaches the cells deeper inside the body.

b) i) It means Marie can stay in the sun 25 times longer without burning than she could without any cream on.

ii) 30 mins × 25 = **750 mins** (= 12 hours 30 mins).

Q3 a) It absorbs some of the UV rays from the Sun, reducing the amount reaching Earth.

b) They used lots of different equipment.
They carried out many different studies.

Section 9 — The Universe

Page 147 — The Greenhouse Effect

Q1

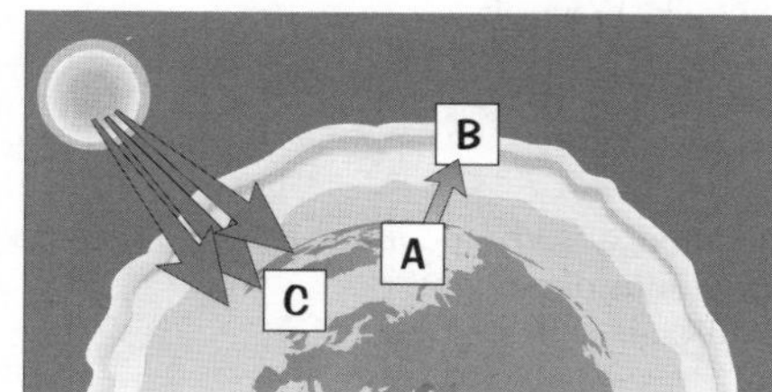

Q2 water vapour, carbon dioxide, methane
Q3 B
Q4 a) i) E.g. respiration in plants and animals / volcanic eruptions.
ii) E.g. burning fossil fuels / chopping down and burning trees.
b) E.g. Natural: volcanoes / wetlands / digestion in wild animals. Man-made: cattle farming / waste in landfill sites.

Page 148 — Global Warming and Climate Change

Q1 temperatures, greenhouse, carbon
Q2 a) False
b) True
c) False
d) False
e) True
Q3 a) The coastline has changed and the amount of land has decreased.
b) Global warming might cause a rise in sea level, flooding low-lying land.
c) E.g. More extreme weather. Food crop failure.

Page 149 — Seismic Waves

Q1 **Earthquakes** produce shock waves. These **seismic** waves can travel inside and on the surface of the Earth.
Q2 a) P-waves travel faster.
b) S-waves cannot travel through the outer core.
Q3 C
Q4 a) P-waves change direction because there's a sudden change in properties as they go from the mantle to the core.
b) i) S-waves don't reach the other side.
ii) This tells us that part of the Earth's core must be liquid.

Pages 150-151 — Mixed Questions — Section 8

Q1 The following three boxes should be ticked:
B represents ultraviolet radiation.
A represents infrared radiation.
A has the largest amplitude.
Q2 a) reflection
b)

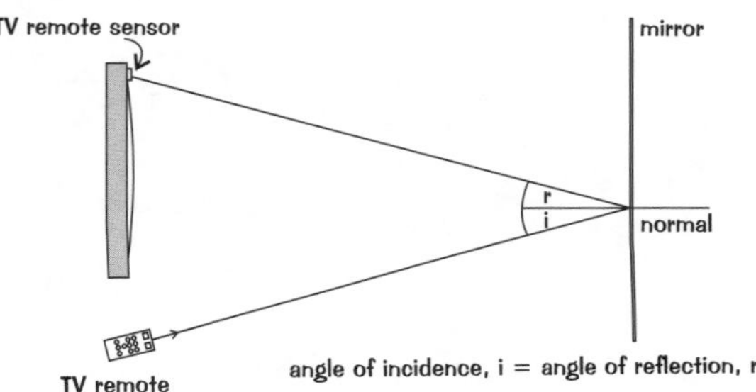

Q3 a) respiration, burning trees
b) Climate change can affect weather patterns, so some places could be too wet or dry to grow food.

Q4 a) i) First convert minutes to hours: 45 ÷ 60 = 0.75 hours.
Sander A: Energy (in kWh) = Power (in kW) × Time (in h) = 0.36 × 0.75 = **0.27 kWh**.
ii) First convert minutes to hours: 30 ÷ 60 = 0.5 hours.
Sander B: Energy = 0.4 × 0.5 = **0.2 kWh**.
b) 4p (0.27 × 15 = 4.05p)
Q5 a) 3 — Microwaves
1 — X-rays
2 — Infrared
b) Metal case — reflects microwaves
Food — absorbs microwaves
Plastic container — transmits microwaves
c) i) E.g. Ionising radiation **is** dangerous.
ii) E.g. Radioactive materials give out **ionising** radiation all the time.

Section 9 — The Universe

Page 152 — Galileo and Copernicus

Q1 a) Ptolemaic
b) Copernicus
c) Sun
d) circles
e) Galileo
f) geocentric
Q2 a) Telescopes
b) The moons of Jupiter, The phases of Venus
c) Jupiter, Earth, Ptolemaic, Venus, small, big

Page 153 — The Solar System

Q1 1. Mercury
2. Venus
3. Earth
4. Mars
5. Asteroids
6. Jupiter
7. Saturn
8. Uranus
9. Neptune
Q2 a) Bits of rubble and rock.
b) dust, debris
c) Objects orbiting the Sun far beyond the planets.
Q3 a) an ellipse / elliptical
b) i) C
ii) A

Page 154 — Beyond the Solar System

Q1 a) quickly
b) light years
Q2 The distance that light travels through space in a year.
Q3 a) Our Sun is one of thousands of millions of stars in the **Milky Way galaxy**. / Our Sun is the **only** star in the Solar System.
b) The Milky Way is a collection of **stars**. / The Milky Way is **one** galaxy.
c) There are **thousands of millions** of galaxies in the Universe.
Q4 A
D

Section 9 — The Universe

Page 155 — Looking into Space

Q1 a) i) We can tell a lot about stars by studying the **radiation** coming from them.
ii) When we see things in space we are looking **backwards** in time.
b) i) Light from street lamps and other forms of lighting.
ii) It makes it hard to see dim objects.
c) It absorbs some of the electromagnetic radiation/light from space.
Q2 a) all, visible
b) structure
c) X-ray
d) microwaves
Q3 It takes time for their light to reach us. / We see them as they were when the light first left them.

Page 156 — The Life Cycle of Stars

Q1 a) nebulas
b) gravity
c) hydrogen, helium
d) energy
Q2 hydrogen, red giant, unstable, nebula, white, fades
Q3 a) heat (from fusion)
b) gravity
c) The force pulling the star inwards and the force pushing it outwards are equal, so they balance and cancel out.
d) A main sequence star.

Pages 157-158 — The Life of the Universe

Q1 The Universe is getting **bigger**. Almost all its galaxies seem to be moving **away from** each other.
Q2 a) The following two boxes should be ticked.
The wavelength of the sound seems longer to Francesca as the ambulance moves away.
As the ambulance moves away, the frequency of sound seems lower to Francesca.
b) As the ambulance moves towards Francesca, the frequency of the sound will seem **higher** to her and the wavelength of the sound will **decrease**.
c) Doppler effect
d) false, true
Q3 a) The light from distant galaxies has longer wavelengths than it should. / The light is shifted towards the red end of the electromagnetic spectrum.
b) Light from distant galaxies is red-shifted because they are moving away from us (the Doppler effect). The more distant the galaxy, the greater the red shift, so the faster it is moving. This shows that the Universe must be expanding.
Q4 energy/matter, matter/energy, explosion, expand, Red-shift
Q5 a) False
b) True
c) True
Q6 E.g. It can't explain observed speeding up of the expansion of the Universe. / It doesn't tell you anything about the Universe before the Big Bang. / It doesn't explain what actually caused the explosion.
Q7 a) How objects in the Universe move. The distances between objects.
b) It's hard to measure the large distances in space accurately. It's difficult to observe the motion of objects because they're far away and pollution gets in the way.

Page 159 — Mixed Questions — Section 9

Q1 a) B
b) the Milky Way galaxy
Q2 a) False
b) False
c) False
d) False
Q3 a) radiation, absorbs, pollution
b) Thousands of millions.
c) CMBR, red-shift, expanding